£3
.50

D0414319

Studies in Twentieth-Century Literature

Series Editor:
Stan Smith, Professor of English, University of Dundee

Published Titles:
Rainer Emig, *Modernism in Poetry: Motivations, Structures and Limits*
Lee Horsley, *Fictions of Power in English Literature: 1900–1950*
Peter Brooker, *New York Fiction: Modernity, Postmodernism, The New Modern*
Richard Kirkland, *Literature and Culture in Northern Ireland Since 1965: Moments of Danger*

Literature and Culture in Northern Ireland Since 1965: Moments of Danger

Richard Kirkland

Longman
London and New York

Addison Wesley Longman Limited,
Edinburgh Gate,
Harlow, Essex CM20 2JE, England
and associated Companies throughout the world.

*Published in the United States of America
by Addison Wesley Longman, New York.*

First published 1996

ISBN 0 582 238854 CSD
ISBN 0 582 238846 PPR

British Library Cataloguing in Publication Data

A catalogue record of this book is available from the British Library

Library of Congress Cataloging in Publication Data

Also available

Set by 5 in 10/12pt Bembo
Produced by Longman Singapore Publishers (Pte) Ltd
Printed in Singapore

Contents

Acknowledgements

This book began as research undertaken while I was holding the position of Teaching Fellow in the School of English, Queen's University of Belfast. For their help and encouragement, I am indebted to all the staff of the School and the students I was fortunate to teach during my two years in post. Queen's University has two very good critics of Irish writing, Eamonn Hughes and Edna Longley, and their unfailing support throughout the writing process was immeasurably affirming. Neither could this book have been written without the support, advice, and friendship of – among others – Tony Canavan, Emma Clery, Colin Coulter, Colin and Amanda Graham, Conor Hanna, Edward Larrissy, Declan Long, Michael Longley, Matthew Martin, Colm McGivern, Eileen McIntyre, Aislin McKeown, Robbie and Fionula Meredith, Paul C. Muldoon, Tom Paulin, Shawn Pogatchnik, Marilynn Richtarik, Stan Smith and Ramona Wray. I am also grateful to the staff of the Department of English at Keele University, Staffordshire who have encouraged me in the completion of the project. Finally, my greatest and most incalculable debt is to Michael Allen whose insight, critical generosity and patience has inspired not only me but many of the writers featured in these pages.

The publishers are grateful to the following for permission to reproduce copyright material:

Derry Journal Ltd for a letter by Edmund Warnock in *The Derry Journal* 9.3.65; Faber & Faber Ltd for extracts from the poems 'Martello', 'To the Linen Hall' and 'S/He' from *Liberty Tree* by Tom Paulin and an extract from the poem 'Whatever You Say Say Nothing' from *North* by Seamus Heaney; Faber & Faber Ltd/Farrar, Straus & Giroux, Inc, Inc for extracts from the poems 'Mossbawn II', 'The Seed Cutters' and 'Singing School I', 'The Ministry of Fear' from *North* by Seamus Heaney (UK title)/*Selected Poems 1966–1987*

For my Mother and Father, with love

CHAPTER ONE

Introduction: The Interregnum, the Institution and the Critic

> To articulate the past historically does not mean to recognise it 'the way it really was' (Ranke). It means to seize hold of a memory as it flashes up at a moment of danger.
>
> (Benjamin 1973: 247)

The Ulster Museum in the heart of South Belfast fulfills its role as the 'national museum for Northern Ireland' (Ulster Museum 1993: 2) with some grace. An elegant mix of architectural styles, its hybrid form reflects the pluralist historiography to which it now aspires and which is testified to by its commitment to the Education for Mutual Understanding programme and its support for the cross-curricular theme of Cultural Heritage. Anxious to 'present impartially the complicated story of Ulster's past' (Ulster Museum 1993: 6), the museum's major exhibits demonstrate a sense of the shared dignity of labour and Northern Ireland's great contribution to the world's industrial development. Met by a series of large static machine plants used in the production of Irish linen, the visitor wishing to follow the recommended tour begins on the ground floor and progresses up the building in a spiral movement. Following the arrows, he or she moves from linen to aeronautics and ship-building, past the reconstruction of a shop window from an indiscriminate age, before encountering what seems like a narrative proper. Starting in 1590 with Sir Arthur Chichester and Hugh O'Neill, plantation is considered with indecent haste and within twenty yards the visitor encounters Henry Joy McCracken's uniform close to that of a First World War soldier of the 36th (Ulster) Division. Soon after, history ends. Moving past the formation of the Ulster Special Constabulary (1920) the narrative of Ulster's past is foreclosed just as Ulster is rendered a politically meaningless framework due to partition. However, as it is the national museum for *Northern Ireland*, the visitor to the institution could reasonably expect some indication of post-partition development in the North. Following the arrows, which after all now suggest

1

a narrative of sorts, one is led directly from 1920 to an exhibition of dinosaurs followed by the micro-colonial instant represented by the mummy of Takabuti. As a metaphor, or even a joke, the resonances are telling.

It would though be unfair to see the Ulster Museum's reticent refusal to stray beyond the post-partition development of Ulster as anomalous. Rather such an absence acknowledges unfinished business just as it bespeaks a form of timidity and no great imaginative leap is required to apply the words of 'Wystan' in Paul Muldoon's '7, Middagh Street' to Northern Ireland itself: 'The roots by which we were once bound/are severed here, in any case,/and we are all now dispossessed' (Muldoon 1987: 39). With this sense of fissure, Northern Ireland as an imagined entity continues to ask radical questions of historiographic procedure and it is through the cultural forms of folk-memory, marginalia and anecdote that such questions are most insistently posed. In 1968 the Dublin magazine *Hibernia* published an article by Patrick Boyle on Northern Ireland – then strictly exotic territory – titled 'Ulster Revisited'. The article was envisaged as humour and the author could not have foreseen the imminent explosion of prolonged violence in the North. As such his depiction of pre-Troubles quietude and silent sectarianism in Dungannon now appears irredeemably ironic:

> Fenian gets, one learned, were heavily built, slow moving people, falling mostly into paunch at an early age. They had high complexions, bulging blue eyes and a rotundity of visage that earned them the epithet 'Bap-face'. Pushed well back on their foreheads, they wore soft hats. They were quarrelsome in drink, foul-mouthed, over-fond of the weemen, but still it could be said in their favour they paid regular and ceremonious visits to their places of worship.
>
> Orange hoors, on the other hand were lean and light-footed. They were pale faced with fanatical, deep-set eyes and thin lips. Pulled well down over their foreheads, they wore dunchers. They were quarrelsome in drink, foul-mouthed, over-fond of the weemen, but still it could be said in their favour they paid regular and ceremonious visits to their places of worship.
>
> (Boyle 1968: 11)

A version of Seamus Heaney's satiric ' "One side's as bad as the other," never worse' (Heaney 1975: 59), the impossibility of writing an article such as 'Ulster Revisited' after 1968 testifies to the fact that, whatever else the political and social crisis in Northern Ireland has done, it has shattered any idea of a solely nativist solution to constitutional settlement. As such the piece presents a society of fixed forms and binarisms, a battered relic from an idea of history as endlessly circular and dependent on an oppositional, rather than dialectic, relationship: 'Another swig of creamy malt. Ah, well! The old ways are undoubtedly the best. Society was never meant to be other than polarised between the two distinct races – the Fenian gets and the Orange hoors.' Such satire exposes the pernicious forms of exoticisation[1] prevalent in many forms of writing about Northern Ireland, and it is through the series of tropes that this concept consists of that history is presented as foreclosed and betraying. The Dungannon Boyle finds in the summer of 1968 relives versions of itself in a manner designed to deny any sense of a developmental history, and locates in that passivity a communal past which renders antagonism as a kitsch folk-memory present in every gesture and at every unfulfilled moment.

Significantly, on 24 August of that year, just one month after the article was published, a march by the Northern Ireland Civil Rights Association from Coalisland to the town highlighted the ongoing process of housing discrimination against Catholics in the area. This was met by a loyalist counter-demonstration which succeeded in preventing the intended culminative rally by NICRA going ahead. The binary social structures of Boyle's article had begun to be remade in terms of a narrative of dispossession, singular and indivisible. Possibly taking cognisance of this, in 1983, Tom Paulin found in the town something quite different again:

> Can you *describe* history I'd like to know?
> Isn't it a fiction that pretends to be fact
> like *A Journal of the Plague Year?*
> And the answer that snaps back at me
> is a winter's afternoon in Dungannon,
> the gothic barracks where the policemen
> were signing out their weapons in a stained register,
> a thick turbid light and that brisk smell of fear
> as I described the accident and felt guilty –
> guilty for no reason, or cause, I could think of.
>
> (Paulin 1983: 55–6)

Perhaps a distinctly Northern Irish reading of (or political response to) T.S. Eliot's epiphanic moment in 'Little Gidding, V': 'History is now and England' (Eliot 1984: 222), Paulin's historical memory conceives of the past as a series of moments, 'accidents', which are inherently resistant to the embryonic meta-narrative he is required to construct. The fine ambiguity playing around the particular 'cause' the narrator might espouse reminds the reader of the oppositional political positions such a reading of the past can engender while all around the textual detritus of an oppressed history ('a stained register') inevitably accrues. This forms a useful illustration of the difficulties surrounding any attempt 'to articulate the past historically', while 'Martello' in its entirety enacts the process of seizing 'hold of a memory as it flashes up at a moment of danger' and reads it as a constitutive paradigm.

It is out of the silences and ellipses signalled by the Ulster Museum's fragmented narrative, and the discontinuity between 'Ulster Revisited' and 'Martello' that a structural principle appropriate to the cultural narratives of

3

Northern Ireland can be constructed. For if, as we have seen, the act of transforming the process of time into a narration is necessarily open to the accusation of deceit, the concomitant belief engendered in the ultimate *telos* of a narrative involves at all points a consciousness of finite time; a structure which insists upon points of departure, digressions from the main strand of the instilled history and the arrogance of the writer's struggle with what Walter Benjamin perceived as that which is 'infinite in every direction and unfulfilled in every instant' (Benjamin 1977: 134). As history imposes itself on the scene of the past, so it grants significance to the primal act through the anterior reconstruction of events. In this way historical time is marked only by the referential absences of its signification, by its blankness. As Benjamin reminds us (Benjamin 1979), the subject lost in the labyrinth of the state is a familiar trope but within the process of history it is equally difficult, although not impossible, to trace an imaginative exit.

Benjamin's denial of an integrated totality to history can offer the possibility of a historical process which harmonises with Roland Barthes's famous definition of the *scriptible* nature of certain textual strategies (Barthes 1990: 3–4), and it is through an acknowledgement of this confluence that the critic can gain an empowered position over the very arbitrariness of heterogeneous data. This, however, can only remain so if the *lisible* (or passive) act of reading is countenanced as an ever-present threat both to a notionally insecure selfhood and a critical position without institutional ratification. For the dispossessed or the non-believer, as Friedrich Nietzsche insisted, 'the entire history of a "thing", an organ, a custom, can be a continuous sign chain of ever new interpretations and adaptations whose causes succeed and alternate with one another in a purely chance fashion' (1967: 77). In these terms the history of Northern Ireland becomes imposition rather than reconstruction: a process struggling with the eternal collision of arbitrary events and even if, following Benjamin, this may hint at the possibility of a historical method, it becomes a method bound to a near implausible level of agonised self-consciousness. To brush history 'against the grain' (Benjamin 1973: 256) is to remain in opposition to the present state of the dominant, only waiting for, or believing in, the messianic happening which marks elimination, not of the subjective consciousness which changes the dialogue from act to act, but of history itself.

For these reasons entering the cultural narratives of Northern Ireland is a task which should be undertaken with understandable care. Edward Said, who has written sympathetically of these kind of departures, has noted that, 'beginning is a consciously intentional, productive activity . . . moreover, it is activity whose circumstances include a sense of loss' (Said 1975: 372). Foregrounding the sense of beginning as conscious allows us to perceive that, just as the act of conclusion is at all times present in any one narrative, so is the point of origin. A text or a community, once having delineated its sphere of existence (and thus provoked the sense of loss to which Said refers), can continually rebegin itself, continually reassess its ending, without gaining freedom from the narrative stricture referred to above. Universal history may remain as a construct without 'theoretical armature' (Benjamin 1973: 254), but at least can be encountered with the real hope on the part of the materialist of 'blasting a specific life out of the era or a specific work out of the lifework' (Benjamin 1973: 254). In such a way, the process of making a beginning, of filling the empty time, requires a definite circumspection towards the significances of previous narratives.

To this end the contesting narratives of Northern Ireland can be considered as strictly mythologised entities with the necessary condition that, as Fredric Jameson states in relation to Benjamin's work on *Elective Affinities* (Jameson 1974: 65), 'we understand myth as that element from which the work seeks to free itself'. Here care needs to be exercised. The litany of dates (for instance 1690, 1798, 1916) and the communal affinities which surround them in Northern Ireland are often taken as evidence of a mythologised community in the classic sense.[2] In these can be found the formation of narratives from primal beginnings and a concomitant belief in the malign nature of atavistic forces. In this reading, history can reassert itself as a corrective force. The narrative which contains the sickness can be cured through a rigorous application of wholesome historical methodology.

This essentially revisionist model of narrative development, which seeks to subtend the narrative singular under the narrative plural, challenges Benjamin's messianic nihilism through its belief in reforming *telos* as cure, by a sense in which the sub-narrative can be framed as temporary neurosis. Such approaches are currently not uncommon within Northern Irish historiography; indeed the myth of awakening has an obvious and understandable appeal yet this should not disguise the potential limits of such an interpretation. For Benjamin the true failure of non-materialist historiography lies in its arbitrary fixing of signification, the necessary result of which is the transformation of empty time into an allegorical landscape sundered from the activity of human existence. As such, allegory becomes the method by which meaning is extended across the diversity of heterogeneous time by the manoeuvres of the dominant authority, the subjective is rendered objective and valorised by the ultimate allegorical concept, history itself. An allegorised landscape therefore has no boundaries, no possibility of escape back to a world of pure matter, and can provoke little more than a longing for a violent dissolution of the totality.

In this way Northern Ireland as a community mythologised through allegory is by no means unique yet such a perception does enable a wider contextualisation of the province[3] along simultaneous time and thereby entail a necessary reading of the area as essentially heterogeneous. Again, with this

5

awareness, it is salutary to return to Barthes who wrote consciously from within such a delineated historical space (albeit with his own irony) and further developed this perception through his own well-known theory of myth:

> Myth is not defined by the object of its message, but by the way in which it utters this message: there are formal limits to myth, there are no 'substantial' ones. Everything, then, can be a myth? Yes, I believe this, for the universe is infinitely fertile in suggestions. Every object in the world can pass from a closed, silent existence to an oral state, open to appropriation by society, for there is no law, whether natural or not, which forbids talking about things.
>
> (Barthes 1987: 109)

It is of interest that Barthes's strategy for survival in a mythologised society is to enter it fully, to be part of the 'oral state'. Under the condition of a historical totality Benjamin seeks elimination, Barthes subversive integration. Throughout his decipherment of societal codes which forms the text *Mythologies*, Barthes exudes a sense of bemused wonder that he too can read the language of myth, that he too is of the historical moment. This may be the last of a series of desperate ironies yet it can also be paradigmatic in its veiled insistence that to escape from the system, the only way is to go in deeper.

Such an approach can inform an individual reading of Northern Irish culture. To reveal the constitutive forces of a myth it is necessary to insist upon its status as understandable, to perceive it as 'universe' and to witness its passing from silence to allegory. In turn, the concept of simultaneity, which is crucial to this critical position, becomes, as Benedict Anderson states, 'transverse, cross-time, marked not by prefiguring and fulfilment, but by temporal coincidence' (Anderson 1991: 24). Although Anderson is concerned with the development of nationalist communities, the sense of an individual imagining her/himself as part of a wider, or more specialised, human activity moving through history (activity which of course – and the distinction is important when considering Northern Ireland – need not be aspiring to the state of nationhood) is a significant one. It fulfills the function of myth precisely because it is imagined; it is not necessary or even desirable for each individual to 'know' personally all or any of the other subscribing members of the group but only to be displaced within a narrative. Barthes's own mythical reputation as heroic semiotician developed from the sense that he was consciously placing himself at the point of 'temporal coincidence', that he was prepared for the sake of identifying myth to imagine his own community as subject.

So how can the narrative of Northern Ireland be read at this point of 'transverse, cross-time'? In what sense, if any, is there a recognisable macro-narrative which is distinctive? Here interesting aberrations from universal models of the historical totality arise. Northern Ireland has often been considered as a geographically and culturally discontinuous community. On the margins of Western Europe and subject both to the effects of exterior influences from beyond its physical borders and interior disturbances of its own internal disputing narratives, it becomes definable only by its heterogeneity: the archetypal 'border country' (Hughes 1991: 3). As I will discuss, the often arbitrary nature of this fragmented communal consciousness and the tensions implicit in the essentially spatial distribution of power in the province have problematised any sense of an easy temporal development of linear narratives. Indeed, as suggested previously, to sense a disturbance in the free flow of teleological history is not necessarily to break free of that history but can equally suggest the backwater of an impasse, to be denied the possibility of resolution within a fictive (and yet ubiquitous) historical totality. It is a sense of being on the borders of history as well as on the borders of spatial development which informs this reading of the current 'position' of Northern Ireland. Within the concept of simultaneous time, to be in doubt of the *telos* is to be in doubt of the primal beginning, to suffer a crisis of confidence in history as formative and therefore to find activity self-consciously performed within the vacuum of a lived interregnum.[4]

This is not an uncontroversial construction. In *Culture and Society* Raymond Williams, faced with a similar dilemma in the anterior reconstruction of a narrative, invokes the concept of interregnum as a pause between the Victorian attitude waning in Britain by 1880 and 'our contemporaries' who appear 'after the war of 1914–18' (Williams 1993: 161). Acknowledging that: 'it is almost true that there are no periods of thought; at least, within a given form of society', Williams still cannot negotiate the breakage in sensibility across this period within a cultural continuum. Instead an interregnum is imagined as a way of maintaining 'certain important links' between the two major periods of cultural activity that more properly engage his interest. In this reading, the presence of interregnum signals instability, flux and 'a working out, rather, of unfinished lines'. The period that it limits gains significance only in relation to what has been and what will yet be and as such it occupies a marginal space, constitutes a disruptive presence that, for Williams, 'suggests brevity'. Such a sense of interregnum is useful to this study in that it signals an absence or a problematic space within linear developments of tradition and continuity. However, in its existence as foreclosed and posthumous imposition the implicit instability the term can engender as a lived condition is naturally restricted; rather Williams's usage gestures to an unease with the historically determined models he is employing. To open out the disruptive features of the concept *as a condition* it is necessary to turn to Nadine Gordimer's 1982 essay on South Africa 'Living in the Interregnum' and her sense of that society as one in which, 'historical co-ordinates do not fit life any longer; new ones, where they exist, have couplings not to the rulers, but to the ruled' (Gordimer 1989: 263). Naturally, this is not to suggest that Northern Ireland is analogous to South Africa under apartheid – despite the fact that one of the functions of the province is to be endlessly analogous – but rather to note that it is in the insecurity of life without teleological guarantee that interregnum gains its full resonance and currency. As Gordimer further states:

> The state of interregnum is a state of Hegel's disinterested consciousness, of contradictions. It is from its internal friction that energy somehow must be struck, for us whites; energy to break the vacuum of which we are subconsciously aware, for however hated and shameful the collective life of apartheid and its structures have been to us, there is, now, the unadmitted fear of being without structures. The interregnum is not only between two social orders but also between two identities, one known and discarded, the other unknown and undetermined.
>
> (Gordimer 1989: 269)

In this struggle between two identities, it is Gordimer's awareness that the conditions and contradictions of the interregnum must be lived through in the present that informs her own potentially dialectic practice. By placing herself at the point of temporal coincidence Gordimer is uniquely qualified to chart patterns of social relations and narratives that now exist 'without structures', without what she memorably refers to as 'the 78 *rpms* of history repeating the conditioning of the past' (Gordimer 1989: 270). Appropriately it is within this sense of a breakthrough that Gordimer finds in Antonio Gramsci's *Prison Notebooks* a model suitable for her own concerns: 'The crisis consists precisely in the fact that the old is dying and the new cannot be born; in this interregnum a great variety of morbid symptoms appear' (Gramsci 1971: 276).[5] In this almost marginal statement, as for Gordimer's work, it is important to note that, for Gramsci, the disruptive energies of the interregnum in social relations have more positive than troubling aspects. While for Gordimer its presence signals the irretrievable breakdown of a historical cycle of oppression, for Gramsci it was a signal that 'the ruling class has lost its consensus, i.e. is no longer "leading" but only "dominant", exercising coercive power alone'. In Gramsci's dialectic practice such a detachment in the hegemony of the dominant (mirrored, as he points out, by a concomitant ideological detachment among 'the great masses' (Gramsci 1971: 276)) reveals the coercive power of the state to the oppressed and so constitutes, at least within the historically conceived interregnum, a possibility close to Benjamin's 'Messianic cessation of happening, or, put differently, a revolutionary chance in the fight for the oppressed past' (Benjamin 1973: 254). In this way the 'morbid symptoms' that appear, the coronachs and myths of possession that dominate aspects of Northern Irish culture, signal a wider fracture and a greater degree of self-consciousness and irony within all cultural performance that gestures to the future; the 'new' that is not yet born. The detachment of the individual from the constitutive ideological formation does not signal the death of that ideology but rather its transformation into tradition and irony.

As this book will insist, it is in language usage where such morbid symptoms can be most clearly identified. In 1984 Tom Paulin cited Estragon's lines from *Waiting for Godot* to express a deeply rooted concern that culture had written itself out of history: 'Nothing happens, nobody comes, nobody goes, it's awful!' (Paulin 1984: 9). The Derry-based Field Day Theatre Company, of which Paulin is a part, has, over the last fourteen years, focused on a Gramscian sense of 'crisis' in its analyses of Irish culture. This 'crisis' is both assumed and yet self-fulfilling; a term invoked to breathe life into history and to aspirate the barely twitching body politic. That the word cannot sustain the linguistic pressure placed upon it in turn forces instability. It is pushed into the realm of the tautological utterance which, as we know from Barthes's own analysis, becomes another aspect of a mythologised society:

> One takes refuge in tautology as one does in fear, or anger, or sadness, when one is at a loss for an explanation: the accidental failure of language is magically identified with what one decides is a natural resistance of the object . . . (It is) a magical act ashamed of itself, which verbally makes the gesture of rationality, but immediately abandons the latter, and believes itself to be even with causality because it has uttered the word which introduces it. Tautology testifies to a profound distrust of language, which is rejected because it has failed. Now any refusal of language is a death. Tautology creates a dead, a motionless world.
>
> (Barthes 1987: 152–3)

In other words, there is a crisis because there is a crisis. In the absence of any self-validating term, Field Day's forced reliance on the structures of language to bypass a historical seizure articulates a desire to enter to a new narrative, and yet this becomes an endlessly circular act of re-beginning based on the inability of language to effect a satisfactory homogenisation across time. Forced to work with the materials available despite the knowledge of their inadequacy, as Seamus Deane comments: 'we could not *but* fail, given all the limitations of the situation with which we started' (Lundy and MacPóilin 1992: 25–6). In turn Paulin has recently noted with some irony in the poem 'Basta': 'Would it – would it ever be/Year One again?/not that nondate no never' (Paulin 1994: 102).[6]

This acknowledgement of the impossibility of a return to first origins is significant not least in the extent to which it demonstrates that poetry in Northern Ireland often prefigures social and political developments. As I write this, the province is in the sixth month of a fragile but enduring peace agreed by all the major paramilitary groupings but initiated by the IRA leadership on 31 August 1994. Applauding 'our volunteers and other activists, our supporters and the political prisoners who have sustained the struggle against all odds for the past twenty-five years', it is hard, amidst the many emotions that such a statement engenders, not to reflect on the elegiac desire for closure that it expresses within the terms of a 'complete cessation of military operations'. While it would be foolish to deny the possibility that within this scenario there is the opportunity for a new historiographic awareness, the very fluidity of the situation, in itself, engenders a desire to return to 'Year One again', to foreclose the confusion of the past through the establishment of a new calendar and to move beyond the detachment of the interregnum.[7] One key aspect of a factional culture is that part which dreams itself as built on grandiose, epoch-making events, and with this is a concomitant sense that it is through slow developmental processes that the possibility of betrayal is likely to assert itself. Caught within the specific momentum of events then, the desire for closure can be understood as part of a narrative of political aspiration which in turn delineates the primary moment of violent beginnings in a manner which accords with Said's formulations on the process I have previously considered. With this desire for recontextualisation, the ongoing transformation of the past into history seeks to reinvent previous acts of violence in a way designed to prevent their consequences reverberating into the present, and one might note that it is at such times that language itself most obviously displaces the disruption of the primary act. It is, of course, the unhappy paradox of such a progression that these developments inevitably insist upon, rather than deny, that sometimes sinister instinct towards 'unfinished business' which typifies much of what passes for political discussion in the North, and it is with such instincts that myths of dispossession assert themselves with their full force and resonance. However, while the concept of a clean break with the past can be seen strictly as an impossibility, this should not be to deny the efficacy of its status as an aspiration, nor to belittle the readily understandable desire for stability and progress which underwrites it. In the same way as Gordimer's formulation, the condition of interregnum as I have identified it in Northern Ireland does not negate the possibility of constitutive (and, of course, constitutional) political action but rather relocates such movements within the concept of a present that remains in crisis.

As this suggests, in invoking the concept of the interregnum as a structural principle care needs to be exercised if only because its usage, in itself, entails a scepticism towards those forms of historical signifying practice that have a basis in actual political narratives. Indeed, in this context even the act of fixing dates or events for its onset or culmination forces a definitional stance at odds with its status as a lived condition. Rather the interregnum is marked by the symptoms of detachment, plurality and temporal coincidence which can incorporate the nihilistic constructions of mythology as codified by Barthes and the radical questioning of historiographic practice signalled by Benjamin. In my study of Northern Irish cultural activity through this period then a cohesive narrative structure does not appear, instead there are ellipses, gaps, discontinuities and silences. Voices and arguments disappear or trail off into incoherence as the undetermined identities to which Gordimer refers find in their Northern Irish manifestation foreclosed or tautological patterns of response from which there are no exits. This is not to imply that all such cultural activity undertaken in Northern Ireland can be tidily catalogued under the label of 'morbid symptom', but rather to note that the ongoing struggle to determine individual or communal cultural identity in the North is part of a process of reconstruction which has far more recent and contingent origins than the pervasive strategies of 'tradition' imply. In turn, and more positively, this awareness allows for, or insists upon, a critical dialectic stance that cannot restrict or delimit the full range of cultural possibilities inherent to any gesture. In acknowledging the varied and heterogeneous forces that constitute identity, the contradictions that are lived through in the present remake Northern Ireland as an area of interaction and plurality in which even the manoeuvres of reaction are forced to operate in a dialectic. Despite the voices and actions of those who insist on the archaic nature of Northern Irish society, culturally if not politically the province has resisted such monolithic readings. Here, as elsewhere, there is no such thing as a truly nativist tradition; even labelling it as such indicates a dialectical relationship with other cultural forces that continually remake the univocal and uni-accentual traditions with which they are in perceived opposition.

Despite these necessary provisos it is, however, possible to locate certain systematic tendencies inherent in the interregnum, and it is these paradigms that structure this work. Developing Gramsci's sense of detachment within social relations as the central symptom appropriate to the condition, this work is centred on the deformations and explications of aesthetic liberalism in response to social violence and breakdown and what we have seen Gordimer refer to as 'the unadmitted fear of being without structures'. As this suggests, the final ideological positions that this liberalism can adopt are often far from the original intent as the stylised discourses available to particular groupings are found to constitute inadequate modes of response. In the desire to reformulate what has gone before and the concomitant pressure to locate, if not a point of origin at least one of security, at times only traces remain of the original desire. It is in this way that the phrase 'moments of danger' that engages Benjamin and which I have used for the title of this book gains added resonance and emerges as a structural principle. While, in my adaptation, it refers literally to the violence of chance or intentional sectarian collision in the North, it also, perhaps more properly for the purposes of this study, demarcates the moments when communities or individuals that had previously been able to follow cultural practices that were immune, or at least isolated, from social violence had to engage with a factional society which, yet again,

11

was disintegrating into numerous disruptive manifestations – a progression well illustrated by the two versions of Dungannon represented by Boyle and Paulin which I have already considered. As always, within Northern Irish culture it is not the presence of a divided society *in itself* that prompts cultural activity or revision but rather the moments when the paradoxical stability of that division is disrupted and the equilibrium (even an equilibrium of injustice) is lost. In an oblique manner, it is this process that Deane refers to in his General Introduction to *The Field Day Anthology of Irish Writing* when he asks: ' "How, in the light of what is happening now, can we re-present what was, then and since, believed to have been the significance of what "really" happened?" It also makes a difference *which* "then" is chosen to be re-presented' (Deane ed. 1991: xxi).

Although Field Day's own choice of 'then' remains controversial, Deane's sense of re-presentation has found resonances and an ideological presence even among those who would, and do, despair of the Field Day project. With this the systematic analysis that Field Day has undertaken has operated, sometimes uneasily, alongside similar, if more covert, constructions of ideological development. In the act of 're-presenting' lived social relations, intellectual groupings in the North have been forced to engage with a problem markedly similar to the one Gramsci located at the heart of the condition of interregnum:

> The problem is the following: can a rift between popular masses and ruling ideologies as serious as that which emerged after the war be 'cured' by the simple exercise of force, preventing the new ideologies from imposing themselves? Will the interregnum, the crisis whose historically normal solution is blocked in this way, necessarily be resolved in favour of the old? Given the character of the ideologies that can be ruled out – yet not in an absolute sense. Meanwhile physical depression will lead in the long run to a widespread scepticism, and a new 'arrangement' will be found.
>
> (Gramsci 1971: 276)

While a sense of ironic fatalism clings to Gramsci's notional 'arrangement' he also acknowledges that out of the interregnum there exists 'the possibility and necessity of creating a new culture' (Gramsci 1971: 276), and it is from this conjunction that the concept gains its significance for Northern Ireland. With the awareness that the previously dominant, if uneasy, hegemonic formations in the North have broken down irretrievably the new detachment, or rift, between the ruling ideologies and the masses has forced the intellectual class into a dramatic realignment, or polarisation, of interest. As the 'simple exercise of force' has not and could not restore consensus rule so the mediation of power in the province, now operating without hegemonic stability, has left the intellectual class in a vacuum of responsibility detached from the previously stark choice of loyalty to the dominant or to the oppressed. This model is, in turn, complicated by the fact that the dominant formations of power in the province as have existed in various guises since the imposition of Direct Rule[8] themselves form part of a negotiation with Gramsci's conception of the 'old'; which in this instance can be understood as the sentimental connection between the different socio-sectarian interests of traditional Unionism.[9] It is out of the decline of this residual hegemonic position that many of the cultural initiatives central to this book have developed. As the state of interregnum insists that a restoration of this formation is an impossibility so it has been the role of culture, mediated by the hegemonic and occasionally insurgent intellectual classes, to establish the basis of a new 'arrangement' imagined as both within and beyond the existing state of partition.

This has had a particular effect on those intellectual classes specifically involved in the production, dissemination and analysis of aesthetic artefacts within Northern Ireland itself, and it is on these often fundamentally bourgeois groupings that I have chosen to focus. Within the process of hegemony I have been outlining, similar patterns of progression can be traced in the development of these formations as they move from individuated and isolated voices of dissent located in opposition to the dominant hegemony, through a period of coterie and social definition, to their final manifestation as constitutive institutions to some extent implicated in or modifying the existing dominant structures. While this pattern closely follows Gramsci's sense of 'arrangement' as the ultimate role of the interregnum, it also illustrates how the counter-hegemonic role of what are now often termed 'subaltern' formations seek to take over the dominant ideology by 'active or passive affiliation' in order 'to influence the programmes of these formations (and) to press claims of their own' (Gramsci 1971: 52).

As David Lloyd has noted, Gramsci's definition of the 'subaltern' can incorporate 'groups that do not conform to a classical Marxist definition of the proletariat' (Lloyd 1993: 126) while still allowing for a degree of social specificity in its consideration of other minority groupings. With this awareness I will seek to demonstrate how the representation of social groupings analogous to subaltern formations was a process that engaged the particular intellectual classes I am concerned with as a precondition to subsequent counter-hegemonic activity. If this, to some extent, necessitated a rejection of certain complicities with the dominant formation it also suggests the need for a pre-hegemonic classification within this model out of which insurgency could develop. In its initial phase this takes the form of a rejection of socio-sectarian interpellation of the subject as a meaningful distinction of identity and a concomitant insistence on a new opposition predicated on the rights and autonomy of the aesthetic artefact as seen in opposition to social breakdown and the dominant. Seamus Heaney has considered this development in relation to his own work and what I have considered the residual dominant hegemony:

Like other members of the population, young and old, the poets knew the score. Sectarian prejudice, discrimination in jobs and housing, gerrymandering by the majority, a shared understanding that the police were a paramilitary force – all this was recognised as deplorable, and yet it would be fair to say that by the mid-1960s there was a nascent expectation of better things, on both sides. . . .

I think the writers of my generation saw themselves as part of the leaven. The fact that a literary action was afoot was itself a new political condition, and the poets did not feel the need to address themselves to the specifics of politics because they assumed that the tolerances and subtleties of their art were precisely what they had to set against the repetitive intolerances of public life.

(Heaney 1988: xxi)

As the fourth chapter of the book will argue, one of the more unexpected results of this perception has involved the New-Critical paradigm of literary criticism (and its emphasis on 'subtlety') adopting certain insurgent qualities in its construction of a counter-hegemony out of which new alliances, transcending religious division, could be formed. The consistency of this development is all the more remarkable if one takes into account the shifting forms of the dominant formation from the period Heaney outlines to the present. As the dominant formations have changed so the counter-hegemonic strategies of the aesthetic have adapted accordingly, eventually creating a position from the mid seventies onwards where these forces could gradually assume an institutional role within the new dominant formations. The final institutional locations of these forces have been brilliantly allegorised by Muldoon's 'Madoc: A Mystery' (1990) which depicts in the vision of 'Unitel' that which Lloyd refers to as 'the finally universal claims of the hegemonic institutions within which conflicting and contradictory interests are negotiated' (Lloyd 1993: 9). However, this is to run ahead of the argument. In the shifting negotiations between the role of the aesthetic, society, and the dominant hegemonic interests of Northern Irish culture through this period one cannot help but notice the all-pervading sense of desperate and urgent necessity as an aesthetic response to social breakdown was created out of half-remembered analogies, fragmentary critical models and often wildly optimistic parallels. Considering the materials that were to hand the achievement of this ideology was, and remains, remarkable and it would be inappropriate to deny the efficacy of these contingent energies in any consideration of the interregnum as a lived framework of interpretation.

With this acknowledgement the structure of this book charts the progress of these communities through the interregnum and the possibilities and restrictions that became apparent. Chapter 2, ' "In the midst of all this dross": Establishing the grounds of dissent', defines the areas and beliefs through which dissent from the residual dominant could be expressed by demonstrating how tradition has operated dialectically against the contingent and imposed problems of partition. More importantly, the initial institutional forms this codification took express vividly how such dissent could be *contained* within the twin strategies of 'rootedness' and folk-memory, and then mediated through the aesthetic artefact. This reading suggests how tradition in a Northern Irish context becomes a form of betrayal close to Williams's awareness in *Keywords* that: 'Considering only how much has been handed down to us, and how various it actually is, [tradition], in its own way, is both a betrayal and a surrender' (Williams 1983: 319); a point also insisted on by Deane in his essay 'The Literary Myths of the Revival' (Deane 1985: 36). The selective and occasionally arbitrary promotion of traditions as a structural principle is seen to gesture to contemporary absences within history, and thus give a voice to forces that ordinarily would remain silent.

As such this tendency suggests a shift in the dominant paradigm of interpretation of Northern culture and its validating qualities. Chapter 3, ' "This thing could rule the world": Northern writing and the idea of coterie', develops this model and considers how its application allowed individual, predominantly bourgeois, groupings to gain self-recognition through a range of mythologised second-order discourses. This identification was predicated on a sense of opposition to various aspects of the residual dominant formation and prefigures the eventual assimilation of these groupings within institutional forms in the stress laid on the idea of coterie.

The theoretical models employed for this counter-hegemonic activity are the subject of Chapter 4 which finds in the New-Critical literary evaluations undertaken by Northern Irish critics a means of subtending and denying the heterogeneous forces of history that fragment the province. It is through this evolution that the drive towards institutionalisation gains momentum, and as such this marks the ultimate triumph of the literary aesthetic as a paradigm of reconciliation and the decline of the insurgent coterie formation. Moreover, in this methodology are the perceived means to render Northern Ireland as a distinctive and foreclosed area anomalous in both Irish and United Kingdom contexts.

Chapter 5, ' "Nothing left but the sense of exhaustion": Field Day and counter-hegemony', finds in the activities of Field Day a more self-conscious institutional attempt to work within Gramsci's frameworks and to remake not the residual formations of power but the new dominant formation as constituted since the early seventies. This in turn lends itself to a dialectical reassessment of the formations I have previously been concerned with and gestures to a theoretical state beyond the interregnum.

The final chapter and conclusion to the work suggest what this condition may consist of through a consideration of the current possibilities inherent in a reading of Heaney's poetry and the criticism it has engendered. From this position it reads Muldoon's 'Madoc', as I have previously noted, as an allegory of the progression in Northern Irish writing that I have been charting. 'Madoc', then, brings us to a definition of the institution close to that codified by Williams. It represents 'a noun of action or progress which becomes, at a certain stage, a general and abstract noun describing something apparently objective and systematic' (Williams 1983: 168). In the foreclosure of this allegory the institution becomes endlessly capable of absorbing insurgent or dissident elements and thus returns history to its cyclical equilibrium.

Despite this formulation it is necessary to note that the energies of ambivalence and indecision are always stronger within cultural formations than those of hegemony and coherence. Indeed, just as nationalism is seen to be greater, or more effective, than the sum of its parts, so special pleading for the aesthetic at times of social breakdown does not invalidate the coherencies that it can create out of fractured experience. Such an affirmation may veer towards truism, yet in a society 'without structures' of narrative it is salutary to be reminded of its power. That this, in turn, may involve a seeming abdication of social engagement is understandable in a community often assumed to be in the thrall of micro-narratives. The endurance of Derek Mahon's wish to perfect 'my cold dream/Of a place out of time,/A palace of porcelain' (Mahon 1979: 65) engages dialectically with the interregnum just as it denies it. For this reason such a desire for transcendental escape can only ratify a perception of history as sickness and is not analogous, for example, to Benjamin's messianism. Mahon's extended and profound willed subsumption into the totality of history forces an ironical posturing – not dissimilar to Barthes's – which acknowledges the futility of the aspiration. To search for an exit along the plane of aesthetic free play is to display an acceptance of the inevitability of the flawed historical progression, only leaving, in Mahon's case, a hope that something of beauty will remain amidst the rubble.

As an illustration of this, Mahon's 'A Disused Shed in Co. Wexford' (Mahon 1979: 79–80), often anthologised as a seminal act of aesthetic historiography,[10] bears a sense of a communal history yet can be read as paradigmatic in its failure to become epic. Despite the large geographic and historical sweep it attempts, it is self-consciously rooted at the point of transverse time it inhabits and steadfastly refuses transcendence as an escape from the backwater of historical impasse:

> Even now there are places where a thought might grow –
> Peruvian mines, worked out and abandoned
> To a slow clock of condensation,
> An echo trapped for ever, and a flutter
> Of wildflowers in the lift-shaft,
> Indian compounds where the wind dances
> And a door bangs with diminished confidence,

Lime crevices behind rippling rainbarrels,
Dog corners for bone burials;
And in a disused shed in Co. Wexford,

Deep in the grounds of a burnt-out hotel,
Among the bathtubs and the washbasins
A thousand mushrooms crowd to a keyhole.
This is the one star in their firmament
Or frames a star within a star.
What should they do there but desire?
So many days beyond the rhododendrons
With the world waltzing in its bowl of cloud,
They have learnt patience and silence
Listening to the rooks querulous in the high wood.

These first two stanzas question and pull at the first line's 'might' in a desire for historical location. A thought might grow outside the formal limits of the poem, outside history, but only within a narrative which is 'worked out and abandoned'. Images of historical process crowd the poem but, while a lift-shaft may offer a linear development up (or down) history, the echoes which inhabit it can only form a micro-narrative of endless beginnings, cyclic and tautological. Mushrooms, deceptively bearing a sense of instantaneous beginning, frame their teleological vision as 'a star within a star', the micro-narrative of time frozen in the temporal and spatial moment of the civil war. The point of desire looks towards the eternally absent moment of teleological fulfilment, while it is only the inarticulate rooks which mark the passing, and therefore the awareness of, homogeneous empty time.

The poem continues for a further four stanzas, calling for the moment of apocalyptic resolution which is desired despite (or because of) its unknowability. To open the shed door becomes a contradictory act of both release into history and destruction of the micro-narrative, one performed only by the deity who, in the crucial position of *narrator*, can remain free of narrative. Instinctively the community searches to articulate its situation in temporal terms, an articulation which the poem itself formally re-enacts, yet at the point of *telos* the possibility of betrayal remains. The final stanza denies the closure it promises and leaves time balanced on the edge of the void:

They are begging us, you see, in their wordless way,
To do something, to speak on their behalf
Or at least not to close the door again.
Lost people of Treblinka and Pompeii!
'Save us, save us,' they seem to say,
'Let the god not abandon us
Who have come so far in darkness and in pain.
We too had our lives to live.
You with your light meter and relaxed itinerary,
Let not our naive labours have been in vain!'

In this way 'A Disused Shed in Co. Wexford' can be read as a poem not of community, but for the interregnum; a meditation on the frozen moment as a monad. While few writers are capable of Mahon's imaginative conception, the poem echoes through Northern Irish writing with a nihilistic insistence. To return to the formulations of Edward Said, there are perhaps worse places to make a beginning.

NOTES

1. I am here following Roland Barthes's classic definition of the concept (Barthes 1987: 151).
2. See Brian Walker's '1641, 1689, 1690 And All That: The Unionist Sense of History' (Walker 1992: 56–64).
3. The Unionist connotations of this word emphasise the strain that language as definition is placed under when perceived as part of a narrative framework: 'province' here suggesting both the fourth quarter of Tudor administrative division within Ireland and a natural home for an indivisible part of the United Kingdom.
4. This problematic term is here defined according to its fourth reference in *The Oxford English Dictionary*: 'a break of continuity; an interval, pause, vacant space'.
5. As *The Essential Gesture* makes clear (p. 263) Gordimer uses a slightly different translation of this quotation.
6. The poem first appeared as part of a ' "Peace Process" Special Feature', *Fortnight* 326 (March 1994): 42.
7. Only two months after the IRA's cessation of violence *Fortnight* published an article calling for the establishment of a Troubles interpretation centre to be called the 'Crann'. Containing detailed proposals of its appearance and objectives, the article was reinforced by an open meeting in Belfast. As I discuss in Chapter 2, Northern Ireland's headlong rush to embrace the palliative effects of heritage seemingly knows no limits. See Damien Gorman, 'Weaving a Future Story', *Fortnight* 334 (December 1994): 32–3.
8. Since 30 March 1972. The suspension of Stormont ended a fifty-year-long system of government; as with many acts of legislation concerning Northern Ireland it was intended as a temporary measure.
9. '(Direct rule's) introduction represented the definitive end of the "Orange State". It allowed the British government the space to introduce a strategy of reform "from above" ' (Bew and Gillespie 1993: 50–1).
10. For instance, *The Faber Book of Political Verse* (Paulin 1986: 444).

CHAPTER TWO

'In the Midst of All this Dross':
Establishing the Grounds of
Dissent

THE COUNTRY

A few miles outside Belfast at Cultra Manor in County Down can be found the Ulster Folk and Transport Museum: a curious recreation of Ulster society in microcosm. Buildings, selected not for their authentic localised distinctiveness but because of their assumed mundane generality, have been pillaged jackdaw-like from across the nine counties and carefully rebuilt following the shape of a 'typical' Ulster town and its rural hinterland.[1] Entering this unnamed settlement is therefore to experience a keen sense of otherness within the specificity of place as, inevitably, the desire to 'recognise' the area as *authentic* contradicts its standing as museum – its own self-conscious fictionality.

The venture becomes impossibly ironic; in the face of hard physical evidence (the museum takes pride in pointing out that each individual stone from each individual building is carefully catalogued to ensure absolute exactness in reconstruction), the visitor must *imagine* authenticity, agree to be temporarily displaced in order to experience the enrichment of heritage. The artefacts encountered, not just houses and buildings but also spades, kettles and other general agricultural and domestic equipment, are frozen at around the turn of the nineteenth century and have to speak (loudly) for themselves. They must tell their own story, and in this way subtend social division through the processes of assumed communal inheritance.

It is then appropriate that we are given very little information about each building. As the visitor walks around the museum – the exhibits are widely scattered – we must 'discover' them for ourselves. In this there is a certain self-gratifying labour as history is stumbled across almost by chance. The town does not display its own arbitrary narrative but contains it, the 'tourist' (more often than not an inhabitant of Ulster) becomes the active half of the reaction, and if he or she fails to read the signs they are the ones found wanting. Such a concept cannot hope to fulfil the contradictory, although much desired, state of a 'living museum' but instead stands unwittingly as a metaphor for the act of rebeginning in narrative. Qualities of the physical, the spatial, are promoted above the temporal and the historical and yet firmly anchored at a safe distance from the present. Resolution is placed off-stage – perhaps the town will continue to grow until it envelops the settlements on which it parasitically draws – but simultaneity across a community and across time is foregrounded as a curiously self-fulfilling prophecy.

Although the museum cannot recreate the typicality for which it strives, there is in its own history as a Northern Irish state-funded institution a more reassuring and familiar story. Founded in 1958 through an Act of Parliament and subsequently expanded by further Acts relating to financial provision in 1964 and 1967, its creation was indicative of a confidence in the regional status of Northern Ireland within the United Kingdom. This was a confidence strengthened by the failure of the IRA's border campaign to gain widespread support amongst the Catholic minority[2] and, as Sabine Wichert has noted, there was 'a clear indication that the old controversies were taking a rest, or even becoming traditions, less and less relevant in the increasing relative prosperity of the later 1950s' (Wichert 1991: 66). This transformation bore its own resonances for a museum which could encourage such a sense of tradition while containing it within carefully defined geographic and temporal limits and yet this ossification – from lived political culture to self-conscious inheritance – would also cause problems for the museum's social function in the less confident seventies.

Not that there was any freedom of choice for the early Board of Trustees. The unusual legislation that had founded the museum in the initial Act had outlined its statutory obligations: the Folk Museum must explore and demonstrate 'the way of life, past and present, and the traditions of the people' (Gailey 1988: vii). It has been within this concept of a notionally plural tradition that the museum has differentiated itself from similar projects elsewhere; its role becoming one not simply of embodiment or representation but of mediation and education. George Thompson, the first Director of the Museum, was aware of this dilemma, perceiving that 'Ulster may be seen as one of the least fertile areas in Western Europe in terms of Folk Museum growth' (Longley 1971: 154). Unlike similar projects in Wales and Scandinavia, the museum could not be seen as 'a manifestation of a strong sense of national or cultural identity' (Longley 1971: 154); rather it was initiated as a way of neutralising distinctive or even dangerous local cultural activity by a process of rendering such tendencies within a paradigm of tradition.

The underwritten concept behind this project can be defined therefore in Phillipe Hoyau's[3] terms as 'ethno-history', a focus on the details of everyday life which 'derives less from a will to preserve and value a "monumental" and academic past than from the promotion of new values articulated on a largely transformed conception of inheritance and tradition'. The emphasis on a rural, countrified version of history is clearly central to this movement. Political division can be veiled within a *new* discourse which celebrates the vernacular imagination as a form of collective and non-academic identification and through which the inhabitant of Northern Ireland can display his or her best self to the world. In 1971, George Thompson illustrated the museum's belief in this project through an extended article on the development of the museum (Longley 1971: 153–65) and its focus on 'practical methods consistent with the prevailing social situation':

> It is, then, in the history of day-to-day life which has, more often than not, followed its course in spite of political manoeuvring than because of it, that the personality of the community and its people is to be found. . . . The Ulsterman must be made much more aware of a heritage which transcends factional divisions, and that awareness must be developed beyond the level of conscious effort; it should be instinctive, for a sense of cultural identity is a basic, deep-rooted need in the human individual.
>
> (Longley 1971: 163–4)

How a project as artificial as a museum is able to instil an 'instinctive' cultural identity is an issue the article does not address, and yet it is correct to see the museum's strategy, especially after the beginning of the current period of social violence, as formative rather than confirmative. Tradition, envisaged by a later Director of the Museum as 'a means of admitting cultural performances based on precedents coming down to the present from the nearer or more distant past' (Gailey 1988: 64), in turn is perceived as an inheritance that must be obtained, to paraphrase T.S. Eliot, by great labour. In this way the concept of tradition could be saved from those forces of atavism, whether from the loyalist or nationalist communities, that had been seen to hijack it for violent ends and precedents. If history was now in some way a dangerous and betraying concept, then tradition could become a redemptive force reminding 'Ulstermen' just what they had in common.

In many ways such a perception places an intolerable pressure on the actual visitor who through self-conscious effort must strain for the instinctive recognition demanded by Thompson which will validate their own sense of belonging. Walking around the buildings and trying to feel some instinctive bond with them, he or she is caught within the disabling semantics inherent to the process of defining that which is to be considered 'real' and that which is evidently artificial. For this reason then it is not too fanciful to argue that the museum offers its vision of the past as somehow more 'real' than the outside world and concomitantly suggests that it is the present society of sectarian fracture which is now somehow false, somehow imposed. Operating at the level of conscious effort, yet straining for an instinctive

21

recognition, the subject is defined in relation to the object-symbol and as such it is not inappropriate to read the Folk Museum as a postmodern event in its accordance with Jean Baudrillard's theory of the simulacrum and its ultimate divorce from the realm of the actual.[4] In the commodification of the traditional object-symbol – exemplified for Baudrillard by 'tools, furniture, even the house' – traces of 'a real relation or of a lived situation' inherent to those objects are destroyed by the act of consumption (Baudrillard 1988: 22). The object 'must become sign; that is, in some way it must become external to a relation that it now only signifies'. While the museum wishes to preserve above all else the lived values and relations inherent to the artefacts it displays, the new context of display as a consumed object ironically erases any sense of this original value; the objects can only signify something that was once assumed to exist. With this process the new frame of reference – the museum's relationship to the 'real' Ulster – can only confer meaning on the symbol-objects that it displays by an eternal play of difference. The materiality of those artefacts is both proclaimed and questioned as 'human relations tend to be consumed in and through objects, which become the necessary mediation and, rapidly, the substitutive sign, *the alibi*, of the relation' (Baudrillard 1988: 22).[5]

It is in the inevitable interpretative vacuum left by this process that tradition asserts itself. If it is the role of the museum as simulacrum to replace and *determine* the real, if, in other words, the flow of meaning is running in the opposite direction envisaged by the initial Act of Parliament, then similarly it is the role of tradition (and with it, its less respectable alter-ego, nostalgia) to mediate this new relationship in terms of strategic contemporary needs located in the present. This point is fundamental to a reading of the museum as an aspect of of ethno-history which, as Hoyau insists, is able to: 'adjust ethnological and historical research to the ideological demands of the time . . . and above all rationalise nostalgias, offering them "real" contents. By revaluing "poor" forms of knowledge and despised objects, ethno-history affirms its spirit of openness, and at the same time makes its appeal to as widespread an audience as possible' (Wright 1991: 25). This democratic appeal is in itself symptomatic of a nervous condition. In the act of giving nostalgia a physical legitimacy its efficacy as a lived system of values is simultaneously denied as its new-found dominance signals an insecurity in that very realm of the real that it seeks to support; as Baudrillard has noted, 'When the real is no longer what it used to be, nostalgia assumes its full meaning' (Baudrillard 1988: 171). With this awareness nostalgia is rendered as a proactive force operating in the dimensions of the present moment and forming a dialectical relationship with a perceived crisis in human relations as they, in turn, negotiate a connection with the objects of the past. As Baudrillard develops his thesis: 'There is a proliferation of myths of origin and signs of reality. . . . There is an escalation of the true, of the lived experience; a resurrection of the figurative where the object and subject have disappeared. And there is a panic-stricken production of the real and the referential, above and parallel to the panic of material production' (Baudrillard 1988: 171).

Such recourse to the concrete actualities of production to effect a displacement of history – which in turn becomes synonymous with betrayal – can be read as one of the dominating tropes in recent Northern Irish culture and constitutes perhaps one of the more obvious 'morbid symptoms' that Gramsci perceived as part of life in the interregnum (Gramsci 1971: 276). While, in his model, the 'old' is dying, its symbiotic relationship with the as yet uncreated 'new' necessitates that it lingers on with a stubborn irascibility. For all the brave statements of support for the poor despised forms of knowledge the museum is protecting, its actual function can be understood as an attempt to subtend a received sense of history as official state gravitas by artificially aspirating a much older ideology: nature as redemptive force. Physical images of origin and unity can foreclose history by an appeal to timelessness *and* placelessness against which it offers only the assurance of the physical and material. For this reason the artefacts in the museum do not stand in the present moment of time but must be encountered on more-or-less arbitrary terms at a date which is vague and yet securely pre-partition. Any attempt on the part of the visitor to gain a more certain historical fix is not only frustrated but should be seen as strictly contrary to the spirit of the institution. On entering the replica of the Northern Bank building, the observant will notice a calendar displaying bank holidays for the year 1920, a short distance away a gravestone proclaims someone's death in 1922. In the desire to represent the typical Ulster, the museum effortlessly enters the vacuum of interregnum and indeterminacy: a permanent monument to the perceived betrayal of the Ulster people by an illogical and sundered sense of inevitable narrative development.

With this awareness, it is hard to avoid the irony which clings to these images of transposed permanence, especially when the artefact under examination owes its existence to those forces of schismatic breakdown that the museum is usually silent about. For this reason, perhaps the most incongruous exhibit within the anonymous country town which forms the main part of the museum is the presence of a full terrace of high density housing from the Sandy Row area of Belfast.[6] In what sense can they still be perceived as 'part' of Belfast itself? The visitor from the city must fit them into a narrative of Belfast which, crucially, places dislocation at its locus. As Patrick Wright has stated in relation to the housing of Hackney in London, the preservationist attitude that deems such objects worthy of retention has

> . . . a more subjective side as well, involving as it does a contemporary
> *orientation* towards the past rather than just the survival of old things. As so
> few guide-books ever recognise, this is not merely a matter of noticing old

objects situated in a self-evident reality: the present meaning of historical traces such as these is only to be grasped if one takes account of the doubletake or second glance in which they are recognised. The ordinary or habitual perspectives are jarred as the old declares itself in the midst of all this dross.

(Wright 1991: 229–30)

Wright's recognition that in the socially determined present self-evidently 'old' artefacts are granted a value above and beyond their actual historical worth orientates the preservationist drive embodied by the museum's strategies towards a specific articulation of needs, desires and contemporary absences. To 'read' the history of a settlement is therefore an interpretative skill dependent on a shifting, negotiated, identification with the community which is to be recognised; a circular argument which avoids problematic issues of communal loyalty by saturating the merely old (and unpleasant at that) with arbitrary narrative meaning. The 'cottages' of Sandy Row speak to us and proclaim the primacy of the physical actuality over the assumed strangeness of history written as a discourse of social breakdown. Culture, henceforward defined as 'everyday life' (Wright 1991: 253), celebrates the material over the temporal and disguises its own displacement (which is all the more noticeable in the now ruralised locale of the Sandy Row terrace) through a reliance on the fixed essence of the 'old': a space that can only exist a safe distance from the present.

It is then sadly appropriate to note that, in line with the political developments of Northern Ireland since that founding 1958 Act, the museum does not democratise history but instead seeks to erase it by foregrounding the politics of identity as central through the process of grounding, an occurrence defined by David Lloyd as 'the act of fostering, by which a people "separated from their forefathers" are . . . given back an alternative yet equally arbitrary and fictive paternity renaturalized through the metaphor of grounding: through its rootedness to the primary soil' (Lloyd 1993: 16). With this, Northern Ireland, a construct which of course had temporariness needled into its very existence,[7] is displaced by the (ironically) Tudor-established nine-county Ulster in an attempt to perceive the past as established touchstone rather than as a narrative of schism and fracture. The difficulties of this, as I have demonstrated, are manifold but were ably encapsulated by John Hewitt who voiced unease after a visit to the museum in the poem 'Cultra Manor: The Ulster Folk Museum':

What they need now, somewhere about here,
is a field for the faction fights.

(Hewitt 1991: 187)

There is, of course, nothing anomalous about the role of the museum in this regard. In offering symbols of embodiment and representation, its perception of identity is one that has also nourished a number of pervasive literary strategies in the North. To escape the tautology of a betraying language the writer who seeks (and of course will inevitably achieve) transcendence through the efficacy of location must also negotiate an embodying role within an assumed community and landscape. To speak legitimately about the area delimited the writer must, paradoxically, be typically of it and yet be privileged in being able to effect the transcendence of its typicality in order to demonstrate it, like the museum, to the public. It is here that the function of the writer as paradigmatic becomes significant. To navigate a route through often arbitrary shifts in narrative, the concept of intentionality rewrites the text as autobiography so that closure can only be achieved when it aspires to express, in the absence of political discourse, the fulfilment of the human subject. The achievement of the text becomes the physical actuality of the text and the unseen labour behind its production. In *Ian Paisley My Father* (1988), Rhonda Paisley addresses these issues directly through a text which manifests an extraordinarily personal meditative philosophy. To reclaim her father as the true leader of a lost tribe in the face of previous biographical attacks,[8] Rhonda Paisley's revisionist urge incorporates the personal reminiscence, the accusation of betrayal by the outsider, and, most importantly, the constant restatement of the Ulster narrative as a justifying litany:

> For a child, things of great consequence always have a beginning and an end. 'The troubles' began, to my mind as a child, one morning when I learnt that the Rt Hon. Bill Craig, then Minister of Home Affairs, had been sacked by the Northern Irish Prime Minister, Captain Terence O'Neill. It was the late '60s and O'Neill, a liberal Unionist, had been pursuing a policy of appeasement with the Roman Catholics. . . . That day for me was when 'the troubles' began. Regrettably, my childhood brought no memory which signalled an end to this event of such consequence.
>
> (Paisley 1988: 31)

Here, as elsewhere in the book, Rhonda Paisley's style evokes irresistibly the Protestant confessional novel of nineteenth-century England, so that, at times, she can sound like an Ulster Unionist version of Esther Summerson. In the muddle of a narrative which has a clear beginning but no perceivable end (again a parallel with the labyrinthine plot structure of *Bleak House* is possible), she seeks to perfect the individual life as one dedicated firstly to her father and secondly to God; a work of justification which promotes the quotidian aspect of Ian Paisley's life[9] over the failed and increasingly schismatic political vision. With this, the fluid prose she adopts seeks a point in space which is securely pre-twentieth century and rooted in a common inheritance of Protestant political values unified around the totality of the islands. As the tension between this pre-lapsarian technique and the betraying history from which it seeks to remove itself grows greater, Rhonda Paisley can only bear witness to the individual leader as a man for all time; an absolute entity whom the reader must necessarily acknowledge as such or be condemned as a sceptical 'outsider' (possibly the most extreme label of condemnation Northern Irish culture can envisage). Again, theoretical explanations become undesirable and are foreclosed by the pervasive influence of the primary soil:

> To know a person, that is to know them genuinely and not just be acquainted with them, you must understand their heart. It is a process which takes time. To know Ulster and comprehend the situation here you must understand the beat of the land and the rhythm of its music. It is a process which takes time. Outsiders do not usually give the time. . . . Often I have sat alone on a hillside close to the beach which I love to walk along and tried to take in, to absorb into my being the beauty of this land. . . . It permeates my blood and the bond created can never be broken. The rhythm of the land will be part of my pulse forever. Its influence cannot be taken away – it is too late for that.
>
> (Paisley 1988: 42–3)

By reading such a declaration as coherent with nationalist discourses, one can argue that such rootedness is placed in doubt simply through it being given a voice. *Ian Paisley My Father* acknowledges failure and despair through its declarative tone. Its status as text is forced to make conscious the relationship between object and subject that ideally its author would subtend under a universal paternalism. With this Rhonda Paisley inhabits a landscape where it is perpetually 'too late' to initiate a political strategy. The land is given a voice as disillusionment with Westminster becomes overwhelming yet the history of betrayal by England,[10] which her brand of Loyalism proclaims, becomes endlessly cyclical. Through the course of *Ian Paisley My Father* the imaginative sweep of the vision gestures towards the final betrayal of the Ulster Protestant as a political subject, a goad to the imagined concept of a British nation-state which has long since lost interest. This messianic concept of final destruction leaves the text, and possibly the Democratic Unionist philosophy it embodies, faltering on the final precipice of history and calling sado-masochistically for the final act of humiliation which will free it. Seemingly this humiliation will always come but it can never be enough. The politics of despair are always inarticulate and offer only the sign, the analogy (Ian Paisley as Moses) and the eternal opposition of the outsider as a theoretical framework. Despite Rhonda Paisley's stated wish to demythologise her father he is displaced through the work as an endlessly metaphoric figure embodying the feeling of the land and the 'common man in the street' through the silence of his rhetorical and figurative tropes.

It is in this way that Rhonda Paisley's unwilling commodification of seemingly natural impulses and emotions defines her position within disabling semantic arguments and oppositions. In a later article for the *Irish Times*, 'A Struggle about Identity, Loyalty, Government and, above all, Territory' (28 October 1993), the function of the Union and with it the possibility of democratic exchange is located at the centre of the now familiar disjunct between nature and culture:

> We have been fed in our state schools the English version of our Irish history. We have been called British first and Irish as a sub-title, a geographic addition. We have been weaned from an organic and beautiful Ulster heritage and fed the synthetic, over-ripe (or half-rotten) heritage of a British empire that is no more and which also was broken by betrayal on betrayal. Now we are chained and fettered by direct rule. . . . To be a part of Ulster is not to be a geographical term nor a subtitle. It is an inheritance. It pulses through the landscape and the veins, we are born to it.

Read alongside *Ian Paisley My Father* such statements provoke certain questions about the author's belief in the desirability of the state democracy to which the rest of the article nominally adheres. Coherent with her previous views on the essentially problematic nature of any artefact marked by artificiality, the article's lines of enquiry are a logical extension of the issues that play through the representational contradictions of the Folk Museum as outlined by Thompson. Finding in Ulster an 'organic' inheritance and sentimental connection to the land, the politics of betrayal by the British Empire become simultaneously the politics of artificiality. Any attempt to separate the idea of representation from that of embodiment, or indeed any attempt to privilege culture over heritage as a lived system of values is rendered, by an intriguing twist, un-Irish and alien. To return to *Ian Paisley My Father*, it is through this instinctive connection of inheritance that totalitarianism enters the social framework of values as the only natural and intuitive response to betrayal.[11]

Of course neither Rhonda Paisley's *Irish Times* article nor *Ian Paisley My Father* should be perceived as unusual in their reliance on grounding to circumvent political stasis. Indeed, while her particular political philosophy prompts her ambiguous stance towards any form of social settlement not predicated on an organic connection, the issues of embodiment and representation with which she is engaged have had a distorting effect across many aspects of Northern Irish culture. Such arguments have often been identified in relation to writers such as John Montague or Seamus Heaney who have consciously felt able — although not always comfortably — to draw on a tradition of rural, Gaelic poetry in their work (Lloyd 1993: 16), and have thus been able to accept the mantle of 'singer' appropriate to their community. Yet it is in the areas of instability, the torn, divided city or the fractured, displaced tradition, where these aesthetic manoeuvres become most fascinating. John Hewitt, famously of 'Planter stock' (Hewitt 1987: 146), spent a long and uncertain writing career agonising over the politics of identity from a historical position which needed constant examination, constant rebeginning:

> To return for only a moment to this question of 'rootedness'. I do not mean that a writer ought to live and die in the house of his fathers. What I do mean is that he ought to feel that he belongs to a recognisable focus in place and time. How he assures himself of that feeling is his own affair. But I believe that he must have it. And with it he must have *ancestors*. Not just of the blood, but of the emotions, of the quality and slant of mind. He must know where he comes from and where he is: otherwise how can he tell where he wishes to go? The overtones and implications of this would, however, lead us beyond the limits of these pages and must be left over for another more spacious occasion.
>
> (Hewitt 1987: 116–17)

That 'another more spacious occasion' was never found was perhaps not a coincidence, the terms invoked here form an inadequate point of beginning but are significant in that they illustrate the particular type of impasse into which Hewitt's epistemology was inexorably heading. Realising both the potency and despair implicit in the concept of a received history, Hewitt reinterpreted narratives of possession as formulated through the region and was prepared to apply European models of regionalism to Northern Ireland as a specifically mythological system. As the ineffable statement 'how he assures himself of that feeling is his own affair' indicates, this is predicated on an individualism too vague to be supportable and, again like the strategies of Ulster Folk and Transport Museum, the subject is left having to be already inherently part of the system in order to identify with it. His later short essay, 'Regionalism: The Last Chance' (1947) polemically restated this difficulty and emphasised the centrality of narrative development to his vision through a belief in pre-lapsarian wholeness:

> Threatened by over-centralisation, already half subdued by a century of increasing standardisation in material things, rapidly losing his individual responses in the hurricanes of propaganda, political, commercial, ideological, western man gropes instinctively for the security of a sheltering rock. Many in these islands seek among the rubble of once valid religions for that shelter. Some believe that a wise psychology, aware of many-faceted human nature, will serve. Others, that in achieving a proper relationship with organic nature they may be saved. . . . One other approach remains, to my mind more urgent and no less valuable because it does not exclude any of the foregoing, rather, indeed, would provide circumstances to which they might be more readily applicable; one which, although it begins with the individual, must immediately pass beyond the individual and react upon the community – another word which to live must become flesh. This word is regionalism.
>
> (Hewitt 1987: 122)

As the reference to 'these islands' suggests, Hewitt's regionalism was not necessarily a direct attempt at changing the constitutional position or existence of Northern Ireland as a political entity. As the examples of successful regionalism he later cites[12] demonstrate, the concept becomes at best a way of decentralising small amounts of power to the provinces. Indeed he goes on to admit that regionalism can only benefit Ulster if it remains, in turn, part of a larger association, his preference being for a federated British Isles. The precarious post-war political situation of Northern Ireland makes such reasoning understandable yet, even then, there is something too comfortable in Hewitt's belief in a pre-twentieth-century individualism which returns, before the 'hurricanes', to a myth of first beginnings pure and unalloyed. As a narrative which seeks to undercut the primary narratives of Irish or Ulster nationalism, it offers a resolution which is predicated on the reconciliation of previous individual liberty with a form of communal association. Hewitt's methodology is here on uncertain ground; while the polemical drive of his prose and his seamless syntactical shifts between the (assumedly) individual 'I' and the communal 'we' indicates a paucity of any theoretical basis for an application of regionalism to Ulster,[13] it becomes clear that the work stands as an angry cry from the provinces desperate to find significance amongst the atavisms of a failed political concept.

In this way, to return to the work of Lloyd, Hewitt's regionalism becomes interesting not through the political initiative it spectacularly failed to deliver, but through the way it allowed him to imagine a community based not on history but along aesthetic and geographical guidelines. It was a myth which idealistically claimed individual loyalty through the tropes of rootedness to the primary soil of Ulster[14] as a 'natural', organic allegiance, and by so doing placed centrally the artist as crucial arbiter of communal judgement:

> But if the approach were merely to be on the economic level a long period of time must inevitably elapse before an *emotional unity* could emerge. To quote Mumford further: the 'process begins rather with a dynamic emotional urge, springing out of a sense of frustration on one hand and a renewed vision of life on the other. Only at a later stage does the movement achieve a rationale, a systematic and economic basis. Regionalism, as one French observer points out, begins with *a revival of poetry and language*: it ends with plans for the economic invigoration of regional agriculture and industry, with proposals for a more autonomous political life, with an effort to build up local centres of learning and culture.' [Emphases added.]
> (Hewitt 1987: 123)[15]

By subscribing so closely to Mumford's thesis, Hewitt allows the problematic relationship between the individual – who after all is central to his beliefs – and the communal 'emotional unity' to be reconciled only through the paradigmatic figure of the artist: an ideology which accords at least as well with the nationalist thinking of the nineteenth-century Young Ireland journal the *Nation*[16] as it does to any of the regionalist thought to which he more obviously subscribes. The writer becomes saturated with meaning and must mediate the relationship between the individual and the territory in such a way as to propose language as a force of unification rather than division. While Yeats, in obviously differing circumstances, was capable of occasionally fulfilling these conditions on his own eclectic terms, it was a task beyond Hewitt's more limited intellectual grasp or affiliations. By never clearly recognising which community he was serving[17] or writing for, the absolute concept of Hewitt's Ulster regionalism was always open to the misreadings and political appropriations that its ambiguity sought to foreclose. As his contemporary Roy McFadden noted, 'I suspected that the Ulster Regionalist idea could be used to provide a cultural mask for political unionism or a kind of local counter-nationalism. I was also troubled by Hewitt's use of the word "Ulster", which he did not clearly define' (Dawe and Foster 1991: 176).[18] Hewitt had moved from a period of studying the works of C.G. Jung during the forties (Dawe and Foster 1991: 174–5, 303): a move which suggests a further Yeatsian trope in the opportunity it afforded him to find a personal myth again predicated on the individual subject. Certainly it is significant that this interest waned when he became fully conscious of the regionalist agenda. Whatever regionalism might have been in Northern Ireland, it seems clear that for Hewitt at least it was a mode of evasion: a way of posing delusory ethical debates on the question of bourgeois identity in his work while avoiding any attempt to address political or *territorial* schism.

As has often been the case in Northern Irish culture, it has been within the structures of the aesthetic artefact itself that such practices have been most effectively interrogated. In John Montague's 1961 collection *Poisoned Lands and Other Poems*,[19] the poem 'Regionalism, Or Portrait of the Artist as a Model Farmer' (Montague 1961: 56)[20] effectively condemned regionalism as provincial, nativist and insular. While this critique was one Montague would later modify after his collaboration with Hewitt on 'The Planter and the Gael' Arts Council tour of 1970,[21] his accusations were well aimed and clearly had Hewitt – and through him Kavanagh – specifically in mind:

> Wild provincials
> Muttering into microphones
> Declare that art
> Springs only from the native part;
> That like a potato it best grows
> Planted deep in local rows: . . .
> Shield from all might harm her,
> Foreign beetles and exotic weeds,
> Complicated continental breeds:
> And when my baby tuber

To its might has grown
I shall come into my provincial own
And mutter deep
In my living sleep
Of the tradition that I keep.
My tiny spud will comfort me
In my fierce anonymity.

Although the nature of this satire allowed Montague to construct himself in opposition as a sophisticated internationalist, the poem's presence within a collection which sought to identify those symptoms which had 'poisoned' Ulster indicates a more serious critique. As Montague recognised, for Hewitt the conflation of regionalism and formal poetic achievement became a way of containing and controlling dangerous passions; the literary equivalent of the 'little towns to garrison/the heaving country' which appear in his poem 'The Colony' (Hewit 1991: 78).[22] As a reading of this poem indicates, Hewitt's poetry through this period is obsessed with the concept of the enemy both as external force and internal temptation. Desperate to protect a notional selfhood from the corrupting influence of passion, even his interest in Jung, to which I have already referred, can be seen, not as an exploration, but as a schematicisation of troubling impulses and desires into a readily understandable epistemological framework. The pattern of his intellectual life that begins to emerge is one in which methodology seeks to restrict the chaos of sensory impression. In opposition to the Joycean model of aesthetic detachment invoked by Montague's title, Hewitt as 'model farmer' seeks to cultivate, contain and catalogue the discordant and anomalous voices which continually interrupt his work, disrupt the steady flow of his neo-dialectic method and escape into print.

Read in this way, Hewitt's writings appear as nothing less than wagers with heterogeneity: if his analytic method cannot prevail, sensory impression and prejudicial emotion will inevitably break through. Moreover, there is evidence that Hewitt was aware of this dilemma. An interesting, although little cited, sonnet 'Aquarium' (Hewit 1991: 225) takes as its theme agency and representation and notes, with some exasperation, that 'the old obsessive search/for binding epithet' will lead to nothing 'riper' than '*striped* Perch/or *pink-finned* Rudd'. The aquarium itself represents a 'challenge to my verbalising mind' although does not entail 'the risks of dialogue' as the fish who inhabit it are merely subjects to be represented. As Hewitt perceives the danger and inevitable confrontation of agency the poem's thematic concern oddly resembles Paul Muldoon's later 'Chinook' which similarly seeks to contain within a metaphor the disruptive energies of language: 'I was micro-tagging Chinook salmon/on the Qu'Apelle/river' (Muldoon 1987: 9). The analogy is telling. In its reluctance to enter language, to give voice to the 'dumb' fish, 'Aquarium'

31

recognises that all such codification can be seen as fundamentally reductive and aesthetically inadequate: 'to drag my leaky net to land' is not to bring to a successful conclusion a well-turned sonnet but to sense impending despair.

The neo-Georgian forms and belief in regionalism which haunt much of Hewitt's work can be seen then as self-conscious admissions of defeat; methods of strategic containment and a buttress against the centripetal energies of modernism and the formal chaos which can follow. While Montague's critique of regionalism and formal insularity is important if only because there was little effective criticism of regionalism as a political or aesthetic practice at this time, it required Seamus Heaney, responding to Hewitt's regionalism and to 'Portrait of the Artist as a Model Farmer', to suggest through a poetic dialectical method the ultimate universalism of a carefully applied regionalist agenda in his poem 'The Seed Cutters' (Heaney 1975: 10):

> . . . The tuck and frill
> Of leaf-sprout is on the seed potatoes
> Buried under that straw. With time to kill
> They are taking their time. Each sharp knife goes
> Lazily halving each root that falls apart
> In the palm of the hand: a milky gleam,
> And, at the centre, a dark watermark.
> O calendar customs! Under the broom
> Yellowing over them, compose the frieze
> With all of us there, our anonymities.

The seed cutters' dissection of the seed potatoes as locations of meaning – the point at which growth will begin – ultimately reinvigorates the 'anonymity' that Montague condemns through his 'spud' in the final word of 'Portrait of the Artist as a Model Farmer'. With this 'The Seed Cutters' moves from an image of communal anonymity to a parable of the literary self-conscious that can transform the 'wild' provincial stance offered by Montague into a repetitive, calendrical, aesthetic practice. However, this is not to suggest that Heaney's covert defence of regionalism entailed that he would fall back to the overtly deterministic strictures of 'Regionalism: The Last Chance'. While in the later essay 'The Regional Forecast' (Draper 1989: 10–23), Heaney acknowledges the importance of regional cultural activity as a precursor to political identity in a way which accords with Hewitt's previously stated arguments, he is concomitantly aware that 'it is necessary to beware of too easy an assumption that the breaking of political bonds necessarily and successfully issues in the forging of a new literary idiom' (Draper 1989: 12). By drawing attention to the conflict of interests between 'the imaginative and activist wings' of regional development, Heaney seeks to disentangle those impulses that Hewitt had deliberately unified through a belief in an 'idealised past' (Draper 1989: 12). Heaney's regionalism then stops short of Hewitt's call for a 'more autonomous political life' perhaps because it would be through such a manoeuvre that Ulster would dissociate itself from the rest of Heaney's imaginative hinterland. Instead he is content to perceive the phenomenon as a means of raising 'our subcultural status to cultural power'; a strategy that can continue to contain and demonstrate the subversive discourses of Irish nationalism that other Heaney poems (collected alongside 'The Seed Cutters' in *North*) express.

It is through these attacks that the limits of 'Regionalism: The Last Chance' are contextualised. As Montague reads the concept as cravenly provincial, so Heaney, like McFadden before him, finds in its polemic bluster a covert expression of unionism. With this, the essay stands as testament to an ideology which was essentially despairing of history and the political subject and which sought to foreclose such forces within the landscape and within silence. As a poet, however, it allowed Hewitt to grant contemporary significance to his own essential instincts which lay in the foundation of a writing coterie as social force (Dawe and Foster 1991: 179) – an obsession which, as I will demonstrate in Chapter 3, haunts writing in Belfast and Derry even now. In his later years the recognition Hewitt sought as paternal head of such a movement was finally fulfilled and his memory exists as a mythological phenomenon; the benign protector of a poetic tradition in Ulster at a time when it was near total eradication.[23]

THE CITY

I have considered the Ulster Folk and Transport Museum, *Ian Paisley My Father* and Hewitt's regionalism not because of their individual importance but because they demonstrate a crucial tendency in Northern Irish culture to subtend the force of a betraying history as political motivator under the urge to return to physical actuality. With this, the landscape becomes a mode of redemption through which the writer can mediate the politics of identity to his/her community. In this manner the city, the contemporary shape of settlement, lies in opposition to history, the frozen immutable polarity, in that its fragmentation is not to be interpreted but is contained in its procedures. The alienated individual internalises that fragmentation in relation both to the rural myth of continuity[24] and to a displaced sense of narrative; a problematic opposition perhaps most clearly illustrated within the literary artefact, as Burton Pike has revealed:

> The image of the city in a literary work occupies a peculiar position. Since its empirical referent is a physical object in space, the word-city is an inherently

33

spatial image. But this unavoidable association with spatiality conflicts in modern literature with the dominating convention of time. Perhaps this explains why so many cities in contemporary literature are etherealised or disembodied, like Biely's St Petersburg, Musil's Vienna, or Eliot's London. This etherealisation reduces their spatial presence so that they appear as dependencies of time; they become images which reflect transitoriness rather than stable corporeal places.

(Pike 1981: 120)

Although Belfast could hardly take its place alongside Pike's list of canonical cities, the modernist distinctions he draws are important. As a conductor of the uneasy shifts between rural and urban geography, between fragmented and betraying histories, Belfast has been, until recently, an *unwritten* city placed beyond the process of metaphoric displacement by its own self-evident physicality. A disembodied terrace from Sandy Row forms its own signifying system and must proclaim aloud the values it embodies precisely because the city from which it has been taken occupies a paradoxical intersection in spatial and temporal development most clearly marked by silence. To write the city, to make it *visible,* is to stress its place in spatial territory yet also to perceive its contemporaneity through narrative within the process of a fragmented history. In *Images of Belfast* (1983), a visual and textual impression of the city, Robert Johnstone's fluid prose enacts this contradiction through its own (not entirely successful) desire to avoid tropes of sentimentalised nostalgia:

But if the past is a doubly foreign country, in some way Belfast remains a mysterious place. Its dark hearts lie unexplored in my cognitive map like old charts of Africa. Terrible and dramatic crimes occur obscurely in places one has no reason to visit and every reason to avoid; civilised and measured lives carry on in unremarkable streets. Belfast is an incorrigible extra parent or shady uncle, who shaped one's life but whose doings only filter through in news reports or rumours. If asked, large numbers of its citizens will profess to love the place. They do so with such alacrity that you begin to suspect they don't think you believe them. The city remains a member of the family, from whom you might at times want desperately to escape, but with whom there is an unbreakable bond.

(Johnstone and Kirk 1983: 1)

By placing the city in opposition to an unknown and alien history, Johnstone's urge to root Belfast within a metaphoric structure of recognition is destined to failure. Spatial mystification overplays temporal mystification through the labyrinthine qualities of the unknown and it is no coincidence that the alienated individual is left only with the metaphor of familial belonging. As with the 'extra parent', Belfast is recognisable in its silence simply because it is *there*, because recognition is predicated on an identification with the self as part of the physical fabric of the city which forecloses history through a literal re-enactment of the grafted arbitrary paternity central to David Lloyd's interpretation of grounding. Again the issue becomes purely circular; in the absence of a narrative linear thread to history, the self can only 'read' the story of Belfast by first being part of it and by further recognising the futility of separation from its organic psychic wholeness. The weight of the 'unbreakable bond' actually removes the potential of historical possibility and reasserts a warm atavism as the governing concept of settlement.[25]

The agenda of *Images of Belfast* is then both crystalline and contradictory. Interspersed with photographs of disembodied images juxtaposed with recognisable landmarks, Johnstone's text plots an uneasy path between fragmentary, distinctly modernist, experience and communal wholeness searching for, and eventually finding, that image of the city which allows transcendence. By the conclusion of the work, and placed next to a photograph of a new-born child, Johnstone reasserts narrative as the structurally organising principle and from the elevated point of Cavehill re-imagines the labyrinth as an area of humanist potential:

> Looking over the city and feeling the old puzzlement that so much passion should burn in such a beautiful setting, it is easier to reflect that we are, after all, human beings in Belfast as much as in Paris or Jerusalem. Jesus rejected dominion over the earth: some of his most ardent followers in the Holy City, or in the hundreds of churches and gospel halls below us now in another very holy city, would not, I fear, have agreed that there is no final solution to the problems of living together, however simple it seems from an eminence. The spires, like signposts or periscopes, point to the sky, and eyes are fixed on a notional millenium or a sweet and equal republic where everything will suddenly be all right. The hills are for dreaming, the occasional holiday from reality. I think that for most of us, most of the time, it should be enough to carry on amongst all the other anonymous ants, where reality is rich enough to sate the hungriest senses, catching in the corner of the eye, at the end of a street, the hills that are always promising something.
>
> (Johnstone and Kirk 1983: 174)

It is worth noting that Johnstone can only depict the contained city through analogy; the point of unification between the temporal and the spatial occurs off-stage in the heady ether of the transcendent moment and so remains eternally unfulfilled. Perhaps Cavehill is the suitable location for such wish-fulfilment. The passage cited alludes to the poetry of Derek Mahon and, more significantly, the Protestant republicanism of Tom Paulin[26] through which Wolfe Tone and Henry Joy McCracken's famous Cavehill proclamation of independence is evoked. History is compressed into the simultaneous moment, the point of frustrated aspiration with which Johnstone, sympathetic to the ideals of the United Irishmen, can identify. Perception of Belfast as an organic whole within a spatial parameter, simultaneity across history, and an aspiration for a collectivist transcendence fuse crucially as the city's very physicality becomes life-affirming. A broken and schismatised Belfast can be reconstructed by the individual who privileges the spatial, quotidian actuality over a reading of history as missed opportunity – an interpretation consistent with both regionalism and ethno-history. Significantly, one year after *Images of Belfast* was published, Stewart Parker's *Northern Star* similarly took the McCracken myth and, in a play which is resolutely contemporaneous in its historical methodology, again located a desire for a frustrated wholeness within the geography of the city in McCracken's final impassioned speech:

> And yet what would this poor fool not give to be able to walk freely again from Stranmillis down to Ann Street . . . cut through Pottinger's Entry and across the road for a drink in Peggy's . . . to dander on down Waring Street and examine the shipping along the river, and back on up to our old house . . . we can't love it for what it is, only for what it might have been, if we'd got it right, if we'd made it whole. If. It's a ghost town now and always will be, angry and implacable ghosts. Me condemned to be one of their number. We never made a nation. Our brainchild. Stillborn. Our own fault.
>
> (Parker 1989: 75)

Again Belfast has to operate under the sign of frustrated aspiration. For Parker the agony of the missed historical opportunity signals the onset of a growing inarticulacy; a silence soon to be given physical form by McCracken's death. Within the opposition of 'what it is'/'what it might have been', the shipping which McCracken would carefully 'examine' (as one would scrutinise anything that was strange) allows a glimpse of the actual future of the city as mercantile and based on the economics of the Union; the awareness of the other which disturbs the organic rhythm of the litany of naming. As the structure of the play and the recognisability of the landscape McCracken describes suggest, this is a contemporaneous moment, a moment of betrayal forever rewriting the future of an organic Belfast in terms politically mundane rather than aspirational. The city becomes a place eternally at the point of missed opportunity and always in danger of lapsing into silence as the defeated partner within a loveless Union.

In locating centrally the McCracken myth and the future of the organic settlement to Belfast, Johnstone and Parker are continuing a longer debate about the significance of a city anxious to struggle from silence into a parochial condition of self-worth. Part of the difficulty within this debate is that 'rootedness' (a typical Hewitt word) carries within its organic design some sense of self-growth, albeit a growth predicated on the ubiquitous myth of belonging. The point where organic growth becomes the infringement of the alien is, in turn, highly arbitrary and one reliant on the signifying potential of the lost leader (Rhonda Paisley's father; McCracken) to embody the displaced point of discontinuity. This analogous figure leads the community through the seismic shifts of historical discontinuity and is at all times considered in the present tense. In this way the 'history' of Belfast can be read as a series of betrayals within a permanent state of crisis which leaves the city forever poised on the precipice of narrative determinism. How this narrative is established becomes a point of instability central to an understanding of the city as a mythologised landscape embodying the signs of its own distortion. It is in these terms that much of the earlier writing about the history of Belfast can be understood: a crucial readjustment in the perception of the civic development of the town determined according to the religious and societal background of the writer.

To trace this disjunction it is necessary to return briefly to the nineteenth century and the attitudes of the Protestant community of the city to the history of their settlement. In 1841 the reactionary Presbyterian fundamentalist Henry Cooke, responding to the visit of Daniel O'Connell to Belfast, wrote of the city:

> Our town was merely a village. But what a glorious sight it now presents . . .
> new streets and public buildings – numbers of new manufactories . . . signs of
> increasing prosperity . . . and to what cause? Is it not the free intercourse
> which the Union enables us to enjoy with England and Scotland – to that
> extension of our general commerce which we enjoy through that channel?
> . . . I see the genius of industry . . . which looks down upon our lovely town
> . . . accompanied by the genius of Protestantism.
>
> (Goldring 1991: 26)

Similarly a 1902 guide to the city claimed: 'Belfast as a town has no ancient history and does not lay claim to remote origin like so many towns in Ireland. Its record is simply one of industrial progress' (Goldring 1991: 34). By depicting the development of Belfast as one of almost miraculous growth, the conflation of unionist politics with an essentially Presbyterian sense of being blessed as a member of God's people allows the city the simultaneity of a mushroom: an aesthetic miracle of sudden creation which organically bears witness to its own values. That the town has 'no ancient history' becomes a cause of celebration within a pre-partition view of Anglo-Irish relations where such terms required antiseptic handling suitable to that contaminated by exclusive nationalist politics. The narrative extended temporally no further back than the foundation of the linen industry and spatially to no point beyond the conurbation; as Cooke perceived, prior to the city there was 'merely a village'.[27]

This discontinuity between two forms of settlement, one at best a military garrison or at worst simply rural, and the other a manifestation of civic pride embodying inherent values, informs this reading of Belfast, and again it is at The Ulster Folk and Transport Museum where a reconciliation is attempted. By seeking a continuity in the juxtaposition of blacksmith's foundry, water mill and industrial terrace, the imagined settlement positions contradictory signals in continual organic harmony retelling a story of the industrialisation of Northern Ireland which does not accord with the principle of displacement which underwrote much of the enterprise. As always the belief in a communal past will triumph over the assumed intellectual process of history as the past is conceived within, to use Patrick Wright's term, 'present social reality' (Wright 1991: 142). In this way it is appropriate to see this progression as part of the gradual assimilation of what Gramsci terms the 'fragmented and episodic' (Gramsci 1971: 54–5) histories of subaltern social groups into institutional forms of containment located, by strategic necessity, in the present.

However, it would be misguided to suggest that this imaginative hegemony has only recently been challenged. The writings of Cathal O'Byrne, an extended series of *Irish News* articles collected in the volume *As I Roved Out: A Book of the North* (1982),[28] offer an antidote which is so neatly oppositional as to strengthen the grounds of the argument as one rooted in a late nineteenth-/early twentieth-century struggle for historical legitimacy:

> Belfast, according to the paid boosters, must have sprung up full grown and tall, a very Adam at its birth, and a marvellously prosperous Adam at that. Belfast never knew a poor day, at least by inference – that is what the paid penny-a-liners would have us believe. The reverse of that, however, is the truth.
>
> The North, laid waste by the Planters of James and Elizabeth, was for many years after their coming steeped in abysmal poverty and degradation, for which state of affairs the English hold-up man, Chichester, and his gang of thieves and murderers were entirely responsible.
>
> (O'Byrne 1982: 133)

O'Byrne's work is suffering a slump of critical fortunes at the moment. Patricia Craig, in her anthology *The Rattle of the North* considered his writing too 'unacceptably banal' (Craig 1992: 10) for inclusion, yet his reclamations of history place the entire city as subject for appropriation. Suitable to this embattled position, the absolute opposite position to the views of the 'paid penny-a-liners' is always likely to be the truth, and in this way his work becomes a polemic form of defiance unafraid of trampling on historical particulars in order to be heard. In this way all aspects of the city's history need to be rewritten. The significance of the McCracken myth as O'Byrne repeatedly returns to it arises not from McCracken's Presbyterianism (as with Johnstone, Paulin and Parker) but from his essentially Catholic longings: 'The plain truth of the matter is – and the explanation will be readily understood by any Catholic – Henry Joy McCracken, the Presbyterian, in his last hour on earth, was anxious to make the affairs of his soul right with his Creator; in other words, and quite naturally, he wanted to go to Confession, and this he did after his own fashion . . .' (O'Byrne 1982: 128). For O'Byrne the Reformation was at best a basis for negotiation as within every Protestant he saw a good Catholic trying to get out. It is in these terms of essentialist unity that he places his hope for the future of the island. As McCracken is Catholicised so is Belfast and with this what he considers as the city's 'worthwhile Irish history' is often favourably considered against the British side of its past:

> There is an old homely saying to the effect that ''Tis easy baking beside a full flour bin.' And so it is. And for the same reason it was easy for the Planters, be they English, Scotch, or Welsh, to wax fat or grow prosperous on the rich lands on which they were 'planted.' Little thanks to them if they did – when they got everything for nothing – the houses and lands, the cattle and crops and cornmills, and all the broad acres of the real and original Irish owners, who, dispossessed by some hungry and greedy adventurer, and to make room for his rabble of hungrier parasites, had to fly to 'Hell or Connacht'. So, the next time you are obliged to listen to that hoary and threadbare old myth anent the industry and the thrift and the dour determination of the 'Ulster' farmer being responsible for his prosperity, by remembering a few of the above facts you will be able the better to appraise it at its proper value.
>
> (O'Byrne 1982: 241)

The vernacular and anecdotal style of this writing is repeated throughout the book as are many facts, stories and opinions to form a litany of oppression composed in a style which, wittingly or not, writes against a sense of history as received gravitas. With this, the book's subtitle, 'Being a Series of Historical Sketches of Ulster and Old Belfast', gestures to a state of impermanence within the textual medium that effortlessly remakes history as a series of disconnected yet paradigmatic tableaux. As the dust jacket notes to the second edition of the book (1957) point out: 'Cathal O'Byrne did not profess to be a historian . . . he was a story teller in the old tradition.' This is an opposition that Ciaran Carson's poetry would later explore, yet in O'Byrne's work the two poles are brought into a compelling and yet ultimately inconclusive opposition. The lengthy and awkward sentence structures he employs attempt to capture lived speech patterns and bring the city within his remit as a mythology of the private, yet throughout the work there is a longing to return to first-beginnings and a concomitant desire to find the moment of epiphany which will bring the fourth green field into harmony with the other three:

> During our visit to the Lagan Village we left the main thoroughfare and got lost in a maze of streets – streets that ended in blind alley-ways and culs-de-sac, or led us to the entrances of great yards, through the open gateways of which we caught a glimpse of green fields that sloped away to the edge of the Lagan water, with the seagulls wheeling and screaming under the grey sky, and the great masses of the gas-tanks on the farther side looming dark and ugly beyond.
>
> (O'Byrne 1982: 162)

As with *Images of Belfast*, the trope of the labyrinth is again invoked as an image of the city yet unlike Johnstone's liberal form of transcendent release, escape can only be in the form of a glimpse which will be immediately overwhelmed by a vision of the creeping industrialism to which it cannot be reconciled. For this reason O'Byrne's work is remarkable in that it displays an entirely totalitarian procedure; historiography, whether 'respectable' or constitutive of Hoyau's 'despised' forms of knowledge becomes completely beholden to the machinations of imperialism in which there are no imaginative enclaves. The deliberately informal humanity of O'Byrne's prose is continually placed in opposition to the impersonal forms of hard Protestant industrial development which he abhors and wilfully misunderstands. Despite the fact that *As I Roved Out* attempts to maintain a humorous and informal tone, at the centre of the text is an absolute insistence on establishing a communal past to which O'Byrne is the sole heir and from which history as institutional narrative discourse is excluded. As I will demonstrate, aspects of his narrative style and emphasis on repetition can be found in the poetry of Ciaran Carson, yet perhaps the true continuation of O'Byrne's vision can be found in Gerry Adams's work *Falls Memories* (1982). While employing O'Byrne's essentially and deliberately ahistorical methodology as his major theoretical procedure, Adams also inherits O'Byrne's particular stylistic rhythms of litany, so that, for instance, Thomas Russell cannot be cited without the constant acknowledgement that he was 'the man from God knows where'. However, in paying his dues to O'Byrne, Adams is not merely citing a nationalist historian as his textual predecessor but locating a primary difficulty in the writing of the past where the urge to establish difference has to be grounded in the present of opposition. Anecdote and an artificially respirated sense of folk-memory must bear witness to the truth of oppression and in that the individual fable or story becomes archetypal as a general paradigm of the failed English intervention in Ireland unfolds. With this, extended narrative becomes untrustworthy, remote from the concerns of Patrick Wright's sense of 'everyday life', and received history as a means of expressing the dilemma of silenced social groupings is again discredited. Certainly teleologic narrative cannot be an adequate descriptive form for a process which clearly represents unfinished business and if history is the domain of the 'paid boosters' the most potent approach available remains the individual as examplar and the myth of personal and communal recollection.

Such means of defining opposition are, of course, not confined to Belfast. Seamus Deane, considering his Derry birthplace in an autobiographical essay, 'Why Bogside?' (1971), more self-consciously deploys these techniques in locating his own sense of place and community while remaining constantly aware of the possibility of betrayal:

> The Bogside in Derry was a street, now it is a condition. Many who aspire to the last never saw the first, and many who did see it responded with

visible distaste. The Bogside and its neighbouring streets lay flat on the floor of a narrowed valley. Above it towards Belfast, rose the walls, the Protestant Cathedral, the pillared statue of Governor Walker, the whole apparatus of Protestant domination. *History shadowed our faces.* Behind us rose the middle class Catholic quarter, no Bogsiders in those days. The drifting aromas of poverty were pungent and constant reminders to the inhabitants of those upper heights that, if the Protestant Ascendency was justified by the *freaks of history*, class distinction had the merciful support of geography. We lived below and between. [Emphases added.]

(Deane 1971: 1)

Although Deane's prose has often been structured around a strict binary framework[29] it is, perhaps, particularly appropriate that images of siege should form his essay on Derry. Again history as a concept is associated with Protestant unionism; a restrictive force that not only prevents an unequivocal view of the situation but which can be blamed for the disastrous presence of the Protestant Ascendency. In this totality Deane's Bogsiders function as disruptive elements in that they constitute a marginalised grouping 'below and between' the dominant power relationships of class and religion. This position is amenable to Gramsci's sense of the subaltern classes as interpreted by Lloyd in that they can neither be represented within a 'classical Marxist definition of the proletariat' or within the existing state formation (Lloyd 1993: 126–7). As such, the 'condition' the Bogside becomes is one that offers itself as a perpetual and unrepresented instability within historiography. As Lloyd notes, this subaltern position can 'be read as the sign of another *mode* of narrative, rather than an incomplete one, of another *principle* of organisation, rather than one yet to be unified' (Lloyd 1993: 126–7). A later essay on Derry by Deane, 'Derry: City Besieged Within The Siege',[30] restated this disjunct but more forcefully and pessimistically insisted on the geographic reinforcement of the betrayal: 'The people of Derry are, in effect, locked into the city and its history. Ringed by the border, they are cut off from Donegal to which the majority Catholic population looks as its natural hinterland. Ringed by the walls and by the zones of their housing estates, they are cut off from one another' (Deane 1983: 18).

In is in these ways that the Derry Catholic is constructed as the archetypal alienated city-dweller (a point emphasised by the fact that it is through essentially Protestant constructions of civic stature that Derry becomes more than the small town it initially appears to be), removed fundamentally and irreversibly from any sense of organic community and destined to consider his/her fellow Catholic with little more than bruised bewilderment. Deane's Bogsiders are marginalised both temporally and spatially, in class terms and in religious terms, but recourse to the kind of collective folk-memory that Adams can find on the Falls Road is impossible. The Bogside as 'condition' – as a silenced or subaltern formation – denies the physical actualities of

41

being that are central to a formulation of a notional communal past and leaves the community 'below and between' narrative significance. As the subaltern definition denies representation within dominant state formations so it becomes unrepresentable to itself: Deane's sense of being 'cut off' becomes Lloyd's assertion that the subaltern classes are 'occluded by their difference from dominant narratives and forms'. History may be tangible; the past is less so.

It is these difficulties which the Belfast poet Ciaran Carson has also addressed in his recent poetry yet in its mode of construction is suggested an almost startling potential for the recontextualisation of the temporal and spatial polarities I have outlined previously. After a poetic silence of a decade, Carson's *The Irish For No* (1987) and *Belfast Confetti* (1989) defiantly returned Belfast to the state of a *scriptible* city, and in so doing fundamentally questioned the status of the inchoate narrative as the governing principle of historical existence. With this Carson can be seen as exploring the possibility of a Northern Irish poetic aesthetic which might be amenable to, if not complicit with, postmodern frameworks of narrative.[31] By refusing to consider the rural as a psychic hinterland and maintaining a resolutely urban vision of human development, the labyrinthine, ephemeral vision of the city as modernist trope is allowed to function as a muse, thereby challenging a construction of the writer as saturated in the primordial past of an essentially agrarian continuity.[32] The effect of this can be a profound alienation of the writer as charismatic figure within the text. In Carson's work, as in the poetry of Tom Paulin's *Fivemiletown* (1987), the poetic self as foundation of the lyric convention dissolves on the page as the city becomes an area of discontinuity and fracture far from the preordained certainties of, say, Johnstone's *Images of Belfast*. Again Pike's analytic search for a logical New Critical explanation (what Jane Tompkins (1985: 125–6) terms the 'modernist reading') of such mysteries can illustrate this difficulty:

> The inhabitant or visitor basically experiences the city as a labyrinth, although one with which he may be familiar. He cannot see the whole of a labyrinth at once, except from above, when it becomes a map. Therefore his impressions of it at street level at any given moment will be fragmentary and limited: rooms, buildings, streets. These impressions are primarily visual, but involve the other senses as well, together with a crowd of memories and associations. The impressions a real city makes on an observer are thus both complex and composite in a purely physical sense, even without taking into account his or his culture's pre-existing attitudes. 'Observer' is a slightly awkward term to use here since it indicates a person who is, with some awareness, looking at the city from a detached viewpoint. 'Observer' applies better to the writer and narrator than to the citizen.
>
> (Pike 1981: 9)

It is at the point of tension between observer and inhabitant that Carson's poetry has located itself. Taking as its epigraph Benjamin's assertion that 'to lose one's way in a city, as one loses one's way in a forest, requires practice', the first section of *Belfast Confetti* places itself at the moment of temporal coincidence, and acknowledges that it is only through the methodology of fragmentation that coherence can reassert itself. In this way it is in the modernist sense of the labyrinth invoked by Pike that the possibility of creating new aesthetic wholes remains. The poetry engages with the idea of inhabitance as a lived strategy and finds in that 'fragmented and limited' vista a structuring principle. As Carson realises in the prose piece 'Revised Version' (Carson 1989: 69), the writer cannot be a part of the whole *and* survey its form. Displacement of the self becomes a mode of deceit and only '*the city is a map of the city*'.

This is a construction that bears comparison with the argument forwarded by Baudrillard in 'Simulacra and Simulations', who notes that 'counterfeit and reproduction always implies an anguish, a disquieting foreignness' (Baudrillard 1988: 182). With this Baudrillard takes as his allegory the Borges tale 'where the cartographers of the Empire draw up a map so detailed that it ends up exactly covering the territory'. As the Empire declines so the map dissolves and fades back into the soil of the territory it once signified; for Baudrillard it has 'nothing but the discreet charm of the second-order simulacra'. It is then necessary that Baudrillard must dismiss this allegory as it suggests the idea of a model with referential purpose – a nostalgic return to a fixed origin which does not accord with his belief in first-order defining simulacra of the hyper-real. Carson's poetry too, we might note, enacts a similar dismissal of second-order simulation yet in its insistence on the signifying structures of the city as unreproducible site of origin the realm of the 'real' which Baudrillard sees as 'slowly rotting' must assert itself. As *Belfast Confetti* insistently reminds the reader: 'No, don't trust maps, for they avoid the moment: ramps, barricades, diversions, Peace Lines' (Carson 1989: 58).

It is this awareness of the potential deceit implicit in the idea of second-order simulation that informs Carson's poetic practice and his argument with Heaney. If, for Heaney, myth allowed the possibility of understanding the historical nightmare (a belief which locates Heaney in territory now shared with Brendan Kennelly), for Carson it is 'falsifying issues . . . applying wrong notions of history, instead of seeing what's before your eyes' (Carson 1975: 186). In this way Carson attempts to allow the confusion to speak for itself: a process of continual reinvention in which the temporal moment perpetually gives way to a new version of itself. If such a method can be categorised perhaps it is best seen as a neo-modernist statement of faith in the belief that the 'nowness' of the living situation will continue to extend over the historical debris necessary to its condition; that even the poem which makes such a proclamation

43

exhibits its transitory nature through its own desperate rhetoric:

> The maps are revised again, as a layer of toxic spoil would have to be removed from the whole site and the view across the Lagan from the Ormeau embankment completely transformed by the obliteration of the gas-holders. The jargon sings of leisure purposes, velodromes and pleasure parks, the unfurling petals of the World Rose Convention. As the city consumes itself – scrap iron mouldering on the quays, black holes eating through the time-warp – the Parliamentary Under-Secretary of State for the Environment announces that *to people who have never been to Belfast their image of the place is often far-removed from the reality.* No more Belfast champagne, gas bubbled through milk; no more heads in ovens. Intoxication, death, will find their new connections. Cul-de-sacs and ring-roads. *The city is a map of the city.*

Carson's work often seems located in the idea of residency and the negotiations inherent to an idea of rootedness; dense geographic and etymological linkages are hinted at and psychic journeys are conducted through the local speech idioms, yet despite this Carson does not suggest that the inhabitants of the city can actually know its 'reality'. Carson's home ground of the Falls Road is, after all, very different to Gerry Adams's vision of the same place, in that in Carson's work the actuality of folk-memory to shape the communal present is denied. Folk-memory is present in the poetry but is handled as 'quotation' and operates perpetually under the sign of potential erasure. As a weapon of the dispossessed, however, Carson demonstrates its linkage with the now potentially murderous ideology of 'belonging':

> The map is pieced together bit by bit. I am this map which they examine, checking it for error, hesitation, accuracy: a map which no longer refers to the present world, but to a history, these vanished streets; a map which is this moment, this interrogation, my replies. Eventually I pass the test. I am frisked again, this time in a regretful habitual gesture. A *dreadful mistake*, I hear one say, *has been made*, and I get the feeling he is speaking in quotation marks, as if this is a bad police B-movie and he is mocking it, and me, and him.
>
> (Carson 1989: 63)

The exhumation of history will always signify danger within Carson's poetic landscape and its invocation necessarily involves the dramatic, the displaced quotation, as the community relives the myths of its own existence. With this the narrator disappears into the narrative as it, in turn, seeks to function as paradigmatic and timeless. However, this is a gesture necessarily entailing a self-conscious failure for, as the poem 'Turn Again' suggests, to 'turn into a side-street to try and throw off my shadow' will in itself change the constitutive historical process. It is in this way that we can locate Carson's work within the specific oppositions of empowered discourses with which I have previously been concerned as the poetry offers a similar conflict between communal history, in this case represented by the tradition of the *seanachie* or the storytelling of John Campbell of Mullaghbawn,[33] and a fierce nihilistic insistence on the physical temporal moment as the one point of surety. Again folk-memory belongs to an (alienated) community while history belongs to the oppressor. There seems little that can be done as regards changing this relationship save to understand and commit to paper the capabilities of the British Army's '30,000,000 candlepower gimbel-mounted Nitesun' (Carson 1989: 78) in the hope of finding some textual security which will weather the revisions of history.

Carson's belief in the absolute spatial and temporal present as the only point of faith in the city does not accord with *The Irish For No*'s dust-jacket assertion that 'What is and what was are lovingly minded in Ciaran Carson's novel work.' Instead it appears that Carson is involved in a desperate gamble against history: preparing to commit the assertion to print but holding an awareness that to so do may only increase the historical lumber on an already overburdened sense of the past. As narrative technique and desperate irony come into conflict a poem such as 'Queen's Gambit' (Carson 1989: 33–40) loses all sense of a writerly presence and seeks to enter the communal past of 1969:

> The ambient light of yesterday is amplified by talk of might-have-beens,
> Making 69 – the year – look like quotation marks, commentators commenting on
>
> The flash-point of the current Trouble, though there's any God's amount
> Of Nines and Sixes: 1916, 1690, The Nine Hundred Years' War, whatever.
>
> Or maybe we can go back to the Year Dot, the nebulous expanding brain-wave
> Of the Big Bang, releasing us and It and everything into oblivion;
>
> *It's so hard to remember, and so easy to forget* the casualty list –
> Like the names on a school desk, carved into one another till they're indecipherable.

As an elegy for the dead the text fades into itself; language is inscribed into language and the poem enters a world of pure silence where the competing (re)visions of the past become lisible quotation. Simultaneous time holds the point of the 'Big Bang' in constant balance with 1916, 1690, and although these myths might outlive the memory of the human dead (again as with *North*), at least the threat or promise of messianic oblivion is within reach. From this point in the poem the writer emerges from the text and with heavy self-irony is remade in the reflected images of the Falls Road barber's shop he enters. His 'newly-lowered' ears have a 'furtive look', his face seems 'Born Again', he looks like 'someone else' and begins to feel a 'new man'.

As the barber begins a submerged narrative about paramilitary activity, the 'poem' becomes dramatic monologue, the poet is remade as function of the text, and history and myth have blended indistinguishably. It is only with the final stanza that release, rather than closure, is suggested, and with it the reader is encouraged to revisit other parts of *Belfast Confetti* as the volume increasingly gives up on a notional direct referentiality and begins repeating versions of its own textual procedure:

> Turning into Tomb Street, I begin to feel a new man.
> Perfume breathed from somewhere, opening avenues of love, or
>   something déjà vu.

Ultimately, however, we should be wary of seeing Carson's poetry as anything other than second-order *simulacra* as, for all its referential procedures, it insists upon the idea of defining moments and territories. The city is *there*, in the dimensions of the present moment, and it is only somnambulistic reading habits which allow it to be anything else. If the city is a map of the city the poem is a version of the same self-fulfilling purpose; a paradigm of the victory of displaced myth to be endlessly repeated. The methodology of the text contains the awareness of displacement as sickness, but both *The Irish For No* and *Belfast Confetti* allow for the possibility of defeating a Benjamin–like nihilism by offering their own route to Barthes's scriptible state. This though is a possibility based on an extreme internal scepticism. Unsure of its occupancy of the site of second-order simulation, the poetry will nevertheless affirm this position if it confirms the presence of the first-order of the 'real' within hierarchies of power.

If Carson's poetry is distinctive in its fusing of geography and communal perceptions of the past, a similar interest in the manipulation of homogeneous narratives can be found in the work of two young Belfast novelists: Glenn Patterson and Robert McLiam Wilson. Although it would be premature to endorse the opinion that posits these writers as leaders of an Ulster fiction revival,[34] the appearance of their books has allowed the debate on Northern Irish identity to be relocated, albeit briefly, in discourses other than the poetic and to suggest other forms of cultural expression. Prose fiction has been a much-practised although long-neglected form of writing in the North, with written expressions of cultural identity tending to favour poetry or drama, so it is perhaps appropriate to conclude a discussion on this theme with reference to the novel as communal form.

In *Imagined Communities* Benedict Anderson (1991: 25) suggests that the novel form marks a particular stage in the development of homogeneous communities in that 'it is clearly a device for the presentation of simultaneity in "homogeneous, empty time," or a complex gloss upon the word "meanwhile" '. With this, it is important to note that Anderson does not link nationalism to this tendency explicitly, but rather constructs it as a 'precise analogue'; the primary significance of the form remains as a means of illustrating anonymous yet shared cultural activity through a reimagining of historical progression as communal apprehension. Anderson's definition is useful then as it allows the possibility of homogeneity to express itself within the form without foreclosing the resistant strategies of disruption that can remain. In McLaim Wilson's ironic *bildungsroman, Ripley Bogle* (1989), a Bakhtinesque carnivalism reduces and inverts the significance of the macro-narrative for the despairing character of Ripley Bogle until the whole notion of homogeneous time and its implicit teleology is reduced to the level of incomprehensible farce:

> Picture it. The mid-sixties, the birth of Maurice and myself. There aren't actually very many bombs and guns around as yet – just a lot of jobless Catholics getting the shit kicked out of them and having their homes burnt down on Protestant feast days, adding to their well-stocked catalogue of hatred and injustice.
>
> Soon, however, will come the Civil Rights marches. The Protestant lot will get annoyed. They (reasonably, I feel) would rather like their civil rights to remain exclusively Protestant. So, the British Army will be drafted in to protect the Catholic minority from the brutality of their Proddie countrymen. Maladroitly enough, the British Army will then shoot a little bunch of unarmed Catholic civilians, clerics and toddlers on Bloody Sunday. In their turn, the Catholics grow rather peeved and start exterminating a whole plethora of soldiers, policemen, prison officers, UDR men, Protestants, Catholics, English shoppers, Birmingham pubgoers and men who make the mistake of editing the *Guinness Book of Records.*
>
> Tsk, tsk, tsk! What chance did we ever have? For a piece of normality? Not much.
>
> (McLiam Wilson 1989: 83)

This is not simply an example of revisionist satire designed to barb both Nationalist and Loyalist alike but is instead suggestive of a genuine ambivalence on the part of the novel towards any signifying structure: a process that confirms rather than subtends the hierarchies of power with which it is engaged. Certainly it is possible that the Christ-like Bogle can only express such apparently reductive insensitivity because his credentials as Belfast Catholic are secure (he would pass Rhonda Paisley's 'belonging' test), yet in the manner in which the narrative voice trails the narrative event down (or up) history lies a desperate awareness that the clichés of historical abuse are inadequate to define the predicament of a poverty-stricken Irish tramp surviving on London streets. As the character Ripley Bogle is displaced geographically so is he placeless through history. In the same way as Deane's Catholic Bogsiders, he is 'below and between' all forms of significance and is reliant rather on a subversive rhetoric designed to confuse issues of national and class loyalty. In *Ripley Bogle,* we might argue, reduction becomes a weapon of the dispossessed. This allows the heterogeneous nature of the past to free itself from homogenising narrative, and in such a way enable what are essentially subaltern positions outside of both folk-memory and history to claim an identity in the present. The novel extends from an anonymous Thursday to Sunday, and through its progression narrative is gradually purged from the text through the exorcism of repetition until, at its climax, the awareness of nihilistic actuality allows a quotidian peace to be found at a point beyond history yet surely within the text:

> That's it. The end. I'm glad it's over. I was running out of evasion. I've sown up all my pockets and I've nowhere left to put my bullshit. I produce the last of my cigarettes. I take it slowly, savouring the process. My last match flares bright and sudden in the mist and I ignite successfully. My exhaled tobacco breath is indistinguishable in the moist fumes of the coiling, weary air. I sit up a little and press my eyes into gazing service. Empty-bellied, I tremble with meagre content. I smile without reason. Things aren't so bad.
>
> (McLiam Wilson 1989: 272)

If McLiam Wilson is determined to remove the pressure of history from the text in order to achieve his own epiphanic moments, Glenn Patterson is more subtle in his invocations. Patterson's second novel *Fat Lad* (1992) analyses the legitimacy of the idea of Protestant settlement in Northern Ireland within a history of received barbarism that is not too far from either Robert Johnstone's work or the proud reclamations of Henry Cooke. Again the focus is on the self-evident reality of the city as justification, but if territorial conflict in Northern Ireland is often predicated within societal terms, Patterson is keen to remind the reader of its more heroically humanist attributes:

> The battle between *de*struction and *con*struction, Kay told him, warming to her guide's role, was the oldest battle in Belfast. The congenital predisposition of various of its inhabitants for periodically dismantling the city had been matched at every turn by the efforts of those who, against this and other, even more elemental enemies, had struggled throughout its history to build it up. Men (for men, in the past they invariably were) who had looked at mudflats and seen shipping channels, looked at water and seen land. Belfast as a city was a triumph over mud and water, the dream of successive generations of merchants, engineers and entrepreneurs willed into being. . . . These were Kay's ancestors. Their struggle was her struggle, and it was a struggle, moreover, which she had internalised and ritualised; a struggle she re-enacted in miniature several times a week in her own life, hurling herself on dissolution in the bar-dark hours, piecing herself together again the next morning (as Drew had seen her do many times), then increasing in vitality as the day progressed, as though energised rather than sapped by prolonged exposure to the city.
>
> (Patterson 1992: 204–5)

Although the plot device that allows this intervention creaks alarmingly, it is prompted by a silent off-text accusation which echoes through much of Patterson's work. History is marked by silence in *Fat Lad*, textual narrative is intercut and fragmented and, like the novel's title, exists only in shorthand as a kind of referential mnemonic. The real focus in the work is on geography and the spatial positioning of Patterson's alienated characters. Kay, as the inheritor of the traditions of Edward Harland, serves to remake the city for every moment; an ahistorical presence within a text where action (usually sexual, familial, or alcoholic) only gains significance according to its location. In this way Drew Linden's frustrated sexual affairs in London, Belfast and Dublin chart the political territory of possibility for the Ulster Protestant male in terms of betrayal, recognition and aspiration. Although such analogies may seem trite it should be noted that Belfast itself becomes through *Fat Lad* a city of flux and commercial modernity displaced within itself by multinational trading interests and observed with the sour dislike of an exile. The city no longer represents essence but becomes a constant second-order simulacra of itself alive to the inadequate linkages of what Marshall McLuhan has defined as 'the highways of the mind' (McLuhan 1994: 102). In short, Patterson allows into the various possibilities marked by the idea of Belfast the particular semantic pressures engendered by the concept 'anywhere'.

No great leap of intuitive reason is needed to connect the ghost-ridden attics of the Ulster Folk and Transport Museum with the glass fronted facades of Glenn Patterson's vision of modern Belfast: each is a necessary although complicated function of the other. The authenticity of the museum is tactile, a contract in history witnessed by its own physicality and the self-referentiality of the belonging/recognition cycle which evades schismatic historical breakdown. Belfast, as Patterson and Carson recognise, is *no place*; displaced by the all too evident signs of social disruption it becomes endlessly open to appropriation and analogy. Because of this it is perhaps no longer possible to follow Rhonda Paisley into a bonded and familial relationship with the territory of the city. The great leader of the lost people shows no sign of appearing and the eternally present possibility of betrayal may just have been passed with no great revaluation or indeed any great awareness.[35] If Belfast used to function under a sign of perpetually missed opportunity it now, as *Fat Lad* demonstrates, operates within a specious internationalism which questions perhaps the most important affective myth of its inhabitants: that Belfast is a special place *apart*. In this sense the city and its discordant relationship with its territory is, as Eamonn Hughes points out, 'a modern place with the pluralities, discontents, and linkages appropriate to a modern place' (Hughes 1991: 3), yet it is also thereby a city haunted by myth, a city anxious to find significance in narrative, and a city condemned to endlessly reconstitute its past.

NOTES

1. '[Folk] museums do not look for the unique building having no historical or cultural significance other than as the manifestation of its builder's eccentric ideas. The criterion of typicality is all important, for the individual building chosen must represent something more than itself.' Trefor M. Owen, 'The Role of a Folk Museum' (Gailey 1988: 76–7).

2. This is significant if one credits the assertion of George Thompson, the first director of the museum, that funds intended for the development of a National Museum were 'diverted to defensive measures against militant anti-partitionists' in 1921 (M. Longley 1971: 153).

3. 'L'année du patrimoine ou la société de conservation', *Les Révoltes logiques*, 12 (Summer 1980): 70–7 (cited in Wright 1991: 25).

4. Care has to be exercised with such a model as, despite the strategies inherent to the Museum, I wish to maintain that there is still a distinction between the 'real' and the 'fictive' within socio-cultural discourse; a distinction that Baudrillard in his reading of Disneyland ultimately seeks to deny. See Norris 1990: 174.

5. The relationship of the subject to this play of difference is illustrated by the distance which the visitor must cover to 'find' each artefact in its physical setting. The individual labour required to 'discover' the inherent bonds between the subject and the object–symbol conceals the actual process by which the closed and self-referential system of relationships between the signs is consumed.

6. 'Tea Lane (Urban terrace). From Rowland Street, off Sandy Row, Belfast. Six terrace houses built in the 1820s representing the oldest surviving terrace housing in Belfast. From the 1820s until the 1880s the street was known as Tea Lane.' From the Visitor's Broadsheet (Ulster Folk and Transport Museum, 1994).

7. See Foster 1989: 526: 'Partition was now a fact, though its British architects had expected it to be temporary, and built in several unrealistic inducements to future unity.'

8. For example, Patrick Marrinan, *Paisley: Man of Wrath* (1973) or Ed Molony and Andy Pollak, *Paisley* (1986).

9. 'Whatever you may think of my father's political aims or religious beliefs, I trust that you will not permit those views to rob you of the view of him in the softer tones of a husband, father and friend' (Paisley 1988: 147).

10. It seems necessary to quality the use of 'England' in this context rather than 'Britain'. Loyalism, in the face of renewed calls for Scottish self-determination and the strong historical links between Scotland and Ulster, would seem to accept, and despair of, the essentially Anglocentric composition of the British constitution, and therefore to locate the prospect of betrayal as coming from a (largely despised) Westminster intent on denying the destiny of the imagined Union.

11. 'I always remember when he (Ian Paisley Junior) was younger he was having an in-depth discussion about the troubles with Mum, Sharon and me. With the clear and confident logic of a politcally-aware eight-year-old he affirmed, "What this country needs is a dictator, and I'm the man to do it!" His political awareness is no less astute but his logic, I'm glad to say, has matured somewhat' (Paisley 1988: 3).

12. Such as, for instance, The Tennessee Valley Authority (Hewitt 1987: 123).

13. It is worth noting that Hewitt, again like The Ulster Folk and Transport Museum, establishes his proposals from a (presumably) nine-county Ulster rather than from the administratively convenient Northern Ireland. This is possibly because, despite the specious modernity which clings to the essay, it was and is easier to give individual loyalty to a concept of Ulsterness. See Whyte 1991: 69–70.

14. 'Ulster, considered as a region and not as the symbol of any particular creed, can, I believe, command the loyalty of every one of its inhabitants' (Hewitt 1987: 125).

15. Lewis Mumford was central to Hewitt's thinking on this issue, for a useful example of his belief in settlement as organic creation see *The City in History* (1961).

16. In relation to this point it is worth noting that Hewitt, despite his refusal to the accept the reality of partition, recognised Dublin as 'our literary capital' and was encouraged in his urge to write by letters and comments from AE (Hewitt 1987: 150).

17. See Hewitt's 'The Colony' (Hewitt 1991: 78), which can be read either as a masterly lesson in the use of contradiction and reduction within the poetic artefact or as quite confused. In the absence of arguments to support the former I would suggest the latter.

18. It is worth noting that McFadden had no better ideas.

19. My reference copy of this work was inscribed with the hand-written dedication 'John Montague for John Hewitt; some Ulster poetry'.

20. The poem reappeared in the 1977 edition of this volume divided into six-line stanzas and shorn of the title 'Regionalism'.

21. See Chapter 3.

22. See note 17.

23. See Tom Clyde, 'A Stirring in the Dry Bones: John Hewitt's Regionalism' (Dawe and Foster 1991: 249–58). Clyde is perhaps the chief promulgator of this pervasive mythology.

24. In the context of Northern Irish writing this remark needs some qualification. Patrick Kavanagh, perhaps the most important recent writer in this tradition, conclusively destroyed any vision of the Irish agrarian environment as redemptive or as lying in benign opposition to the urban; yet underwriting and reinforcing the harsh sterilities of a poem such as 'The Great Hunger' is the irony of Maguire's fate as main character in an inverted *bildungsroman*. His place in society is tied to the societal narrative of continuity, and thus his tragedy enacts the consequences of a one-for-one relationship with history *and* location. Later writers such as John Montague or Seamus Heaney have further perceived dislocation within a contemplation of the rural landscape yet have often located that dislocation through a complex oppositional structure (see Montague's 'Home Again' (1972: 9–17) or Heaney's 'Land' (1972: 21)) which protects the referent (landscape) by a focus on the sign (place name, metaphor).

25. The desperate unrequited love that Johnstone perceives as part of the Belfast condition could possibly be read as an assertion of a parochial mindset in the face of provincialist pressure. The silence surrounding such affection suggests a willed unconsciousness, a silence, towards definiton which invests significance in the physical environment simply *because it is there*. The fact that Belfast is geographically marginalised in an Irish, United Kingdom and European sense of space may be a contributory factor to this, as may the ideology, typical to Johnstone and Kirk's book, which insists on an absolute identification of the self with the settlement.

26. See Mahon's ironically aspirational 'Everything Is Going To Be All Right' and

'Spring Vacation' (Mahon 1979: 107) and Paulin's 'The Book of Juniper' (Paulin 1981: 21).

27. It is perhaps worth noting in addition that the two names most commonly associated with the development of Belfast as an industrial centre, Edward Harland and Gustav Wolff, were both fiercely against Home Rule and committed to the Union as the only foreseeable way of maintaining such progess. Harland would become a future Lord Mayor of the city in 1885 yet was still prepared to relocate the shipyards to the Clyde should Gladstone's 1886 Home Rule initiative have proved successful, while Wolff felt such pride in the development of Belfast he was moved to versify:

> You may talk of your Edinburgh and the beauties of Perth,
> And all the large cities famed on the earth,
> But give me my house, though it be in a garret,
> In the pleasant surroundings of Ballymacarrett.

This extract is taken from Robert Johnstone's invaluable history of the city, *Belfast: Portraits of a City* (Johnstone 1990: 113).

28. This edition is worth considering if only for the troubled and slightly sniffish preface by John Hewitt.

29. Perhaps the best-known example of this oppositional tendency is his (in)famous response to the hunger strike crisis of the early eighties, the aptly titled *Civilians and Barbarians* (Deane ed. 1985).

30. The exhausted fatalism of this essay provides a rationale for the fetishisation of the city that Deane's embryonic Field Day movement was promulgating at the time.

31. For a useful if inconclusive speculation on this issue, see Neil Corcoran, 'One Step Forward, Two Steps Back' (Corcoran 1992: 215–16).

32. Carson's long-standing opposition to such assumed myth-making can be traced back to his review of Heaney's *North* (Carson 1975: 183–6), in which he perceived the collection as based on a fundamentally mystifying principle that obscured rather than clarified the roots of violence in Northern Ireland. It is also interesting to note in relation to this urban–rural polarity that John Hewitt found his aesthetic home in the Glens of Antrim rather than in Belfast or Coventry.

33. 'The author is grateful to John Campbell of Mullaghbawn whose storytelling suggested some of the narrative procedures of some of these poems', Acknowledgements (Carson 1987: 6).

34. Candida Crewe, 'Belfast Slabbers Pave a Literary Way', *Guardian* (18 February 1992: 32); Francis Spufford, 'Patchwork of Ulster Memories', *Guardian* (20 February 1992: 23). The realisation that a Protestant novelist and a Catholic novelist from the North of Ireland can not only agree on many issues but actually appear to like each other seems a source of endless fascination to the author of the former piece.

35. There is something perennial in the comments of a mystified Seamus Deane on the hunger strikes of the early eighties when he writes, 'The point of crisis was passed without anyone seeming to know why the explosion did not come. Perhaps the truth is that both sides had played out their self-appointed roles to such a literal end, that there was nothing left but the sense of exhaustion' (Deane ed. 1985: 42).

CHAPTER THREE
'This Thing Could Rule the World': Northern Writing and the Idea of Coterie

NORTHERN MYTHS AND COMMUNAL SATIRES

> Or more fancifully, we could take Dineen's *poem* and let Belfast be the *mouth of the poem* – surely Farset is related to the Latin turn in the furrow known as *versus?*
>
> ('Farset', Ciaran Carson 1989: 49)

'Communities', writes Benedict Anderson in his famous formulation, 'are to be distinguished, not by their falsity/genuineness, but by the style in which they are imagined' (Anderson 1991: 6). As I demonstrated in the previous chapter, the various visions and revisions of Belfast provided an affective system of creative oppositions which enabled the writerly self to find expression of the humanist subject. The struggle to emerge from a provincial nightmare into a condition of parochial worth was enacted through the affirming qualities of the city's physical fabric which, in turn, served to displace the perceived broken and schismatised historical legacy of the province.

There are clearly many necessary reasons why such a manoeuvre occurred. The ongoing appeal of John Hewitt's regionalist agenda (since developed as a lived system of political thought) that made this tendency explicit had the concomitant capability to transcend the essentially bourgeois world of values appropriate to an increasingly institutionally-based aesthetic practice while being able to comment indirectly on the sectarian strife of another (assumedly) different section of the community. Emphasis on a shared and recognisable cityscape allowed and allows this implicit condemnation to function, and in so doing could offer at least the opportunity to subtend both sectarian and class difference. Imaginative diversity might then restate itself and flourish amidst the sometimes dangerous but always fundamentally honest environs of the Belfast landscape. Through this everyone could find their own particularised psychic hinterland, and 'identity' as a key aesthetic determinant

.could gain its fully realised (and now central) resonance.

Crucially, this tendency is classically mythic (from the Greek *muthos* denoting both mystification and message) in that it is an emanation of bourgeois ideology into hostile territory and can be described, using Roland Barthes's formulation, as *the privation of History*: 'Myth deprives the object of which it speaks of all History. In it, history evaporates. It is a kind of ideal servant: it prepares all things, brings them, lays them out, the master arrives, it silently disappears; all that is left for one to do is to enjoy this beautiful object without wondering where it comes from. Or even better: it can only come from eternity' (Barthes 1987: 151). In this way, as with Carson's playful analysis of the etymology of 'Belfast', the city creates both the possibility for text and the possibility of audience, and so becomes the 'mouth' of the poem. The self-identification of this audience as bourgeois is discreetly overplayed by an identification predicated on a physical actuality, and thus the potential for a 'writing community' which superficially appears to be above the bearpit of sectarianism arises. Indeed it may be the *only* way in which Belfast can support a non-religiously aligned writing community.

That said, although through this approach an uncharted mythic landscape may seem to spread in all directions, it would be a shallow choice simply to attempt a rehistoricisation of these myths in the hope of finding truth. They are myths chiefly because they fulfill an affective need as *messages* requiring interpretation and as such their demolition would leave little amidst the ruins. Moreover, as Benedict Anderson recognised in his analysis of nationalism, such an approach cannot be resolved in terms of a true/false opposition nor can a linear narration quantify that which is 'unfulfilled in every instant' (Benjamin 1977: 134). Northern Irish writing and culture, to step beyond the confines of Belfast, has long been developed according to a number of mythic scenarios and within a number of oppositional relationships. Without recognising the validity of such myths as *actual* social determinants the astonishing rise of Northern writing, and poetry especially, is not determinable. Such an acknowledgement then should not serve to belittle the significance of this cultural activity or its efficacy as an effective means of voicing concerns and issues which had previously lacked expression. The most striking aspect of the work undertaken through this period is the ever-present sense of individuals constructing out of the analogies and models available to them an aesthetic that was both responsible to, and independent of, the unprecedented political and social crisis. To an extent there are now more sophisticated analyses to hand, and in retrospect much of this early theorising has been criticised thoroughly, yet the essential coherence of the dominant positions as they were formulated through this period is, in itself, a remarkable achievement.

As a framework to these manoeuvres perhaps the most pervasive narrative mythic structure of the province's cultural fortunes has been that which charts an irresistible development from philistinic backwardness to a sense of hyperborean renaissance, all conducted against the background of the most prolonged conflict in Europe since the Second World War. With such a reading the covert implication of this progression stresses the inexorable triumph of bourgeois values through the process of Barthes's sense of *identification* (Barthes 1987: 151). The bourgeois mindset allows assimilation of difference (Belfast as mythic territory) or exoticisation of difference ('the troubles' as irreducibly alien and therefore suitable only for bemused observation) creating a structure of opposition which does not require an actual understanding of the relationships within the tensions of society based on any form of relativism. Perhaps for these reasons it is logical that the rise of Northern culture is most clearly identifiable in terms of poetry.

Anderson, writing on the nation-state, considers the novel as the true formal expression of national consciousness, in that it is immersed in the concept of a 'sociological organism moving calendrically through homogeneous, empty time' (Anderson 1991: 26). By citing examples of how this functions in relation to the development of print-capitalism his argument is persuasive yet, crucially for the example of Northern Ireland, such reliance on submerged heterogeneous narration can only be ascribed within a society which already has confidence in the idea of shared, simultaneous activity. Northern Ireland is no such community and displays no possibility that it will attain such a status in the immediate future.

Indeed as W.J. McCormack has pointed out (McCormack 1986: 16), interpretative models of Northern Ireland itself are often analogous to the methodology of Practical Criticism: the 'text' of the province is immune to the extrinsics of context and contradiction and bears physical witness to its own values in a manner which resists any analysis of its lines of torsion. In this way it exists as the self-evident equivalent of the verbal icon embodying the 'integrity of that cultural artefact'. That poetry, then, has become the dominant cultural manifestation of the province suggests both a fundamental, if little recognised, difference within societal structure which prevents the novel charting the progression through empty time of a self-identifying people, and also distinctive factors within the model of poetic use which has been predominantly employed by Northern poets that prevents self-recognition of itself as a bourgeois activity. For the purposes of this argument this language usage refers, following Balibar and Macherey, to a social *contradiction* 'perpetually reproduced via the process which surmounts it' (Balibar and Macherey 1978: 6). Such poetry can be termed the poetics of identity.

John Wilson Foster, a critic moving to a position of complex right-wing radicalism, perceives just this scenario not only favourably but from within a narrative of structured time suitable to his own rationalising instincts: 'Besides, the autonomous individual may be a bourgeois humanist fantasy, but many of us in Ireland would like to enjoy that fantasy, thank you very much. We have had the psychological feudalism, as it were, of nationalism and oppressive religion: it would be foolish for us to embrace the psychological socialism of poststructuralism before reaping the rewards of psychological *embourgeoisment*' (Allen and Wilcox 1989: 101).

Analysis of Foster's combative rhetoric throughout this 1985 conference paper bears its own reward, and a consideration of the role of post-structuralism as the eternal other to a fledgling Northern Irish writing will have to wait until a later chapter, yet it is worth noting that if bourgeois humanism can be perceived as fantasy, even a useful fantasy, then it has failed fundamentally as an agent for mythologisation and as such becomes internally self-defeating. The autonomous individual must be essentially that alone and cannot be contextualised within a narrative which denies the subject's right to self-determination. Rather, Foster's narrative model speaks loudly of the inexorable triumph of bourgeois values central to its conception, to which I have made earlier reference.

Indeed, within the structures of Anderson's model, nationalism is not a precursor to bourgeois models of thought but can be seen as demanding such strictures for its own success – an awareness complicated although not contradicted by the fact that the rise of the Northern Irish middle class in both communities has been accompanied by a decline in effective democratic institutions over the same period. Such a reading therefore problematises Foster's belief that nationalism is a 'feudal' phase in the development of Irish culture, as it is precisely within the development of *embourgeoisment*, contingent or otherwise, that it is likely to reassert itself.

However, for all Foster's protestations of clear ideological vision, the model is, in itself, a useful example of authentic bourgeois mythologising in its reliance on *identification*. As an individual member of the Northern Irish bourgeoisie Foster can identify fundamentally with other humanists while filtering out the elements of nationalism and oppressive religion which necessarily constitute the other. Religion and nationalism are no longer simply alternative systems of thought but are irreducibly alien and suitable only for observation from a hermetically sealed point of shared security.

'The Critical Condition of Ulster', however, aspires to the status of an anomaly within bourgeois Northern Irish ideology through the almost clinical self-awareness which it displays. The negotiations implicit to the formation of identity are naturally covert: reliant on an unconscious yet assumed shared system of values which cyclically insist on a recognition of the self as autonomous within a common landscape of referents. This is a fundamentally contradictory position, and it is poetry, perceived as a specific form of language usage, which has most ably functioned as a reconciliatory medium. The form, as David Lloyd has noted in relation to the work of Seamus Heaney, has prevented any thorough consideration of the bourgeois subject and yet still enabled the sounding of an illusory note of analytic scruple suitable to the concerns of the community (Lloyd 1993: 15). That poetic models in Northern Ireland have often chosen to carry this burden derives, we can argue, from a subtle warping of a bourgeois sense of the aesthetic as classically defined by Raymond Williams in *Keywords*: 'It is an element in the divided modern consciousness of *art* and society: a reference beyond social use and social evaluation which, like one special meaning of *culture*, is intended to express a human dimension which the dominant version of *society* appears to exclude' (Williams 1983: 32).

It is an indicator of such distortion that Michael Longley's response in a remarkable article from 1969, 'Strife and the Ulster Poet', to the jibe that the 'Malone road fiddles while the Falls Road burns' (M. Longley 1969: 11) could be (perhaps *had* to be) framed in terms poetic rather than societal. Although he admits to 'having been caught out by events', he nevertheless employs a range of mythological tropes coherent with Barthes's analysis of myth in his desire to render the poetic and the individual coherent and autonomous:

> I accept, as I must, the criticism of the slogan 'Malone Road fiddles while the Falls Road burns', the implication that the still and heartless centre of the hurricane is the civic inactivity of liberals like myself. Nevertheless I have to insist that poetry is an act which in the broadest sense can be judged political, a normal human activity; that my own poetry, if any good, will be of value in Ulster more than anywhere else. . . . As a poet I insist that the imagination has a life of *its* own, a life that has to be saved: if it isn't everything else will be lost.
>
> (M. Longley 1969: 11)

There is an absence at the centre of this justification that suggests a tautologous and universalist structure. Although courageous in its engagement, Longley's protestations have to become articles of faith because any analysis of *why* imaginative autonomy is central to a conception of civilisation, even if it were possible, would require an acknowledgement that such a verity is an acquired and distinct position open to rational and empirical enquiry. To protect this central truth Longley has to sacrifice his own civic individuality to the requirements of the imagination, yet – and this is where the divergence from Williams's definition of the aesthetic is most clearly marked – he is protected by his own acceptance of the role as custodian of such imagination. His argument cannot uphold a direct correlation between the values implicit to Malone Road life and such imaginative independence, yet it remains a function of it.

As Longley noted in his introduction to *Causeway: The Arts in Ulster*, 'confronted with tragedy in his own community, as he has been in Ulster, the artist might be inclined to question the validity or at least the usefulness of his vocation' (M. Longley 1971: 9). This artificial schism, obvious perhaps to those on the burning Falls Road, becomes naturalised, thereby subtending the class schism to which 'Strife and the Ulster Poet' initially appears to be attending under the more profound relationship of humanity to the aesthetic. Longley has to 'insist' on the primacy of this model because his prose at this stage inhabits a strategic second-order language, whereby the maxim (for example: 'imagination has a life of its own which must be saved or everything else will be lost') is inscribed with a self-evident eternity which disguises the contingent reasons for its construction. By concealing the reasons for its production in this way, Longley's article proffers a methodology for the survival of a distinct, if fledgling, bourgeois ideology in time of crisis.

As I will demonstrate, Longley found a more tangible expression of this belief through his pioneering work with the Arts Council where the development of regional arts could function as a necessary counter to the mainstream cultural activity of the Council as represented by the non–indigenous forms of opera and classical music. However, this institutional position was only one that could be adopted gradually, and it is of importance to note that one of the strategies of 'Strife and the Ulster Poet' was to maintain an oppositional role for the aesthetic in the face of codified and empowered violence. While offering poetry as a dissident discourse the focus of its dissent was left suitably vague, and thus the potential available audience could remain as wide (and, crucially, as *generous*) as possible.

This language of analytic scruple was to be tested many times as the Northern Irish crisis lengthened and extended, and the bare bones of the myth system Longley sketched in 1969 can now be seen to have developed into a fully realised structure of coterie and autonomy with its own self-regulating code of ethics. With this, the establishment of an atmosphere amenable to such coterie-building energies was an achievement in itself and one recognised by Longley as early as 1971, when he contrasted the previously isolated poetic voices occasionally found in Northern Ireland with 'the sort of local coterie or group which, whatever the originality of its individuals, can inspire its different members and help to extend the imaginative estate of the community to which it belongs' (M. Longley 1971: 95). Indeed, it is within the growing efficacy of the fundamentally bourgeois formations of the Northern Irish poetic community to self-preserve and develop that any sense of cultural renaissance has to be placed. The existence of a cultural movement through which poetry in the North need only be answerable to the community through its own values was the ultimate triumph of this ideology and this was, itself, only remarkable in that the presence of such a system in Northern Ireland was so recent a phenomenon.

Again, despite the pervasive strategies of tradition, the justifying precursors for cultural activity in the North can be seen to have contingent origins. Although it would be misleading to offer a point of beginning for such a development, it is acceptable to trace the rise of this tendency as and when it is marked by self-conscious activity leading towards the desired state of poetic autonomy and commitment. Signs of this achievement can be perceived in the creation of a writing community distinct from London and Dublin; a community not primarily defined by sectarian division; and a community strong enough to allow the personal repudiation of its influence on the part of individual members not only to bear witness to the individuated qualities of that writer's poetry but not to seriously affect the overall credibility of a distinct Northern aesthetic.

As a self-sustaining mature mythological system bearing the signs of narrative coherency, certain events within this inexorable progression now gain central mythic importance. James Simmons's pioneering[1] call for cultural revolution through the medium of his literary journal *The Honest Ulsterman*, the formation and dissolution of 'The Group', Seamus Heaney's 'flight' to Wicklow, consistent and determined attacks on the structure of Dublin's literary life and the refinement of the North's own specific brand of poetic begrudgery all now seem clearly identifiable and distinct events. Moreover, as self-conscious activity, the ghost of analogy shadows events: the mature and paternal John Hewitt is reconstructed as W.B. Yeats, Michael Foley is reread as Flann O'Brien, James Simmons looks in vain for the new Ulster Sean O'Casey and John Montague laments that 'we have a Brian but not a William Faulkner' (Montague 1970: 1).

Although the history of aesthetic production cannot be reduced to a pattern of cause and effect, it is testament to the success of Northern Irish poetry that such a sign hunt can be undertaken at this point of transverse time as the past seems to perceptibly move from silence into allegory. Metaphor dominates the interpretation of narrative matter; Northern Ireland as writerly event becomes a world of pure signs coded for posterity through signifying practice. With this displacement, irony, both in response to the violence and in response to what Jack Holland perceived as 'Northern self-consciousness and a feeling of cultural inferiority in relation to "the South" ' (Holland 1975: 19), became the dominant method of defining the imaginative community of writers: an internal satire on the notional idea of a liberal coterie during a time of civil war which worked successfully because it both questioned and confirmed such guilt.

A small man with coke-bottle-bottom glasses is making an earnest speech 'When that army place on Malone Road was blown up you know they were starting to say it was getting a bit near home now so where the hell do you think it's been I said where the hell do you think it's been for the last twelve months' which is greeted with murmurs of 'This is it' and 'This is the thing.' Then someone draws the Berkley [*sic*] – Paris – Ulster analogy, moving a hand across in front of his face to indicate the slow spread of violence. And someone else says it would be great if the ferment threw up an O'Casey which leads on to the cultural Siberia question, a man from the BBC adopting the role of defence counsel, 'I don't know about that, you know', he begins 'we've had Rodgers, you know . . . And we've had MacNeice', a soft palm touching the chair arm each time in emphasis. 'And we have Mary and the Lyric Theatre . . . And we have Seamus, of course.'

Outside later, I am surprised to feel confused and drunk. Am I all wrong? Soft in the head? Should I repent? Sectarian squabble . . . bully boys . . . deplore . . . minority of course . . . moderate men . . . all shades of opinion . . . greatly to be hoped . . . Or should I go back in and try again, with an urbane swill of a cognac glass, beginning 'It's all a question of paradox of course. Paradox and irony are your only men . . . ?'

(Foley 1970: 2–3)[2]

Michael Foley was consistently one of the most interesting satirists of this period, in part, perhaps, because he recognised the gravity of his subject-matter and because he too shared the desires he parodied. With something more than one eye on posterity ('I take a stroll through the Bogside. DERRY-BORN EDITOR TOURS RIOT-TORN CITY flashes through my mind': Foley 1970: 2), Foley reconstructed the urge toward cultural autonomy, delineated and codified through stereotype the contradictory emotions of the Northern Irish bourgeoisie to the events that surrounded them, and, with a naturally analogous turn of mind, foresaw in his own writing a role as the George Moore of the Ulster Revival.[3] By playing through the exhausted tropes of poetic irony and commitment, Foley successfully rewrote the question 'what can be the response of the middle class to this sectarian conflict?' as 'can the violence be of benefit to Ulster literature?': a self-conscious technical manoeuvre aware of its paradoxical position as civil chaos dissolved the ideal of personal opinion into a drunken world of carnivalesque proportions. The middle class had an opinion about the troubles and as such it was ripe for satire.

Foley's next excursion into the world of Ulster bourgeois culture found attitudes substantially changed. In 'This Thing could Rule the World', published exactly one year later, a small group of people at a private party talking intimately about 'Seamus' had been transformed into a movement:

> What seems to have occurred in Ulster is the emergence of an amateur Oscar Wilde-producing schoolteacher class. In the grip of some new enlightenment they are angry at the 'cultural Siberia' insult and demand that something be done about it. At the same time the Arts Council has money to spend and must be seen to be spending it so, the two factions combine to erect the superstructure known as the 'The Ario [sic] in Ulster' . . . but a few tame poets is rapidly becoming a *sive qua non* [sic]. The effect on the poets is that they think they've reached the promised land – they have an audience. The next step is to overreach the handful who can bring out the best and write instead for the Cultural Siberians who hold the key to fame. . . . It's amazing how the idea of an audience has taken root.

(Foley 1971: 20)

In Foley's 'idea of an audience' there exists the possibility of a developing hegemonic practice in the sense of a specific group having a lived system of meanings and values which is 'constitutive and constituting' (Williams 1977: 32): a self-regulating and self-evident state of reality which serves the material interests of the grouping yet remains unconscious. With this the role of the poet in society becomes central. The figure, an archetype of individualised poetic integrity, becomes a paradigmatic cypher for the hopes and concerns of the community he (in this case the masculine gender seems appropriate) nominally serves. 'This Thing could Rule the World' begins with the news of Heaney's departure from Northern Ireland, a move in part blamed on the circumstances which forced him into the role of 'Queen mother of the poetry world'. The quasi-state institutional analogy is fitting. In the foundation of a small but homogeneous poetry-reading audience Heaney could only function as *representative*, only serve a purpose in so far as he fulfilled his function of individualised personality invested with the concerns of the specific grouping to which he was responsible for his success. Necessary forms of exclusion become evident through this; to be part of the community and yet to be able to express a fully autonomous individual life foregrounds the crucial contradiction, as expressed by David Lloyd, as being 'between the ethical and aesthetic elements of bourgeois ideology' (Lloyd 1993: 14). For Foley, Heaney's success is therefore explicable only within the matrix of Northern Irish bourgeois ideology, and indeed (as Heaney went on to demonstrate), such success could continue without ever having to countenance the opinions of the 'Cultural Siberians'. In this way, satire such as 'This Thing could Rule the World' is self-displacing in that it relies on communal recognition by the satirised[4] and thus delimits the extent of that community through its application of recognisable cultural totems. Through this definition it too is 'constitutive and constituting' and is analogous to the poet-figure in its ability to pose delusory moral questions about and to the audience it ultimately relies upon.

While, within these terms, Foley's work functions as an arbiter of a classically imagined community, it should not disguise the fact that through the work of Longley as Literature Officer at the Arts Council of Northern Ireland there was a more distinct cultural practice, which needed to achieve the goals to which Foley alludes were the Council to continue to fund local literature as part of its operations. The annual reports of the Arts Council provide an immediate example of a direct constitutive practice which was required, as might be assumed from the strategy adopted in 'Strife and the Ulster Poet', to explore the *reasons* why an expansion in the imaginative life of the province was a desirable thing while maintaining the impression of its continued success. The origins of this process are visible in the annual report of 1964–65. Although at this stage the Arts Council did not have any specific financial commitment to literature (Longley, appointed in 1970 as an Exhibitions Officer, became the first Literature Officer) the report highlights the growth in Northern poetry and expresses it in terms suitable to the essentially civilising principles of the Arts Council ethic:

> A criticism which has often been made of this Council, and which this Council must unequivocally accept is, that in the past, it has done virtually nothing to foster and encourage the written word. The primary reason for this neglect has been the reluctance of the Council to embrace yet another field of activity when the grant at its disposal is already seen to be inadequate for the work that it attempts. . . . Various suggestions are made, and it is these proposals that are under consideration. Of course they will require money if they are to be implemented, and the money must be found. 'Poets, who are the caretakers of words, are not less needed but more needed in this age of expanding literacy and mass media.'
>
> If, as a people, we fail to foster our writers, we need not complain if they should fail to speak for us in the gate or give us our name and place in history.
>
> (Arts Council 1965: 10)

The crusading tone of this pronouncement did not prove hollow and perhaps the most lasting and substantial achievement of the Arts Council from this period onwards has been its financial support of northern writing guided, in the main, by Longley. For this reason it is difficult to over-emphasise its importance to the development I am attempting to trace. The reports that followed, if necessarily optimistic in tone, reconcile the notion of aesthetic merit with a strategic economic principle and are useful indicators of activity in that through the seventies they illustrate the rise of poetry in the North by the greater amount of space allocated for the report on 'Literature' and its increased overall primacy within the text. By 1971 Longley could write of the 'very considerable literary vitality in the province' without any understatement, a movement which, by 1972, had become 'unprecedented' and by 1973, a 'phenomenon'.

While there is a clear sense of inexorable and unremitting success underwriting these pronouncements it was one which had to be upheld if writing in Northern Ireland was to maintain its often meagre financial support. Certainly, the extent to which Arts Council funding benefited a large number of writers and publications is considerable[5] but this, it would be fair to comment, was shaped by a fundamental belief in a hegemonic process which favoured Northern Irish writing as an expression of a regional confidence; as Longley put it in the 1972 report, 'one chooses one's horse and places one's bet'. Indeed, this instinct is confirmed by his later comment in his lecture 'Blackthorn and Bonsai': 'As I picked my way through the mine-field, I operated intuitively rather than intellectually' (M. Longley 1994: 43).

Such intuitive strategies envisaged the encouragement of regional and traditional arts over international aesthetic practices ('which in their Irish manifestations make comparatively little impact on the world stage'. M. Longley 1994: 46), and so must have had a destabilising effect on the Arts Council as an institution which then, as now, had huge proportions of its grant committed to such bodies as the Ulster Orchestra.[6] Despite this, the Arts Council's support of many publication projects with the Blackstaff and Appletree Presses, its continued backing of *The Honest Ulsterman* and *Fortnight*, and its own series of individual publications and bursary awards fostered a sense of a Northern aesthetic while making its own crucial role in the process as discreet as possible: Longley having to perform the difficult balancing act of validating the Arts Council's work within the community while emphasising that Northern writing was strong enough not to require artificial injections of government money for its continued success. This, though a considerable achievement, is a debatable assertion.

It is salutary to note – lest the idea of a Northern renaissance become too persuasive – that the audience which Foley delineated clearly was not of a size or of sufficient economic power to sustain the publishing and reading activities of the number of writers the Arts Council supported over the period: a situation to which Longley had to admit in the 1973–74 report when his own sense of the extent of the community became clear:

> Over the past few years this has been almost the only section of the Annual Report in which it has not been necessary to register the effects, in practical terms, of the continuing unrest. The solitary trade of the writer and the discreet dissemination of books and magazines seemed less threatened than those activities of the Council which depend on theatres, galleries and concert halls.

Such discretion ensured that Northern writing could maintain a self-reading which granted it the status of indigenous creation even if this was, in itself, often a result of deliberate coterie-building energies. In this way it became the role of the Arts Council not to simply disseminate the best of Northern writing but to contextualise it through a narrative structure of meaning designed to give it added significance: 'Official recognition . . . helps to ensure that the labours of solitude percolate through to the public, and encourages the muse to prolong her stay' (M. Longley 1971: 97). This constant series of negotiations between the public and private aspects of literature, its independence from and answerability to political events became the Arts Council's particular role and one best illustrated by 'The Planter and the Gael' reading tour of 1970 involving John Hewitt and John Montague. In retrospect, it was this event which can serve as a suitable codification for tendencies that are now familiar as it demonstrated an early willingness on the part of the poets

63

concerned to speak from a communal rather than individuated position. As the Arts Council Report for 1969–70 noted, the selection of the poetry performed was intended 'to define the two main strands of Ulster culture which each poet represents and to illustrate how complementary and mutually enriching these can be'.

This was clearly a popular and innovative strategy (signified by the fact the two poets were asked to repeat their act in the following year) and it should not be qualified by the fact that the ideology which drove it has now hardened into an institutional pattern of continual cultural juxtaposition, yet the participation of the two poets at this early stage was still telling. The mode of representation allowed by the 'Planter and Gael' format could address nominal issues of identity and agency whilst preventing any thorough form of internal analysis: the twin issues of subjectivity and collectivist action which play uncomfortably through much of the poetry performed could be reconciled by a stance which contextualised the personal idiosyncrasy into the wider apprehension of a communal characteristic. Heaney was one who responded sensitively to the significance of the event, noting that it represented 'a certain amelioration of local conditions' and commenting that the programme 'was itself symptomatic of a general attempt being made at the time to bring the solvent of concepts like "heritage", "traditions" and "history" into play in the foreclosed arenas of culture and politics. It was palliative, true in its way, but as everybody including the poets knew, it was not the whole truth' (Heaney 1988: xxi). In turn, and more critically, Heaney's fellow Field Day board member David Hammond has commented that 'The Planter and The Gael' tour reinforced 'some kind of crippled vision of what Ireland was. . . . It's to do with the feeling that all Celts are Catholic and all Planters are Protestant' (Richtarik 1995: 103).

However, if Longley's aspirations in this arena were marked by a degree of care and subtlety, elsewhere more deliberate formations were being forged. In 'Ulster Happening', published in 1969, Padraic Fiacc had managed to cite thirty-seven contemporary Ulster writers, many of them by their first name only, against, for the sake of context, one writer from the rest of Ireland (Brendan Kennelly). To establish this community Fiacc was prepared to engage only tangentially with issues of actual technical merit[7] and adopted a style more typical of the social diarist: 'The other day at Mullens' [*sic*] bookshop I bumped into a growing even more expansive (well-tweeded like Sherlock Holmes) Seamus Heaney. Hugging Auden's *Collected Longer Poems* (Faber) in one arm, he hovered over Brendan Kennelly's beautifully produced *Dream of a Black Fox* (Figgis) with the other' (Fiacc 1969: 18). That a Belfast writer could escape into this metropolitan style is indicative in itself of his purpose, while the fact that this appeared in *Hibernia* gestures towards an entirely different impulse.

Until its closure in 1980 *Hibernia* observed the activities of Northern Irish culture from its Dublin base with a subtle mixture of bewilderment, condescension and denial. By regularly publishing articles on the state of Irish letters by Desmond Fennell, Sean Lucy and John Jordan[8] it fought a rearguard action for the forces of national literary tradition and editorially was inclined to co-opt Northern writing into a coherent Irish tradition as a matter of faith. For these reasons *Hibernia* often became a key journal of oppositional definition for Northern magazines such as *The Honest Ulsterman* or *Fortnight*.[9] Within its pages the concept of a Northern writing as a homogeneous entity was initially and most consistently criticised, with Fiacc's occasional articles on the development of Northern Irish writing ending in 1974 with 'Violence and the Ulster Poet': a self-publicising advertisement for his anthology *The Wearing of the Black*. The subsequent publication by Blackstaff of this anthology was the zenith of Fiacc's coterie-building instinct. By grouping together seventy-three poets under the general theme of Ulster violence he attempted to establish an aesthetic based on the pure dichotomy between poetry and bloodshed, formulating, through an elegant introduction, a relationship careful to maintain the autonomy of the poetic calling:

> This anthology, which has been prepared at a certain time – 1974 – in a certain place – Northern Ireland – does not pretend to offer any final statement on such general questions as how deeply contemporary violence can enter a poet's inner being, or how far it should be allowed to do so by the poet himself. Rather it merely poses the question by presenting poets touched by, or involved in, the situation here, and suggests how they have tried to come to terms with it in their poetry. . . . The structure of the anthology is symphonic in form: the first movement serves as a prologue and contains poems which set the scene, starting off with the prehistoric days of the bog people, and moving on to modern times, darkened with the fear that gripped the province during the Second World War and ending on a note of sudden panic after the 1969 upheaval came to a head. The second movement centres on Derry and the smouldering fears which ultimately exploded into hatred and killing. The third movement is the climactic section: the terror and horror of Belfast. Here the poetry is pervaded by the endless bombings, the sectarian bullets, the torture, murders, beatings and maimings.
>
> (Fiacc 1974a: vii)

Fiacc is here on dangerous ground. By using a structural symphonic form the actuality of the often chaotic violence to which the poets attend is subsumed to the requirements of aesthetic coherence, while Heaney's sense of the prehistoric bog ritual/modern-day murder continuum is accepted as an organising principle with an unsettling ease. As a result of this evasion *The Wearing of the Black* proposes a Northern Ireland consisting solely of dark primal forces: fear-grips, notes of sudden panic are struck, and the province darkens for no apparent (other than atavistic) reason. To complement this medieval world-view Fiacc favoured the poetry of teenagers and used the uncomprehending rage of those he included to comment on his overarching vision of the coming apocalypse wrought by elemental passions. That said, the obvious charge of cynical exploitation which such a reading begs, and which the introduction goes on to acknowledge, could be more easily answered had not Fiacc chosen to make himself by far the most anthologised poet in the collection. As the dominating laureate of violence in the book, he and the anthology he edited are perhaps best served by the epigram to his poem 'Glass Grass',[10] taken from Gunter Eich: 'Understand that you yourself/are guilty of every atrocity/howsoever far from you/it seems to be happening': a claim which co-opts (for instance) the analytic interrogation of implication undertaken by the anthologised Derek Mahon into a scheme whereby any treatment of violence by a poet is read as a sign of sublimated guilt inherited through generations.

However, for all its faults, *The Wearing of the Black* should be read as a tract of its particular period driven by the same instinct which led to Heaney's almost hasty polemic 'Whatever You Say Say Nothing' (Heaney 1975: 57–60). The anthology, despite its role in giving the fledgling Blackstaff publishing house a distinct identity, survived only one short reprint, and Fiacc's poetic reputation has not since reached the same level of influence. Moreover, that the book now exudes the slightly musty air of a museum curio is testament to the extraordinary self-assertion of the Northern bourgeois poetic community to which the matter of dealing adequately with the subject of violence is no longer as pressing as the need to be answerable to the community on behalf of its own values. Fiacc does not suggest that the poetry of the Troubles he anthologised formed a satisfactory response – indeed he suggests in 'Violence and the Ulster Poet' that the 'kids of Belfast and Derry were writing better poems' – yet at the centre of the work is a vision of the poet (ideally Fiacc himself) as paradigm for a truly heterogeneous society including and expanding beyond Foley's Malone Road community.[11] It is the fact that this ideal could not be reconciled to the private meditative voice which echoes through the work of so many of the included poets which pushes the text to the point of self-parody. Fiacc was writing for the cultural Siberians long after the cultural Siberians had ceased to matter.

COTERIES AND SCHOOLS

If Fiacc's agenda appears to have been forced upon him by the urgency of events there is in the aesthetic manoeuvres of James Simmons a more considered attempt at referential intervention. From its first issue in May 1968 Simmons's journal *The Honest Ulsterman* proposed itself as a 'monthly handbook for revolution' and, in Jack Holland's words, 'proceeded to throw up the barricades around what was more or less the lifestyle of the hip' (Holland 1976). This strategy, defined by Longley (who was supporting the magazine through the Arts Council) as 'eccentric and outspoken, seldom dull' (M. Longley 1971: 96), could transform the sensitive pleadings for the aesthetic undertaken by 'Strife and the Ulster Poet' into a distinct political practice:

> It is a literary magazine; but literature starts and finishes with men talking to men, and the most important thing for a man talking to men is to be honest. It is the height of human ambition, and from it all good things follow. A man who speaks publicly should try to speak on matters of public interest, but he must only speak what he knows.
> It is good to be able to say something that matters to other people. When something is said that goes on mattering to other people we call it Literature. I am not just talking about novels and plays and poems. What Lawrence is saying applies equally to good living and good literature; but there is a curious reluctance in people to admit this and act on it.
>
> (Simmons 1968: 2)

The Honest Ulsterman's ideological position took more from Lawrentian romantic philosophy than just its epigraph, and in Simmons's essentially Protestant visionary outlook is a provincial world-view centred on the actuality of partition and on the particular realisable perfection of the conceptual 'Honest Ulsterman': Simmons himself. A sense of the poetic self as paradigmatic could not have been made more explicit. Each early edition traced the developmental steps through autobiographical confession that Simmons took to reach the desired form of individuated essentialism. It was only by the replication of this progression among the readers of the magazine that cultural change could be effected. Commenting on this in a slightly underwritten work, *The Outsiders: Poets of Contemporary Ireland* (1975),[12] Frank Kernowski notes that *The Honest Ulsterman* 'obviously purports to be a radical force in Northern Ireland. However, the ethics and the politics are the socialist-liberal ones, that have characterised members of the intelligentsia for most of this century' (Kernowski 1975: 133). Kernowski's comments have a certain validity but his analysis, written six years after the magazine's initial publication, fails to perceive that such 'socialist-liberal' ethics (rare achievements in Northern Ireland in themselves) coexisted with Simmons's essential acquiescence in partition during and after the dominant formation of Stormont Unionism. In this way, Simmons's view of the Republic becomes confused with his view of marriage; a clash of irreconcilable forces between himself and the exotic other which leaves room only for the possibility of betrayal. The many poems which chart the progress of his first marriages[13] and their subsequent decline into misery are typified by an extreme romantic solipsism and a sense of his own visionary martyrdom through the act of cuckolding and being cuckolded. Unable to possess or integrate the sexual other, Simmons has to insist on an absolute difference: an unknowability also found in his attitude to the Republic in the poems 'Existence Precedes Essence' and 'An Irish Epiphany' (Simmons 1973: 24; 1986: 185):

Existence Precedes Essence

Property is theft
writes Karl Marx.
When someone touches up his wife
the faithful husband barks.

Why do TV aerials soar so high
in Dublin? To eavesdrop on
England. That's why.

An Irish Epiphany

Always after the martyrdom
the chip vans arrive.
In the free republic merchants
and visitors will thrive.

This suspicious mythologisation of the other is developed significantly in the early editions of *The Honest Ulsterman* as its editorial principles (absolutely shaped by Simmons) incorporated international agendas in an attempt to disguise the fact that he could not assimilate into his 'socialist-liberal' ideology forces of difference closer to home. In opposition to the perceived innate Catholicism of the Republic, Simmons set his own individuated liberalism and sought to promote himself as an essential embodiment of such forces: a manoeuvre which gained its most achieved textual presence in the poem 'The Imperial Theme' (Simmons 1986: 163), which, partly as a response to Heaney's 'Act of Union', attempted to ironise the relationship of the sexual act with that of the coloniser as it is present in the realm of the personal:

Girls were of course strangers
to a man. We explorers
wheedled intimacy, pretended
ingeniously to speak
their language, exchanging
bright cheap beads of fantasy,
words of love, for delectable
cuntland, free trade and grazing
on breast and belly, rest and shelter
in forests of perfumed hair. . . .

Through a direct transference of this strategy to editorial practice *The Honest Ulsterman* was left in perpetual opposition: exactly where it needed to be if it were to survive. For these reasons it is difficult to accept Simmons's proclamations of himself and his magazine as sole torch-bearers for the tradition of liberal decency in a war situation. Indeed, the more hyperbolic his proclamations became ('I sometimes find it hard to avoid the conclusion that I am the only man in the world who understands the precise value of literature to society'; Simmons 1968b: 3) the more untenable his position appeared. Despite his calls for cultural revolution, rather than appearing as an anomaly in the context of Northern Irish cultural activity, Simmons's manoeuvres during this period followed a paradigm of bourgeois interpellation which accords closely with Louis Althusser's famous work on the ideological construction of the individual as subject. This extended not just from Simmons's own desire to embody disruptive forces through the notional 'honest Ulsterman' but also from a basic recognition theory reliant on the establishment of 'truth' as a critical parameter within the propagandist drive:

> I have often heard literary people speculating as to whether it is possible to produce a decent work of art inspired by Fascism. But they are people bemused by propaganda who ask first if a statement is Fascist or Democratic before they ask if it is true. We can certainly deduce that Shakespeare had seen crowds behaving very badly and that he could imagine Kings behaving very well; but the intelligent reader is more likely to re-examine his labels than to try and fit them on works like these (*Julius Ceaser* and *Coriolanus*). . . . If each of the hostile groups in Ireland is founded on sound ideas, then it will be possible, sooner or later, for them to find spokesmen who will establish their humanity or potential humanity, even to their enemies. Obviously the sooner the better.
>
> (Simmons 1968b: 3)

As Althusser writes: 'It is indeed a peculiarity of ideology that it imposes (without appearing to do so, since these are "obviousnesses") obviousnesses as obviousnesses, which we cannot *fail to recognise* and before which we have the inevitable and natural reaction of crying out (aloud or in the "still small voice of conscience"): "That's obvious! That's right! That's true!" ' (Althusser 1977: 156). *The Honest Ulsterman* (as its name suggests) expounded its critical facility by a constant calling out of the truth and as such could incorporate distinct ideological positions into its pages without any acknowledgement or awareness that such views might contradict the unconscious premises on which the magazine was based. By interpellating the truth of the texts it encountered it prevented any recognition of itself as ideological subject. Indeed the logical conclusion of this strategy accords with Althusser's own analysis: 'one of the effects of ideology is the practical *denegation* of the ideological character of ideology by ideology: ideology never says, "I am ideological" '. The result of this, for those encountering *The Honest Ulsterman* as a reading act, was an individuation of the self as a distinguishable and irreplaceable subject who would encounter Simmons's prose within the desired framework of 'man talking to men': the 'obvious' 'truth' or 'error' of his proclamations defining the self-regulating community of readers attempting to transcend ideological formation. The individual reader is interpellated as a free subject in order to accept the process of subjection to an ideology freely.

As a distinctly bourgeois trope such a reading concurs with Barthes's view of 'common sense'[14] as a second-order language and in a piece which appeared in *Fortnight* in the same month as internment, 'English in Schools' (Simmons 1971), Simmons reconsidered his liberal individualism as social practice through just the same discourse:

> When I was a student at Campbell's College I never learnt a thing that was any use to me in later life. And Campbell's no worse than the rest. My real education ran parallel to what I was being taught, common sense demanding answers to questions that none of my teachers was asking, let alone answering. . . . However, still your envy, the possession of commonsense isn't a guarantee of easy living: muddle is everywhere. Having been forcibly bored and misinformed at school, I was offered a selection of boring and corrupting jobs in adult life, to do most of which it was necessary to impress people you actively disliked. There is little joy in being sane in an asylum. . . .
>
> Well, now we have it, the lies, boredom and evasions of fifty years now manifest themselves on the streets, in Stormont, in the newspapers. What can I say but, 'I told you so, Yeats told you so, O'Casey told you so, O'Connor told you so.' We must use this huge, expensive educational system, not to keep people muddled and quiescent, but to force the gift of freedom on them, oblige them to know themselves and their society, whereupon they will begin to change it nearer to their hearts' (not my heart's) desire.

Continuing in a similar manner Simmons feels it necessary to list individual texts which might help speed the formation of such individuated subjects yet remains silent on the fact that such a strategy contradicts his central policy of finding truth/error judgements in *any* and *every* literary text as a means of establishing one's own full individuation. Here (as elsewhere) his desire to promote his own intellectual development as paradigmatic problematises the right of all subjects to find their own subject-role, a difficulty which his evocation of a literary elite (to which he promotes himself) compounds. However, it is necessary to note that Simmons's utopian designs on education were not only unrealisable but *had* to be unrealisable in that, were they to be achieved, his own essentially oppositional position would become untenable.

With such a reading, and despite the strident polemic tone of the early editions of *The Honest Ulsterman*, the magazine cannot be seen as an anomalous diversion from the primary matrix of liberal reaction to social violence as I have previously outlined it. In setting his own (seemingly) defiant agenda, the contradictions and evasions visible in Simmons's cultural practice are a logical result of the transformation of Longley's pleadings for the aesthetic into a direct signifying practice. Indeed, despite basing his initiative on a (flexible) personality cult, Simmons has been admirably consistent through a long writing career; a consistency which has provoked the most sustained critical vilification of any Northern writer from within Northern Ireland itself.[15] The forms that such criticism has taken are significant to this argument and are to be differentiated from criticism of Simmons coming from the Republic through the same period. In insisting on both an absolute individuation of the imaginative subject and yet the validity of a loose coterie of like minds centred around *The Honest Ulsterman*,[16] Simmons could be attacked as both provincial and aspirationally internationalist without the contradictions of such a position becoming explicit. This, in part, was a result of the oppositional stance that Simmons had tried to maintain while remaining within the parameters of Northern Ireland's small poetry audience. As Foley noted, for Simmons 'the only largish audience is the phoney poetry establishment which regards him as a complete cod' (Foley 1971: 20). Simmons's 1973 collection *The Long Summer Still to Come* provoked from Anthony Weir an attack so vicious that the editor of *Fortnight* felt obliged to commission another review (by Frank Ormsby – a safer, *Honest Ulsterman*-based writer) for the sake of balance. Although, unfortunately, Ormsby's review was nearly as critical, a consideration of Weir's antipathy towards Simmons in part delineates the matrix of a Northern writing community as it existed in the early seventies. For Weir, a novelist with Northern Irish familial connections, Simmons's poetry embodied the archetypal disabilities of a coterie structure: a line of attack which, in turn, implicitly elevated Weir himself to a position of isolated romanticism:

> The second-rate poet always likes to think of himself as 'belonging' to a movement – usually of other second-rate poets. Mr Simmons not only wants to belong to a movement of chatty, honest poets, but actually seems to have started one here. 'The Honest Ulsterman', which he founded, carries on his tradition of misspelt inconsequentiality. . . .
>
> Mr Simmons has read too much English poetry to be capable of anything more than second-rate, derivative expression, and he has simply not the mind to have anything worthwhile to say. In this respect he is of course no worse than any member of the cosy circle of Ulster poets – Messrs Heaney, Longley, Montague, Hewitt and Co. But unlike them he has not passed beyond the stage of getting a pubertal kick out of writing words like 'bum', 'arse', 'fuck', 'prick' and so on – which only an intelligent poet can intelligibly handle. . . .
>
> To this lecturer in English I would say: You have neither talent nor imagination – but boy! you're good at projecting yourself. And God keep poetry out of the hands of shallow academics – however much 'one of the boys' they may be!
>
> (Weir 1973: 19)

In railing so harshly against the process of coterie it is important to recognise that Weir's attack does not challenge the desirability of a northern aesthetic in itself. Rather, as with Heaney's and Longley's later repudiation of the efficacy of 'the Group',[17] such dissent was framed within a matrix of established cultural activity which, by accommodating internal heterogeneity, enhanced its own efficacy. For Weir, the particular provincialism of *The Long Summer Still To Come* functioned as a metonymical figure for the provincialism of literature written in English; a framework which ironically elevated the collection to a position it is unlikely even Simmons would have recognised. In a similar way the 'cosy circle of Ulster poets' becomes an archetypal oppositional structure[18] for the archetypal disaffected outsider (an ideological formation to which Weir aspired): a process which allowed the Ulster instinct towards coterie that he condemns to function as paradigmatic. Although this may make the review appear internally contradictory in that it belittles a formation whose significance it simultaneously acknowledges, such a strategy was necessary if Weir himself was to recognise implicitly his own importance within tropes of stylised romantic essentialism. The aesthetic demerits of *The Long Summer Still To Come* ultimately are metaphorically displaced within a review which has to insist on its own isolation within a hegemonic framework; a strategy which Simmons too could adopt when necessary.[19]

A more thorough, and notorious, critique of northern poetry was Andrew Waterman's 'Ulsterectomy' (1979: 16–17),[20] which, if comparable to Weir's review in its self-regard, more forthrightly condemned a perceived homogeneity within Northern writing from a declared metropolitan perspective. As perhaps the most sustained attack on Northern writers as Northern writers to date, its significance lies in its locating of this metropolitan culture as being ubiquitous outside the boundaries of the province: the writers of Northern Ireland therefore becoming anomalously provincial in any context other than their own. Again such a strategy is more than disingenuous in that it allowed Waterman, an English-born lecturer at the University of Ulster, the freedom to invoke and inherit a tradition of literary excellence he denies to arguably larger poetic talents than himself, such as Seamus Heaney. Attempting to forestall criticism he notes that: 'The expedient defensive evasion of the issues I've raised will be that I have said it because I'm an Englishman, where the truth is I've said it because I'm me. It's useful to know James Joyce would probably be on my side. In reading, one's paramount concern is to distinguish the really good – whether English, Irish, American – from all that threatens to smother or constrain it.' By validating his criticism with the qualities of universalism and posthumous approval, Waterman can promote himself to an elite while relegating the poets he condemns to a disabling provincial tradition without the possibility of a wider approval. With this, Waterman assumes the role of a civilian amongst the barbarians reporting to a metropolitan audience of the aesthetic horrors he encounters with an anthropological zeal:

> Recent Ulster poetry, hitched to the genuinely impressive star of Seamus Heaney and cashing in on sympathy and interest excited by the 'troubles', has secured an indulgent press from commentators in England unaware of something Ulstermen themselves won't acknowledge, the chauvinistic parochialism and complacency afflicting literary life within the province itself. The root cause is that which produces comparable symptoms in every area and aspect of the province's life: with a population and incidence of talent similar to, say, Coventry plus Wolverhampton, Ulster is saddled by history with a need to affect cultural 'nationhood'.
>
> (Waterman 1979: 16)

Here, as elsewhere in the article, Waterman is careful not to be over-specific as to the actual nature of the 'nationhood' to which the Ulster poets aspire, and it does appear that only Ulster writers are afflicted with the obsessions of 'nationalism and cultural allegiance'. Indeed such selective blindness is consistent with the general tropes of exoticisation his writing embodies, and it is relevant to note that the article, despite the casual conflation of Irish and English literary traditions it places in opposition to 'Ulsterness', found a natural home in the pages of the nationalist *Hibernia*. Self-consciously excluded from 'the mutual-admiration society' of Northern poets he instead affected to join a literary elite based on the concepts of 'universal verities' and 'what life's all about' which simultaneously allowed him to stress his own individuation while evoking a common heritage with Joyce, Yeats, Lawrence and Eliot, which Simmons 'can't realise as of vastly larger and more complex dimensions than himself'. Within literary-historical, geographic and nationalist matrices a Northern aesthetic is isolated into a perpetual homogeneous provincialism: the victim of its own chauvinistic practices.

It is tempting to dismiss both Weir's and Waterman's opinions as sour disaffection from two English writers but this would be to obscure the fact, as suggested earlier in this chapter, that such begrudgery can be seen as an integral marker of a developing hegemonic cultural practice. Moreover, Waterman's article prompted some degree of response,[21] although by 1979 the effective myth of a writing community was no longer adequate to the needs of those coterie members he condemned, many of whom had established literary reputations beyond Belfast. However, the concentration on Northern writers, no matter how unfavourably, as a distinguishable entity did allow judgement to be based on spurious aesthetic guidelines, and in this way the bourgeois origins of the phenomenon were disguised while actual questions of cultural nationality became hypothetical and fluid issues.

It is in the response to Northern poets from critics based in the Republic that this latter tendency was most clearly marked, and again it was in *Hibernia* that something close to a consistent editorial policy was developed through the writings of Jack Holland, John Jordan and Sean Lucy. Early editions of *The Honest Ulsterman*, guided by Simmons's innate suspicion of the Republic and the anonymous polemics of 'Jude the Obscure', had insisted on cultural difference (while acknowledging that in many ways Dublin functioned as a paradigm for Northern Ireland's own Revival) to the point where 'Jude the Obscure' could suggest that: 'Literary society in Dublin, with its misogyny and its sentimental male friendships; perhaps, even in its snobbery (the Dublin Sickness), its alcoholism and its churchiness; has traits that may be associated with a homosexual community' ('Jude the Obscure' 1972: 28). The aggressive accusations of this anonymous polemic attempt to provincialise Dublin from the cultural metropolis of Belfast, a conscious act of redefinition invoking the essential otherness of sexual difference as an indicator of aesthetic/moral worth. Indeed, with the same impulse, it is significant that Michael Foley could discuss 'the awfulness of Dublin prose' without apparent irony. Responding to these definitions in *Hibernia*, Jordan in turn rewrote the provincial/metropolitan argument as it appeared from Dublin:

> I have often observed but have failed to comment on indications of an undeclared war between Belfast and Dublin in matters literary and journalistic. . . . Mr Foley's comments on myself I accept as good dirty fun. What is more important is the term 'Dublin prose'. For it implies a subconscious or aggressively adopted provincialism. Mr Foley and others elder [sic] than him appear to see Dublin as a foreign city. (I grant that most Dubliners see Belfast as a foreign city, but I have never seen nor heard tell of 'Belfast Prose'.)
>
> (Jordan 1972: 10)

It is within the framework of an 'aggressively adopted provincialism' that Northern writers could be located by Jordan: an acknowledgement of resistance, not in this case to a homogeneous Irish tradition of letters, but to a hierarchy of cultural excellence in which Foley and other *Honest Ulsterman* contributors functioned as barbarians. However, despite such rebellion, the place of modern Northern writing within an overall Irish tradition was never in real doubt as the development of a movement of writers could equally be perceived within a narrative of national artistic development which could incorporate individual proclamations of dissent by perceiving them as archetypal. As Jack Holland insisted:

> In an age like ours, it is almost inevitable that one of the signs of life in a literary culture will be constant criticism, thrown up by new poets who see the need to challenge or defend previous models; the result of such activity is usually the formation of a 'movement' or school. . . . As Marcus's anthology lamentably reveals, we can look in vain for such a 'movement' in Ireland today. Several years ago something like it got started up North, under the impetus of Heaney, Mahon and Longley. But even it was based more in Northern self-consciousness than in the need to break new ground or

challenge old standards. This Northern self-consciousness was partly a product of a feeling of cultural inferiority in relation to 'the South'.

(Holland 1975: 19)

It is important to recognise that, although *The Honest Ulsterman* did sustain an attack on Dublin writing (seeing it *from* Belfast as provincial), the primary instinct behind its foundation was not as an act of dissent from an overall Irish tradition but was more intimately tied to the canon of British literature and Northern Ireland's problematised cultural relationship with the rest of the United Kingdom. Moreover, the impetus of 'The Group', inspired by the Englishman Philip Hobsbaum, again can be more convincingly interpreted within a matrix of British literary studies and academic institutions which, apart from a developing linkage with Trinity College through Mahon and the Longleys, looked south across the border only sporadically. A sense of 'cultural inferiority' may well have existed,[22] but it was not in relation to the perceived somnambulistic cultural practices of Dublin in the sixties.

However, despite this fact it is interesting to note the way in which this co-option of Northern writers into an Irish literary tradition (an Irish tradition which could incorporate Ulster rather than be redefined by it) was an ongoing process which necessitated a suppression of any mimetic instinct on the part of the critic. To acknowledge that Northern Ireland operated under a different political and social regime than the rest of the island was one aspect of the argument, but to suggest that such difference in turn created a distinct literature of its own was (at least for *Hibernia*) unacceptable. Sean Lucy's review 'Irish Writing: A New Criticism',[23] addressing this issue in 1977, stated in relation to Terence Brown's *Northern Voices*: 'Though sharply differentiated in many ways, the cultural and literary life of the province has at every stage been intimately bound up with that of the whole nation. Ulsterness, willy-nilly, means Irishness; and it is the poets, generation on generation, who have rediscovered and declared this truth in different ways.' This is significant as, while Lucy acknowledges difference, he is ultimately reliant on common sense to force a unity for the imagined nation he cannot bring about by other means: an evasive trope much in evidence in discussions of this issue. The poet remains as the embodiment of truth and as such will only reach a mature aesthetic when that truth is acknowledged through a recognition of implicit Irishness.

This, in turn, has the effect of constructing the experience of Northern Ireland through the seventies as an archetype for the meta-narrative of Irish dispossession. In such a way, those poets who have genuinely 'declared' this identity in different ways are condemned to function as unwittingly provincial. When the Dublin critic and poet Anthony Cronin is forced to discuss the idea of a Northern aesthetic as represented by Tom Paulin he can barely

75

conceal his disgust, and handles the issue gingerly with antiseptic quotation marks: 'For those who do not know anything at all about him, Mr Paulin is a poet, what in some quarters is called "a northern poet" ' (Bolger 1991: 180); he is forced to concede, exoticising both the provincial *and* the recalcitrant fourth quarter of the island state.

The American critic, Dillon Johnston, can state, almost as a matter of faith in his influential book, *Irish Poetry After Joyce*, a homogenisation which denies any sense of internal tension: 'If the partition of Ireland violates the traditional Irish community, then so does the political and journalistic partition of the Irish poetic community, which is based on the argument that the poetic revival is restricted to poets from the North of Ireland. Serious critics make no claims for this superiority, or even existence of a Northern Irish school' (Johnston 1985: 49–50). Despite this bullish assertion, however, it is interesting to note that through the course of the book Johnston only manages to assess in any depth one living writer from outside Northern Ireland, and that being a reading of Thomas Kinsella which, despite a comparison with Austin Clarke, reveals him as oddly anomalous within the tradition to which Johnston adheres. The difficulty of incorporating absolute political and aesthetic fracture into an archetypal historical narrative of fracture is unconsciously foregrounded as dead poets from the post-civil war Republic (particularly Clarke, Denis Devlin and Patrick Kavanagh) are compared in their quietude to the 'desperate ironies'[24] of modern Northern Irish poets. In this way his work demonstrates the 'superiority' he cannot acknowledge. As many writers from Northern Ireland have insisted on the particular deformations appropriate to that location, so the ways in which a northern aesthetic as a bourgeois movement has rewritten and replicated itself have increased. With this the aesthetic principles of tradition and continuum Johnston adheres to in *Irish Poetry after Joyce* are revealed increasingly to be inadequate and foreclosed. A 'Northern Irish school' as a physical entity may be relatively easy to dismiss, but the more complicated lines of influence and development engendered by a sense of a writing community (close to that proposed by Walter Benjamin)[25] provides a framework which, even in opposition, has remained with a stubborn fixity. It is significant, therefore, that Johnston constructs an opposition between the 'political and journalistic'[26] discourse of partition and the work of 'serious critics' in such a way as to echo and reinforce the assumptions of Andrew Waterman and Sean Lucy. Politics, as with Waterman's sense of nationalism, is an affliction confined within the parameters of Northern Ireland, while the truth of Lucy's imagined nation-state is the implicit aspiration of 'serious critics'.

To return to Barthes's definition of bourgeois tropes, it is as a *statement of fact* (Barthes 1987: 154) that this can be most readily understood: 'Bourgeois ideology invests in this figure interests which are bound to its very essence:

universalism, the refusal of any explanation, an unalterable hierarchy of the world.' Johnston's criticism inhabits a world that has already come into being: a world of hierarchical forms that *has already made itself* and which accepts the cultural and (implicitly) political unity of the island by disguising the traces of its own production. 'Political and journalistic' discourse, therefore, although relegated in the hierarchy, gestures towards an active, disruptive, speech, which is sublimated by Johnston's adoption of a second-order language as it strives towards the authority of definition.

Perhaps with this awareness the debate between those who would maintain the efficacy of a Northern aesthetic and those who would deny it can be read as a tautological collision between two second-order languages which, because they inhabit achieved states of existence, cannot be reconciled. For this reason I have left any discussion of what is perhaps the key mythic moment in the literary development of Northern Ireland, the foundation of Hobsbaum's 'Group', until the end of this chapter. Underwriting the sense of a northern renaissance, in various ways The Group as concept occupies purely mythic territory extending beyond its brief history, yet its presence is recognisable as 'a set of fixed, regulated, insistent figures, according to which the varied forms of the signifier arrange themselves' (Barthes 1987: 150). Accordingly some degree of care needs to be exercised in analysis. Although as a metaphor The Group often functions as the locus of primary beginnings in a period pre-'troubles', this has tended to be most vehemently espoused by critics wishing to attempt some form of demythologisation of the entity as in any way a significant catalyst for poetry.[27] In this way, 'revision' has failed to restructure the myth in that The Group as figure supplies an effective need, expressed through a passive second-order language, metonymically representing a coherent Northern Irish school of writing. In other words, it has been those who would denigrate the idea of The Group who have ensured its survival albeit within an oppositional framework.[28] That it has an existence more within archetype than history is relative to the fluidity of the shape it assumes in opposition to other readings of British and Irish poetic tradition.

Understood in this structure, such work is most interesting when it is undertaken by those critics and poets who actually attended The Group in the late sixties and early seventies, many of whom have since consistently reassessed their creative position in relation to it.[29] Most important amongst these revisions has been that undertaken by one of the major talents to emerge from the process, Seamus Heaney.[30] Heaney probably benefited more from The Group's procedures than any other figure and even harsh critics of the Northern coterie formation such as Johnston acknowledge its central influence on the precocious publication of his *Death of a Naturalist* in 1966. Moreover, it has been Heaney who has written most convincingly of The

Group's worth, particularly in the essay 'The Group':

> What happened Monday night after Monday night in the Hobsbaum's flat in Fitzwilliam street somehow ratified the activity of writing for all of us who shared it. . . . What Hobsbaum achieved, whether people like it or not, was to give a generation a sense of themselves, in two ways: it allowed us to get to grips with one another within the group, to move from critical comment to creative friendship at our own pace, and it allowed a small public to think of us as The Group, a single, even singular phenomenon.
>
> (Heaney 1980: 29)

This essay, a slightly rewritten version of a piece incorporated into the 1976 *Honest Ulsterman* symposium, is the clearest endorsement of a coherent writing school in Belfast that exists and was published at such a time as to enter into a debate with the writings of Lucy and Holland referred to previously. At the same time, as Heaney admits in interview (Randall 1979: 10–11; Kinahan 1982: 407), he was much preoccupied with the coterie-building instincts of W.B. Yeats, praising Yeats's great 'organisational energy' in the development of the Revival. In terms of these structures it is then no coincidence that it is in Yeats's essay 'The Bounty of Sweden' that a definition of the ultimate Irish literary coterie gains textual if not physical existence with the evocation to his side of J.M. Synge and Lady Gregory: '. . . when I received from the hands of your King the great honour your Academy has conferred upon me, I felt that a young man's ghost should have stood upon one side of me and at the other a living woman sinking into the infirmity of age' (Yeats 1987: 571). I have already suggested the ways in which Northern writers during the seventies used the model of the Revival as a paradigm for their own hegemonic efforts, but in the particular opposition between the aesthetic approaches of Yeats and James Joyce[31] is an archetype of artistic development through which Heaney could declare his own independence from coterie and therefore, ultimately, from The Group itself. It is in Heaney's long poem 'Station Island' (Heaney 1984: 92–3)[32] where such a progression becomes explicit as the direct intrusion of a ghostly Joyce into the narrative (which can be compared to Yeats's ghost of Synge) indicates not only the disappearance of Yeatsian poetic models in Heaney's work but a growing desire to express a romantic artistic autonomy:

> Your obligation
>
> is not discharged by any common rite.
> What you must do must be done on your own
>
> so get back in harness. The main thing is to write
> for the joy of it. Cultivate a work-lust
> that imagines its haven like your hands at night

dreaming the sun in the sunspot of a breast. . . .

You lose more of yourself than you redeem
doing the decent thing. Keep at a tangent.
When they make the circle wide, it's time to swim

out on your own and fill the element
with signatures on your own frequency . . .

Such a position is far from that of gladly being part of a 'single, even singular phenomenon', and it is in a biographical reading of Yeats and Joyce as paradigmatic functionaries that Heaney finds a voice for his situation. By 1981/2 Heaney was expressing doubts about The Group and could say in interview of Philip Hobsbaum: 'He made the *Belfast Telegraph* believe that they had a literary movement on their hands. Well, those things generate their own power. And then we all got books published here and there; and there was your movement' (Kinahan 1982: 408). In this manner, Heaney's movement away from a group collective ethic is reflected in his growing reliance on the artistic paradigm of Joyce and a concomitant shift from that of Yeats. That Heaney found this a useful myth is, in turn, consistent with the general displacement of events through metaphorical figures that I have identified as a typical aspect of this period and location, while it is perhaps worth noting that it was ultimately Joyce, and not Yeats, who eventually wrote the national epic. Imagined communities do not necessarily have to be formed from the living.

If, for Heaney, Hobsbaum's talents were ultimately little more than those of a good publicist this should not obscure some of the more Yeatsian qualities he also possessed in his coterie-building instincts. The arrival of Hobsbaum in 1962 from a metropolitan cultural centre – he had already been an integral part of a London 'Group' – bore significances of its own, especially in relation to what Edna Longley has defined as Belfast's 'cultural cringe' (Ascherson 1993: 30) of the period. There are many contradictions and evasions evident when reading personal accounts of how The Group operated or what its motives were, but what does appear as a central, if ultimately controversial, conclusion is the dominant importance of Hobsbaum himself as an ideologue. The aesthetic principles he espoused, within a young and ambitious collection of poets, prose-writers and critics, have clearly been formative in establishing a distinctive Northern aesthetic to an extent which is comparable to the more often cited influences of MacNeice and Hewitt.[33] Hobsbaum's own accounts of this period are of little help (his submission to the 'Group Symposium' reads like a statement of evidence in his defence), but it was while at Belfast that he wrote *A Theory of Communication* (1970) which, amidst polemical and wildly aimed attacks on the then new sciences of structuralism and linguistics, outlined his own criteria for establishing a writing group as it had operated in London:

> No effort was spared to find recruits for this Group. It was the reverse of a clique; the only criteria of entry were intelligence and seriousness. Such criteria are personal matters; mistakes, no doubt, were made. And yet it may be held that the truly serious, truly intelligent man will possess those qualities in such measure as to render them far from ambiguous. . . . It is those who are unable to analyse who deprecate analysis. Once we have discredited close critical attention to the text, all sorts of anomalies can arise – biographical criticism, source-hunting, lionising, allusiveness, point-scoring – all of which make a critic's work so much more easy. But there is no substitute for critical analysis: the virtue lies not so much in the conclusion reached as in the reasons evinced for holding it. One may disagree with one's adversary, but at least one knows where he stands.
>
> (Hobsbaum 1970: 165–6)

In Hobsbaum's prose, contained like the lines on a hand, can be read the two major critical influences on his work: F.R. Leavis and William Empson, and it is of significance that it is through Hobsbaum that a direct line of close reading from Leavis's study at Cambridge to Fitzwilliam Street in Belfast can be traced. Hobsbaum has defined his role within any particular Group as 'the chairman, not the leader' (Ascherson 1993: 30), but with his Leavis-like predilection for dogmatic assertion it was not unknown for writers, in Michael Longley's words, to be 'purged, cast out from the magic circle' (Dugdale et al. 1976: 57) for expressing dissent from Hobsbaum's (not necessarily The Group's) dictates.[34] For Mahon this was all 'too Leavisite and too contentious, intolerant' (Scammell 1991: 4) and indeed, as with Leavis's critical methodology, 'democracy' was a concept to be invoked only with caution. However, such authoritarianism, albeit in a quest for 'truth', bears its own resonances within the provincial/metropolitan framework which Hobsbaum's arrival had made explicit. If nothing else, as Michael Longley has noted, such scrutiny did bear its own rewards: 'At these sessions new work was analysed with Leavisite rigour: the atmosphere was electric' (M. Longley 1971: 96).

Because of constant revision, events through this period still remain vague and the critic at this point of time can only guess at Hobsbaum's continued influence on Northern Irish cultural activity, yet the matrix of Leavisite/New Critical models he insisted upon forms a paradigm of interpretation into which can be read the later textual manoeuvres of Edna Longley, Michael Longley, Michael Allen, Seamus Heaney and, through generational dissemination, Paul Muldoon and Frank Ormsby (although it should be noted in this context that dissension from the paradigm is as significant as assertion). As a reading of *A Theory of Communication* reveals, Hobsbaum's own critical instincts at the time of the Belfast Group were veering towards the reactionary, as his fiercely held insistence on a typically British empiricism (mediated through

English Movement poetry (E. Longley 1994: 20) proved inadequate in forming a considered challenge to the structuralist agenda then gaining momentum. Rather, the book displays a deep paranoia about the role of literature in society and is reduced to quoting verbatim lengthy transcripts of (unintentionally hilarious) London Group discussions in a bid to establish close group criticism as a worthwhile alternative to linguistic science. Such an attempt was, and remains, wildly optimistic. Through the activity of the Belfast Group Heaney's work was promoted and Michael Longley's questioned in a way which suggests that Hobsbaum found in Heaney what Leavis found in Lawrence. As Heaney admits: 'He (Hobsbaum) was a strong believer in the bleeding hunk of experience. So there was an edginess therefore, and I was favored and they weren't' (Randall 1979: 15).[35]

However, while these parallels exist, the temptation to read the history of The Group as that of a micro-colonial moment should be resisted if only because Northern Ireland was soon to witness the effects of a much greater example of British-Irish interaction. Indeed, it can be argued that despite Hobsbaum's facilitating role, it is more appropriate to understand The Group as a point of aesthetic contact between Belfast, Dublin and London (E. Longley 1994: 20). The resumption of prolonged political violence in the North inevitably recasts The Group and its activities in a sepia-tint twilight of nostalgia, and it became the task of those poets and critics Hobsbaum left behind to find space for the aesthetic principle in conditions he could not have recognised. Although The Group in Belfast continued after Hobsbaum's departure under the chairmanship of, amongst others, Heaney, its mythic moment as primal beginning had passed while social and political upheaval had made the possibility of formal Group discussion on liberal aesthetics if not unthinkable at least seriously problematic.

One of the difficulties of writing an assessment of the development of Northern Irish writing during this period is that there exists no adequate historical work from which to begin. This chapter has not attempted to fill this absence. Rather the emphasis on coterie and myth I have undertaken provides a structure within which the various scraps of often contradictory evidence can be read as a signifying practice. This is not to deny the possibility of a simultaneous historical process through this period but is rather to note that the preconditions for such a process rarely had constitutive foundations. Despite this proviso it can be seen how the concept of notional imagined writing communities, negotiated through a discourse often unfitted to the events, was an enabling structure in the locating of social groupings rendered invisible by the shifts in paradigm engendered by violence. That these second-order languages survived and indeed triumphed is ultimately astonishing. Although the reconciliations between the bourgeois text and the politically violent were often either dubious or distasteful, the existence of a distinct Northern aesthetic is one achievement left visible amidst the rubble. It is how such a discourse steps out of the passive voice and into the future tense of institutional expression that is the concern of the rest of this study.

NOTES

1. It is necessary to note here that any attempt to enter such a mythology on its own terms requires at times a certain irony. Simmons's work may not in retrospect appear 'pioneering' in that the structural models he was using were largely drawn from a Lawrentian sense of personal sexual liberation, yet it is testament to the effectiveness and strength of this myth that the 'corrective' research of the revisionist will strengthen rather than weaken its overall efficacy.
2. Pointedly rewriting Flann O'Brien's poem 'A pint of plain is your only man', *At Swim-Two-Birds* (1989: 77).
3. When Frank Ormsby in *The Honest Ulsterman* (1972: 2–3) wrote: 'The answer seems to lie in attack through ridicule. The vision switches to a figure on the fringes, roaring with laughter, the possibility of a great comic novel that will be the scourge of and definitive joke on the whole rotten scene', it seems likely he was thinking specifically of his co-editor Michael Foley who was poised to leave Northern Ireland for England. No work by Foley has, to date, actually fulfilled this function, and his literary output has gradually decreased in quantity.
4. *Fortnight*, Foley's publisher in this instance, can well be seen as the unofficial house organ of the 'amateur Oscar Wilde-producing schoolteacher class'.
5. For instance during the ten-year period 1965–75 Arts Council funding was provided for the journals *Northern Review*, *Threshold* (1965–66), *The Honest Ulsterman* (1969–70), *Soundings* (1971–2), *Caret*, *Irish Booklore* (1972–73), and *Lines Review* (1974–75); the writers David McGibbon (1965–66), Derek Mahon, John Montague, Martin Waddell (1969–70), Stewart Parker (1970–71), Robert Greacen, Sam Hanna Bell (1971–72), Anthony West, Maurice Leitch, Florence Mary McDowell, James Simmons, Anthony Weir, John Wilson Foster, Terence Brown (1972–73), Dennis Ireland, Harry Barton, John Boyd, Paul Henry (1973–74), Ciaran Carson, Michael Foley, Robert Greacen (1974–75); and the tours 'Room to Rhyme' (1967–68), 'The Planter and the Gael' (1969–70), 'Life-Span' (1971–72), 'Out of the Blue' (1973–74), 'At Home to the Honourable' (1974–75).
6. According to Longley, this imbalance has remained: 'It took me eighteen years to hoist the budget for literature up to £100,000. The budget for dance got there in eighteen months, or thereabouts' (E. Longley 1994: 60–1).
7. 'Robert Harbinson, a talent too spontaneous for conscious measure, Norman Dugdale, a poet of beauty and excellence.'
8. For example see Fennell's 'Irish Literary Criticism' (1968); Lucy's 'Irish Writing: A New Criticism' (1977); or Jordan's 'Northern Lights' (1972).
9. See Brian Greene's article 'Hadden Hands Over' (1976) which chronicled the recent troubles of *Fortnight* with barely undisguised pleasure: 'it gained a reputation for amateurishness in its early days which it has never quite shaken off, and even

now it is not regarded as required reading by the Northern intelligentsia.'

10. This is the poem Fiacc is most proud of (J. Brown 1988).

11. In the extensive biographies section of the work the phrase 'born of working-class parents' becomes the primary mark of distinction.

12. Glaring factual errors in this book make it a source only to be used cautiously. Kernowski's attribution of Seamus Deane's polemic review 'Mugwumps and Reptiles' (1970) to Seamus Heaney significantly grafts a 'strongly socialist approach' on to Heaney's early collections of poetry.

13. See not only the collection *Ballad of a Marriage* (1966) but the later individual poems 'Husband to Wife', 'Lot's Wife' (1967), 'The End of the Affair' (1970), 'The Silent Marriage', 'Marital Sonnets', 'Protestant Courts Catholic', 'What Will You Do, Love?', 'Cavalier Lyric', 'A Man of Principle' (which contains the now infamous lines: 'Last night the wife was fucked into the ground/by a fat rugby player'), 'We Belong Together', 'The Wife-swappers' (1971), 'Photographs', 'Epigrams' (1973), 'Meditations in Time of Divorce', 'After Eden', 'The Honeymoon' (1980).

14. 'The foundation of the bourgeois statement of fact is *common sense*, that is, truth when it stops on the arbitrary order of him who speaks it' (Barthes 1987: 155).

15. This has continued into the nineties. Simmons's pamphlet *Sex, Rectitude and Loneliness* (1993) was condemned by one Belfast critic as containing 'suspect and cancerous assumptions' which are 'explicitly sectarian'. Patrick Ramsey, 'One-Night Stanzas' (Ramsey 1994).

16. Both Holland in 'Broken Images' (Holland 1976: 24), and Longley in *Causeway: The Arts in Ulster* (M. Longley 1971: 96) have referred to 'The Honest Ulsterman School of Poets'.

17. See Norman Dugdale et al., (1976), 'The Belfast Group: A Symposium' and Frank Kinahan (1982), 'Interview with Seamus Heaney'.

18. A 'circle' of writers enclosing both Simmons, Montague, and the unnamed 'and Co.' could not be described as 'cosy' in any literal or conceptual sense, but rather ascribes a homogeneity to a collection of regional writers which does not explicate the actual and affective forces of coterie and writerly communities which mark this period.

19. Again, see Simmons (1968b: 3): 'I sometimes find it hard to avoid the conclusion that I am the only man in the world who understands the precise value of literature to society.'

20. The poets Waterman considers include Seamus Heaney, Michael Longley, Robert Greacen, John Hewitt, John Montague, Derek Mahon, Paul Muldoon, Frank Ormsby, Tom Paulin and James Simmons.

21. For instance Peter Mangan (1979), 'In Defence of Northern Poets'.

22. See Neil Ascherson's (1993) review of Hobsbaum's group-forming instincts, 'Great Brain Spotter'.

23. Although it is unlikely that the title to this review actually implies a distinct New Critical approach to Irish writing the piece does illustrate, albeit unconsciously, the difficulties of such an approach when forming a national cultural canon.

24. The phrase is Derek Mahon's. See 'Rage For Order' (Mahon 1979: 44).

25. 'The Storyteller: Reflections on the Works of Nikolai Leskov' (Benjamin 1973: 83–107).

26. There is a tradition to this interpretation beginning with Kinsella's definition of a Northern aesthetic as 'largely a journalistic entity' and continued by Peter Fallon and Derek Mahon who endorse this view in their polemic introduction to *The Penguin Book of Contemporary Irish Poetry* (1990: xx).

27. Johnston 1985: 50–1. See also the comments of some of its former members in 'The Belfast Group: A Symposium' (Dugdale et al. 1976).
28. A recent reappraisal of The Group's activities by those involved emphasises this tendency. Edna Longley, ironically if one considers the tensions between writing communities in Dublin and London during the seventies, highlights the importance of the linkage with Trinity while Michael Longley finds in Philip Hobsbaum a more sympathetic reader of his poetry than he had previously acknowledged (Dugdale et al. 1994).
29. 'The Belfast Group: A Symposium' is again a useful illustration of this tendency.
30. It is important to acknowledge that Derek Mahon, a poet whose achievement is comparable to Heaney's, was never a regular member of The Group.
31. This opposition has long been a key model by which Northern writers have defined the predicaments of the aesthetic-social polarity, and has closely featured in analyses undertaken by the Field Day Organisation, of which Heaney is a member. See Seamus Deane's *Celtic Revivals* (1985).
32. This poem was revised by Heaney for the *New Selected Poems 1966–1987* (1990), in this extract the line 'What you must do must be done on your own' is revised to the slightly less portentous 'What you do you must do on your own' suggesting Heaney's own ambivalence towards the differing models of artistic expression available through the Joyce-Yeats analogy.
33. Edna Longley notes the importance of these different influences as part of an ongoing creative dialectic in her introduction to *The Living Stream: Literature and Revisionism in Ireland* (1994: 20).
34. At Belfast two such writers were the critics Michael Allen and Harry Chambers.
35. Despite the recent revision of Hobsbaum's appreciation of Michael Longley's poetry (see note 28), Heaney's comments here seem to confirm Longley's original suspicion.

CHAPTER FOUR

'Unconscious Partitionism': Northern Criticism in the Eighties

CRITICISM AND AUTONOMY

> For the Common Reader represented, not the great heart of the people, but the competent, the cultivated, in general; and these represented the cultural tradition and the standards of taste it informed. And the competent, with their more-than-individual judgement, their better-than-individual taste, *were* common, for to be born into a homogeneous culture is to move among signals of a limited variety, illustrating one predominant pervasive ethos, grammar and idiom (consider what the eighteenth century did with Homer) and to acquire discrimination as one moves.
>
> (Leavis 1948: 105)

It is with a gesture towards that great pre-lapsarian vision of the indivisibly united common culture and its reader that F.R. Leavis in 'How to Teach Reading: A Primer for Ezra Pound' launches his attack on the chaos of a heterogeneous culture consisting 'mainly of individual works'. In the face of Pound's modernistic desire for sensation through the location of individual, centripetal, meaning, Leavis has to insist upon a literary tradition consisting of the 'consciousness and memory of the people' and the 'cultural tradition in which it has developed' in order to re-establish textually the primacy of literature within the ongoing process of the nation and the cultural 'standard of living'. In opposition to this continuum are the forces of current decay, the uneducated readers wallowing in purely textual heterogeneity and 'circumambient confusion'. Such a preoccupation with the cultural and social incidentals hints at the possibility of a provincial anarchy erupting at the margins of a culture (as Paul Muldoon recognises in '7, Middagh Street'), and it is precisely because Pound appears to place this barbarous ideal at the metropolitan centre of the modernist project[1] that Leavis is forced to respond so insistently: 'the main point is that if one is uneducated in one's own literature', he writes, 'one cannot hope to acquire education in any serious sense by dabbling in, or by assiduously frequenting another' (Leavis 1948: 134). That which is rootless and textual is, by its nature, not 'real': a point of artifice and instability within the conglomeration of the canonical state of letters which promises full individuation through a culture constituted in opposition to a state of homogeneous, empty, time.

Read with Northern Ireland in mind, such a position gains greater significance and allows one to suggest tentatively that, while (as many critics and commentators have suggested) there was much that was fraudulent within Leavis's critical project, there was also much that could become constitutive critical activity. Certainly there can be no Northern Irish equivalent of Leavis's disingenuous evocation of the 'common reader' as an ideal illustration of the cultured subject within the homogeneous state. Yet this strategy does suggest the various methods through which Leavis attempted to construct a cultural ideal out of the shattered cultural remnants of Europe after the First World War, and it is in this achievement that his legacy as the presiding genius of the kind of English New Critical frameworks he embodied becomes influential in the development of a distinct Northern Irish criticism.

Indeed, as Ashcroft, Griffin and Tiffin have noted, it is in many ways appropriate to see the development and eventual dominance of New Criticism in essentially post-colonial locations as a considered response to the fractured or even non-existent interpretive paradigms of literary tradition: 'The Americans, lacking tradition, and distrusting literature as an institution, could never believe in the reality of received "categorisations". New Criticism methodised this disbelief, "to force us to begin again with each work" ' (Ashcroft et al. 1989: 160–1). It is through this manoeuvre that the focus on the specific individual features of a literary work, interpreted within a critical paradigm that seemed to subtend the cultural values of the centre, allowed New Criticism to gain a strategic insurgent currency and as such this position is coherent with the reconstruction of the regionally defined aesthetic undertaken by Northern Irish critics and poets from the late sixties onwards.

Moreover, as a paradigm for the act of aesthetic and liberal reconstruction the particular legacy of Leavis's example, if less precisely his methodology, has proffered for critics as diverse as Edna Longley, Tom Paulin and John Wilson Foster a way of re-establishing the seriousness of the interpretative act, the centrality of aesthetic transcendence as a verifiable concept, and the survival of a pluralist literary criticism of poetry under conditions of heterogeneity inimical to an idea of literary tradition. Clearly there is much that is contentious in such a statement: Terry Eagleton's suspicion in *Nationalism: Irony and Commitment* (1988) that 'the liberal humanist notion of Culture was constituted, among other things, to marginalise such peoples as the Irish' (Eagleton 1988: 13) has to be seriously engaged with, yet what Eagleton's argument does not allow – the potential of the marginalised to appropriate as well as be appropriated

– is in itself an implicit act of stealth and resistance which by its occurrence subverts the interpellation of the Irish critic as subject.

It is a totalising imperative similar to Eagleton's, rendering the liberal subject eternally passive while refusing the Leavisite text the notional capacity of 'play' available to other forms of textual expression, that provides Eamonn Hughes's stimulating essay, 'Leavis and Ireland: An Adequate Criticism?' (1988) with its structural energy. Since this essay notes the absence of (but does not undertake) an analysis of English nationalism as it is manifest through critical activity, Leavis functions as a pure metonymy for the type of English nationalism he textually endorsed, and thus enters the argument as a totalised figurative trope incapable of transference across nation-state boundaries, or more particularly, the Irish Sea:

> My point is rather that criticism in Ireland has, for a number of reasons, always occupied a less central role in the culture than has been the case with criticism in Europe or America. Consequently, the massive *corpus* of Irish criticism has never been brought to the point of cohering into a tradition. It is this situation which has left the way open for the application of other, often inappropriate (and appropriating) criticisms.
>
> (Hughes 1988: 112)

There is, perhaps, in this consideration of that which is 'inappropriate' the hint of a Leavisite terminology which suggests that critical interaction takes place on a more microcosmic level than that of the nation-state, and there is much within this essay which seeks to refuse Leavis entrance into the Irish tradition (unformed but stable enough to know what it does *not* want) in a manner that forecloses current critical developments. That said, it is difficult (and unnecessary) to absolve Leavis from the accusations of absolute English nationalism that Hughes levels at him, and yet we should not allow this awareness to disguise the fact that his influence and methodology has been adopted with great enthusiasm by literary cultures far from England;[2] the reasons for which Hughes suggests:

> Leavis's response to this breakdown of civilisation was to replace it with culture. The Empire and its attendant Englishness had represented civilisation as an achieved state, available only for the chosen few, within which culture could act as process, dependent on all, providing an historical drive for an otherwise static system. Leavis implicitly altered this by suggesting that civilisation, now the preserve of the masses, was in decline, while culture was important because it was static, timeless and available only to an elite. By redefining those terms Leavis was engaged in claiming for himself, and for those who 'recognised' him, a true Englishness, at once newly minted and deeply rooted. His project was, in fact, profoundly nationalistic.
>
> (Hughes 1988: 118)

The movement Hughes traces from civilisation to culture as a reformulation of English nationalism within Leavis's critical project required Leavisite elitism, the idea of the 'common reader' as a guardian of the 'standards of taste', to transmogrify into a newly covert and yet insurgent nationalist formation. However, Hughes's insistence that this aspect of Leavis's English nationalism was and remains 'hidden' to critics (such as Francis Mulhern and Perry Anderson) who 'all share with Leavis the exasperating trait of taking for granted the nature of "Englishness" ' ultimately raises serious questions about the possibility of internal models of oppositional analysis being able to escape the totalising aspirations of the ideology under question. While this assertion in itself bears resonances for criticism beyond the English tradition, its potential determinism and textual absolutism is such that it transforms all critics from non-English cultures who have made use of Leavis's work into unknowing dupes absorbing 'residual element(s) of imperial Englishness' when they thought they were locating a 'supranational notion of culture'. It will be the argument of this chapter that such supranational frameworks, while often evoked by Northern Irish criticism as a point of security, also operate within an oppositional dialectic structure which accounts for the specific (and often deforming) contexts of internal cultural debate. With this, the elitist and nationalist stance of Leavis can be seen to contain absences and discontinuities through which the possibility of critical appropriation by non-English cultures has remained. Although such appropriation has taken place essentially through the established New-Critical paradigm it must be seen as involving more than a recycling of 'residual elements' as the heterogeneous cultures it struggles to subtend also involve the dominant forms of present-day oppression within which English Nationalism continues to have its own unique place.

It is for these reasons that the Leavisite influence on what can be perceived as a distinct Northern Irish criticism has positive as well as limiting implications; and it would be restrictive to perceive the extent of that appropriation as being either solely provincial or within a totalised imperial framework. Rather, it is the pervasive influence of Leavis's legacy, which has lingered in Northern Ireland more stubbornly than in other parts of the United Kingdom, which has become this criticism's defining characteristic with Edna Longley, Tom Paulin and, to a lesser extent, Gerald Dawe, John Wilson Foster and Terence Brown[3] all finding in the Leavisite mode a response to Northern heterogeneity and breakdown designed to protect some notional idea of both the aesthetic and a literary tradition. In this way, a Leavisite approach to an idea of the elite and the dialectic it establishes between the concrete actual and the transcendent moment in literature has allowed Northern criticism to maintain the continuum of a civilised and civilising culture across the historical and geographical fracture of partition while retaining an insurgent drive. The codification of Northern Irish criticism into a recognisable series of affirmations and abdications represents then a different theoretical challenge to the codification of Northern Irish poetry; as I have previously demonstrated, the latter relies, to a large extent, on the immediate claims of self-valorisation in order to become established. This is because the critical positions located within and coming out of the North are themselves often products of that cultural heterogeneity that remain essentially inimical to Leavis's notional good critical taste.

What provides a link between Longley, Paulin, Foster and Brown are the various forces of dual inheritance, exile and cultural plurality extending across national borders which find in Northern Ireland the locational and strategic significance to allow such diversity to gain expression within formal limits. This in turn suggests how Northern Ireland itself is an appropriate object of study for the Practical Critical agenda – with it being declared in isolation as a failed or successful entity rather as Practical Criticism declares a poem as a successful or failed experience;[4] a state of being, as W.J. McCormack has recognised, dependent on its unique constitutional arrangement which denies the interplay of extrinsics to the analytic process (McCormack 1986: 16). By acknowledging this impasse, the methodology of Practical Criticism has been worked extremely hard in the North for reasons which can suggest the essential paucity of other theoretical frameworks in Irelands North *and* South. This lack can be perceived in diverse ways but was encapsulated by Robin Wilson, then editor of the Belfast-based current affairs magazine *Fortnight*, who noted during the founding Cultures of Ireland Group Conference in 1991: 'the tendency to be quite happy among ourselves in Ireland with a level of discussion which is anecdotal, which is very superficial, and which, for example, has so far not been participated in by anybody who is a sociologist, who is a critical theorist, social theorist, whatever. This strikes me as absolutely bizarre . . .' (Longley 1991: 45). The context of this despairing statement naturally bears its own resonances, and despite recent developments in the field of Irish cultural studies there still seems no clear substantive evidence with which to question his claims. However, rather than negating the significance of the New-Critical paradigm such absences suggest the appeal that a totalised neo-Leavisite cultural programme, which can require little more than a good grounding in poetic form and a belief in referentiality and transference, might have. This is understandable in that, while Ireland lacks the kind of theoretical and pluralist cultural infrastructure desired by Wilson, a literary criticism based on the aesthetic object rather than a programme of dedicated cultural studies will dominate. Any embryonic discourse appropriate to the forces of cultural heterogeneity will give way in the presence of a containing and homogeneous language.

It is this tendency which can be observed in the socio–literary criticism[5] of Edna Longley, a critic, mostly of poetry, who has probably gone furthest towards establishing a neo-Leavisite agenda in Ireland. Throughout the course of a distinguished academic career Longley, originally from the Republic but with both Protestant and Catholic antecedents, has maintained an astonishingly coherent critical programme, from Queen's University where she is based, concerned centrally with the North as an area of interaction and play set in opposition to what she has often perceived as the monolithic structures of Irish nationalism. Crucial to Longley's manoeuvres, as with Leavis, is the sense of inhabiting a fallen world: a world in which the aesthetic has to operate within the realm of the political for reasons of historical malformation and present expediency. 'Poetry and politics, like church and state, should be separated', she argues in what is probably her most often cited essay, 'Poetry and Politics in Northern Ireland'; 'And for the same reasons: mysteries distort the rational processes which ideally prevail in social relations; while ideologies confiscate the poet's special passport to *terra incognita*' (Longley 1986: 185).

It is around that 'should' that the specific cultural programme Longley has instigated gains its momentum, as her criticism searches the partitioned aesthetic for moments of fusion and transcendence in a way reminiscent of Leavis's desperate sense (after Eliot) of the post-English Civil War dissociated sensibility. This emphasis on borders makes Longley's work clearly distinctive and suggests the ways she has learnt from the tactical manoeuvres of the generation of Northern Irish poets writing since the late sixties. Perhaps anomalous in any context other than Ireland, Longley's work has continually forced the poem as aesthetic object into the bear-pit of the social arena while consistently denying that it should have to function in such a manner. In so doing her work insists on the formal properties of the poem as paradigmatic to the particulars of society while concomitantly formulating a detailed rejection of modernism and its 'parasitic literariness' (Longley 1986: 13). Seeking to reverse British criticism's obsession with poetic content over form (Longley 1986: 170–3), Longley transforms poetic form into 'the binding force of poetry's wholeness . . . the last ditch of its aesthetic immunity', and the beleaguered combative metaphor informs the reader both of the isolationist strategies Longley is prepared to adopt to emphasise the significance of this ideal and a further parallel to Leavis's own vision of the critical act.

There is perhaps much that is disingenuous here and much evidence exists which suggests that it has often been the content of a poem (or rather the beliefs of the poet – thereby qualifying the New-Critical frameworks Longley may adopt) which has ultimately not only informed the judgement of that text's worth but also shaped the assessment of its formal qualities. In seeking to examine and reimagine the aesthetic and historical links between Great Britain and Ireland, Longley's judgements are underpinned by the twin forces of aesthetic 'settling' and 'transcendence' which emphasise the necessary strategic importance of the poem as icon and the one-way relationship of life to art therefore required: 'That Irish history does not march with English history, or in certain respects stands still, does not render obsolescent the *poetry* which grows out of it. Once again, what is alive *cannot* be anachronistic. The creative baton changes hands throughout the English-speaking world and the compost of poetry accrues unpredictably' (Longley 1986: 171).

It is an aspect of Longley's beliefs that the creation of *good* poetry is by no means as unpredictable as she suggests in that it forms a personal canon which cannot allow the 'political', as direct constitutive event, a formative role. Rather, the 'creative baton' of tradition and influence allows for the possibility of a supranational culture within the English-speaking world which, in turn, clearly shares something with Eliot's notional concept of the 'mind of Europe' (from 'Tradition and the Individual Talent' (Eliot 1951:10–18)) embraced by Leavis.[6] For Longley, however, this can only be so if poetry remains a distinct language usage set against the disparate historical narratives of the dominant nation-state, as she insists: 'History marginalises poetry, not poetry history.'

In her pamphlet *From Cathleen to Anorexia: The Breakdown of Irelands* such a strategy enables a direct critique of both Northern Ireland and the Republic which, significantly, also places such 'conceptual entities' in a closed binarism: 'If "Northern Ireland" has visibly broken down, the "Republic" has invisibly broken down. And since 1968 each has helped to expose the contradictions of the other' (Longley 1990: 3). Exposed maybe, but not destabilised. Locked into an eternal principle of opposition, the two entities represent nothing more than a process of endless theoretical referentiality (through which partition becomes a modernist trope), and it is to Paul Muldoon's 'Aisling' (Muldoon 1983: 39) that Longley must turn to find a first order, interventionist, language of resistance. Indeed, in a review of *The Field Anthology of Irish Writing*, she highlights this by noting 'literature's role in the more pluralistic understanding that has slowly started to erode the distorted cultural ideologies propping up our binary politics' (Longley 1992: 21). Engaging with poetry then becomes a way of unifying and transforming sensibility; a civilised activity which continues to live despite the historical debris which continually threatens to suffocate it. Or at least that is how it should be.

While such an analysis of Longley's beliefs seems essentially coherent, it does not allow for the subtlety of an approach which has to accept that such a gold standard of reading does not exist: that the forces of social and historical deformation are in fact stronger than the transformative effect of the aesthetic. No Irish critic has been more aware of the many variations in the ways poetry is read (Longley would say 'misread') across the island, nor has any critic pleaded as eloquently for tolerance in the face of such variety, but it is only by insisting that this is a fallen state of existence that good poetry – which offers a mode of redemption – can become the paradigm she so earnestly wishes it to be.[7] It is here that Longley's sense of 'settling' becomes relevant, a method by which good poetry is differentiated from that which is mundane: 'Most critics of contemporary poetry neglect form. By form I mean the musical shape into which all the "sounds of sense", syntactical and rhythmical, finally settle. Many poems lack such finality and stay a little unsettled. The formal completeness of a George Herbert is rare indeed' (Longley 1986: 170).

Such a definition can, of course, tend towards the ineffable: a statement of self-evident truth which stops on the arbitrary order of the utterance thereby preventing either analysis or progression, yet it is precisely by such a method that poetry can insist on its difference, its ability to inspire and instruct. For Longley, such poetry, especially contemporary Irish poetry, is rarely found and the canon thus formulated – some but not all of Paul Muldoon, most of Derek Mahon except that which goes 'though the motions' (Longley 1986: 171), and increasingly small amounts of Heaney – represents a tiny caucus of excellence which takes from life its content and function and gives back nothing but its example. As a literary critic rather than as a reader, part of the problem with such work for Longley is that, once defined, it is literally *beyond* criticism as it operates within a language system which cannot intersect with any other. Poetry which has 'finally settled' is, by definition, dead; beyond social usage, it must often remain, as with Mahon's 'Preface to a Love Poem', 'a half-way house of un-utterable feeling' (Longley 1986: 174) stranded in limbo between this world and the transcendent other. This is as close to perfection as is possible within the realm of the fallen that Longley must concomitantly insist upon. In her detailed analyses of Mahon's poetry (Longley 1986: 170–84) intense discussions of form and the 'singing line' construct their own hypnotic cadences through strategies which, ironically, remind the reader of the debt structuralism owed New Criticism at its most incisive. As the essay gathers its own momentum we are afforded the briefest glimpse of a state beyond criticism in its discussion of Mahon's poem 'Tractatus' as the reader, the poetry and the poet fuse momentarily in a discourse which collapses the oppositions that for Longley ordinarily impose themselves on the scene of writing: 'Mahon's aural imagination also outflanks more prosaic historians, or perhaps anyone whose definitions limit history as well as philosophy, by conferring validity on Tacitus's poetic error. Stress and assonance celebrate the limitless horizons of the imagination working in its own terms, by making us "hear" the sun sinking, the steam rising' (Longley 1986: 184).

If, to some extent, this suggests a critical blind alley it is when considering poetry which has neither settled nor obviously wishes to do so that Longley's criticism regains its direction and is more sure of its ultimate destination. While Longley's writing has aspired to, and I think achieved, a mode of criticism which envisages itself as highly serious, and engaged with promoting the ideal of poetry as a gold standard, this should not disguise her considerable skills as a polemicist nor her use of rhetorical sleights of hand in order to convey her opinions. These qualities are identifiable in her consideration of the early poetry of Paulin in her review of *Liberty Tree* (Longley 1983: 19), later developed in *Poetry in the Wars*. For the purposes of the review Paulin's work was set against the poetry of Mahon and the play *Across the Water* by David Rudkin; a determined strategy for, although *Liberty Tree* avoids the worst excesses of Rudkin's 'ludicrous realms of sado-masochistic fantasy', it cannot comprehend Mahon's 'subtle register of involvement and responsibility'. With such a comparison *Liberty Tree* becomes 'phoney', a text of 'linguistic self-consciousness' which, however, cannot be considered formally (despite the fact that 'most critics of contemporary poetry neglect form'). Such use of a potentially positive (or at least neutral) critical term as disapprobation can also be found in her perception of Paulin's poetic historical and literary cross-referencing as 'Eliotesque'; the modernist disease typically found amongst exiles.

Nominally it is Paulin's textuality, his artifice, which angers Longley, but whether we should blame for this his exile, his presumed nationalism, or, more simply, *Liberty Tree*'s refusal to privilege the potential of the aesthetic over competing and quotidian historical discourses is not revealed. While 'Sweet Dreams or Rifles' maintained a tone of good humour, its rewrite in *Poetry in the Wars* is more sternly condemnatory and finds through Paulin's involvement with Field Day an essentially sinister framework of nationalist theorists through which his poetry could be read. Consider her analysis of 'Black Mountain Jacobin', a review of *Liberty Tree* by Seamus Deane (Deane 1983a): 'Deane's review finds Paulin's counterpoint between "stage Ulsterism" and "a kind of academic surrealism" "ironic". It seems to me deeply affected and patronising: a talking-down to people whose own talk ("dunchered") he misappropriates in order to despise them. Paulin's version of two-language polarity epitomises how politics abuses poetry: by an intellectual bullying of subject matter, by exploitation akin to what the poet deplores' (Longley 1986: 197).

In the slippage between the figure of the poet as paradigm and the actual example under consideration Longley has structured an argument using criteria that neither Deane nor Paulin would recognise. As Paulin's work has not 'settled', the distinctions between the different aspects of the political and the aesthetic cannot be reconciled by an emphasis on the way the formal properties of the poem engender a literary criticism which is essentially *unfinished* and which has to deal with the raw data of text rather than the finished poetic artefact. With such an interpretation Longley reads *Liberty Tree* not as poetry afflicted by bad politics but as politics itself as, ironically, the self-conscious textuality of the work allows it the status of a transitive speech act: in this sense at least it becomes the genuine article.

As this suggests, a problem with such a development is that by this stage the reader of 'Poetry and Politics in Northern Ireland' may well be quite confused as to where these borders between language usage actually lie (they could indeed be entirely arbitrary) so, as clarification, Longley's next paragraph establishes a new binary relationship designed to present the real enemy: 'Another bully, the structuralist levelling-word "discourse" (much favoured by Deane and *Crane Bag*) fits Paulin's approach. "Discourse" abolishes any boundary between poetry and prose, poetry and politics, in the same spirit as "comrade" abolishes class distinctions. The only casualty is imagination.' If Longley had not stated her position so clearly previously in the essay her lines of reference here would make the use of discourse as a critical term oddly appealing,[8] yet in so far as discourse can contain all that is not poetry there is a certain circular logic to the argument. That said, 'discourse' with its grounding in different language usage insists on, and *has* to insist on, boundaries within textuality. However, because these boundaries are the result of explicit ideological formations and are not transcendentally conceived, there can be no recognition of this within an argument which, if it loses the ineffable dimension of aesthetic transcendence, is rendered inert.

Perhaps surprisingly then, Longley's definition of discourse becomes similar to the post-Foucauldian usage employed by David Cairns and Shaun Richards in *Writing Ireland: Colonialism, Nationalism and Culture* which reads the concept as one which 'constitutes groups, or peoples, as those acted upon, defined, and frequently rejected by the articulators of the dominant discourse' (Cairns and Richards 1988: 16). The only difference is that while Cairns and Richards seek the materially constituted aspects which lie behind the term Longley seeks an imaginative exit from history into poetry as a form of personal liberation which forecloses the sense of a social subject. Such a comparison is not fanciful in that it goes some way towards explaining why, for Longley, discourse is a structuralist 'bully'. *Poetry in the Wars* considers the humanistic and essentially liberal criticism of Stan Smith[9] as 'Marxist-structuralist', and indeed any critic concerned with the material aspects of literary production is liable to be catalogued in much the same way: structuralism being, after all, 'merely a further twist' (Longley 1986: 13) of the real enemy, modernism and its 'philistine hostilities' (Longley 1986: 14).

The logical development of such a position therefore suggests that the overwhelming majority of contemporary literary criticism must be to some extent structuralist which in turn enhances the isolationist position Longley, in a similar way to Leavis before her, is anxious to claim for herself.[10] Once such an opposition is established Longley can move between the modes of professional critic and private reader with ease and thus is able to align herself more closely with the poetic imagination which can 'understand cultural trauma better than the intellectuals' (Longley 1986: 196). Just as *Poetry in the Wars* is markedly reluctant to accept modernism, so its relentless inveighing against what it terms 'academic criticism', modernism's unfortunate progeny, reveals only the slightly anachronistic nature of Longley's ideological position.

There are then strong elements of an isolationist mentality in this; Longley's critical position insists on an extreme subjectivity which prevents actual literary debate while still allowing the full force of polemic to be used against any potential enemy (of which there are many):[11]

> So the Irish poem resembles the Flying Dutchman, as it endlessly circumnavigates in search of adequate criticism: semi-protected at home, neglected or selectively privileged in England, enshrined in Boston or Philadelphia, back home again only to find a post-structuralist invasion killing off indigenous evaluation before it has got properly underway. Alas, where poems become texts, theoretical rather than critical rigour prevails.
>
> (Longley 1990a: 56)

Irish criticism in its embryonic state faces a rigorous development: caught between the rock of Eamonn Hughes's 'appropriate' and the hard place of Longley's 'adequate'; at Queen's University[12] much will be asked of it.

There is, ultimately, a crystalline quality to the structure of Longley's polemics. Carefully organised around a series of interlinked oppositional concepts, as the sum of its parts it appears impregnable. The individual oppositions which form the whole, however, cannot be interrogated without the possibility of absolute collapse, so a certain rigidity remains in place. The principle of criticism as an invocation of the real must continually be defined against the theoretical as abstraction; poetry must function against discourse and the interior against the exterior (only real, empirically proven objects can have a third dimension). This latter concept becomes another way in which Paulin's work fails to make the grade when tested against the crucial arbiter of aesthetic worth: the poetry of Mahon. As Mahon's 'Courtyards in Delft', 'defines and exemplifies the subtle posture of Mahon's poetry' so Paulin's work is marked by its 'flailing at exteriors' (Longley 1986: 203). That some acknowledgement of the exterior may be of certain worth in itself cannot be considered. To recognise the interior within the poem becomes an act of witness, a way of establishing a reading community nominally above and beyond the present limitations of political and religious schismatic discourses. Longley's criticism can only recognise itself when mirrored in the image of the poetic artefact; its mission is not so much to explain as to display, as its concern with formal wholeness forces it into an opposition with its own status as criticism. In this way *Poetry in the Wars* is continually trying to escape from itself and into the focus of its concerns; it engages with criticism just as it rejects it and establishes

95

arguments which simultaneously insist on their own status as self-evident. As she notes: 'to recognise poetry as soon as possible, and to go on recognising it, is a social as well as aesthetic act' (Longley 1986: 14). To raise the kind of issues I have outlined, or to put it another way, to treat this criticism as criticism, is to fail the central test Longley sets her readers and is thus to avoid the major component of her work which can be ultimately summarised by the famous Leavisite maxim: 'don't you find it so?' (Leavis 1937: 63).

This seems appropriate. As Leavis, in debate with Rene Wellek in 1937,[13] insisted on criticism as something other than philosophy or indeed theory, so *Poetry in the Wars* mounts a critique on forms of methodological enquiry without actually establishing a new paradigm for reading poetry. Set against the abstraction of philosophy is the real, or rather the act of making real, and as Leavis suggests, this becomes the role of the literary critic:

> By the critic of poetry I understand the complete reader: the ideal critic is the ideal reader. The reader demanded by poetry is of a different kind from that demanded by philosophy. I should not find it easy to define the difference satisfactorily, but Dr Wellek knows what it is and could give at least as good account of it as I could. Philosophy, we say, is 'abstract' (thus Dr Wellek asks me to defend my position 'more abstractly') and poetry 'concrete.' Words in poetry invite us not to 'think about' and judge but to 'feel into' or 'become' – to realize a complex experience that is given in the words.
>
> (Leavis 1937: 60–1)

What was at stake for Leavis, as for Longley, is not the division of philosophy or theory and literary criticism into separate discourses but rather the relativist assumptions that such a position might engender. Relativism, for both critics, is a sign of cultural breakdown: an indication that the disinterested common reader has a civic as well as personal function and that such a function is under threat. When *Poetry in the Wars* attacks Seamus Deane's 'polarised vista of endlessly "competing discourses" – rival propagandas? –' which 'frighteningly rules out any objective language of fact or value' (Longley 1986: 193) it is not so much Deane's quantification of opposition that antagonises Longley but the necessarily concomitant denial of a higher judgement based on (in this case) aesthetic truth value. Ultimately, as with much of Longley's work, such a concern is expressed through the early twentieth-century debate between modernist texts and modes of counter-modernism. Leavis, though a follower of modernistic precepts in his championing of Eliot, found the alienating techniques of the modernist aesthetic promoted the rise of the disconcerting word 'highbrow', and in the same way (remembering both that Longley can align herself against the 'intellectuals' and that structuralism is merely a 'further twist' of modernism) literary theory undermines the possibility of Longley's notional reading community as it could exist in

Ireland. In this aspect, that such theorists also often have nationalist tendencies[14] is strictly incidental although, as Leavis might have said, it *is* significant.

However, while it cannot be denied that this system of reading, as Leavis demonstrated, allows for a robust and self-generative critical practice, problems have occurred for Longley when attempting to adapt it to the demands of historical research: a development that takes her beyond the more limited reading strategies of Leavis. As Barra O'Seaghdha has noted, 'what she does not always acknowledge is that there is a semi-political, and certainly a literary-political, strategy behind many of her interventions' (O'Seaghdha 1989–90: 19). As a defender of a closely defined empiricism, Longley does not, nor would want to, subvert historical process as a way of understanding the present: there are facts in the past and as such they can be made evident, but in this lies a conflict between the poem as evidence and the poem as an achieved state of knowledge. The former speaks of the contingent forces of contemporary affective need while the latter enacts the desire, achieved through the existence of the poem itself, to be 'through with history' (Longley 1986: 204).[15] This is, as Longley admits, 'an impossible condition and a salutary irony', yet is still (has to be) the ultimate desire 'since poetry cannot be the "creature" of politics'. Ultimately this takes us back to the concept of settling. When reading an essay by Longley such as 'The Rising, the Somme and Irish Memory', her contribution to Field Day's analysis of the seventy-fifth anniversary of the Easter Rising (Ni Dhonnchadha and Dorgan 1991: 29–49), Longley's absolute emphasis on poetry as documentation forces the reader to adopt an elaborate system of guess-work in order to deduce which poets were writing necessarily partial evidence (by my reading Pearse, some Yeats, F.S. Boas, Rupert Brooke), which should be treated as such, and which had 'finally settle(d)' into the poetry of embodiment and exemplification (Heaney, other poems by Yeats, Charles Sorley, Joseph Mary Plunkett, Owen). As much of this poetry is formally Georgian in mode, and none of it modernist, Longley's preferences are all the more difficult to detect.

It is in these ways that Longley can be seen as adapting an essentially Leavisite aesthetic to the demands of social interaction without retreating strictly into Leavis's ideal of a notional elite. For this reason its ultimate manifestation is one that Leavis might not have recognised: Longley throws up the barricades around her own critical practices but always leaves a door slightly open for the late repentant. Her work is a constant and ongoing negotiation between the idealism of truth as it is located in the poetic and the rationality which (in an Irish context) seeks to disrupt the monolith or the definitional. The strategy which allows this is a reading of the aesthetic as transformational; the poem as paradigm signals the diversity of the aesthetic will and enables the 'witnessing (of) the last spasms of the Green and Orange state-ideologies which literature long ago found unworkable' (Longley 1987:

25). Such a reading depends, of course, on being able to clearly identify that which is monolithic – the 'Green and Orange' binarism of symbiosis – and that which is literary, and a keen eye on the poetic micro-climate which can determine when a poem by Yeats (for instance) remakes itself, through its own strategies, as propaganda.

If Longley's own Leavisite concerns have allowed a distinct form of New-Critical activity to be discernible in Northern Ireland, it also suggests ways in which critics either from or concerned with Northern Irish culture have displayed an adaptability in handling European or American critical models which emphasises the uniqueness of post-partition cultural development. While the roots of this development can be traced back to the influence of Leavis's propensity towards provincialism, to Hewitt's regionalism, and to the particular aesthetic interactions which shaped the poetry and criticism of Louis MacNeice, one could argue that it was not until the eighties that such difference was recognised and ratified. The formation of the Field Day Theatre Company in 1980, and the later co-option onto its board of Seamus Deane, Tom Paulin and Seamus Heaney, prefigured this awareness with its stated aim to 'contribute to the solution of the present crisis by producing analysis of the established opinions, myths and stereotypes which had become both a symptom and a cause of the current situation' (Deane ed. 1985: vii). The emphasis on crisis is significant. Although Field Day's work has stressed its pan-Irish context, its particular focus on the North and the board members' own positions within it as organic intellectuals developing a counter-hegemonic strategy arose from a sense of crisis designed to rebegin history after the long hiatus of the seventies. As hegemonic practice the pamphlets thereby produced by the company[16] sought not so much to respond to a sense of crisis but to establish its veracity as a point of potential and to extend its existence after the hunger strikes of the early eighties (which galvanised Field Day's early activity).

Although I will consider Field Day's manoeuvres in greater detail in a later chapter, for now it is relevant to consider that it was an aspect of the binary thinking which typified much of Field Day's early work which perhaps led to a series of other polemically titled critical texts during the decade. Not only did the title of Longley's *Poetry in the Wars* (1986) carry a fierce edge to its otherwise studied considerations, Paulin's *Ireland and the English Crisis* (1984), John Wilson Foster's 'The Critical Condition of Ulster' (1985; Allen and Wilcox 1989), McCormack's *The Battle of the Books: Two Decades of Irish Cultural Debate* (1986), Deane's *Celtic Revivals* (1985) and Denis Donoghue's *We Irish: Irish Literature and Society* (1986) all sought to foreground a statement of credo within the work and its title. That said, for those critics who came from Northern Ireland, linkages other than a common teleological drive to their work are appropriate. The eighties constituted a period of time in which

Northern Irish academics whose further education had benefited from the
Butler Education Act (1944, but extended to Northern Ireland in 1947)
reached a confident critical maturity and although it is difficult to assess the
precise significance of this, it was certainly important to the development of
Deane, Foster and Heaney.[17] For Foster, especially, the context was clear:

> My doctoral dissertation was a minimalist effort, but back in Northern
> Ireland I began afresh and quickly wrote *Forces and Themes in Ulster Fiction*
> (1974), the first word of that title acquiring special meaning in Belfast, in
> which, even in the University district, one would lie abed and hear nightly
> gunfire and explosions. If that was stimulation of a rather desperate kind, a
> quieter kind was the awareness that almost all serious criticism of Ulster
> literature was pioneering; for a couple of years, it seemed as if Seamus Deane,
> Terence Brown and I were writing all of it. Indeed, it is easy to forget that
> less than twenty years ago most criticism of Irish writers was written by
> Americans, and that 'Irish writers' meant almost exclusively the Big Names
> of the Revival.

(Foster 1991: 3)

Foster's urge towards critical autobiography – also indulged in by Deane,
Donoghue, Heaney and Paulin – speaks of his desire to find an autonomous
Northern Irish criticism located in the generation of critics born in Northern
Ireland from 1939–55. This in turn can override the particular theoretical
and strategic positions adopted by those critics (Deane is an interesting example
in this instance) who may not recognise Foster's own partitionist instincts or
their own role within them. For this reason Foster is perhaps the most intriguing
Northern critic to consider within this context. A self-proclaimed unionist
working in Canada, much of his work is marked by a desire to establish
communal modes of critical identification that can allow debate without
threatening the contextual stability of the Union. Foster's 1985 paper 'The
Critical Condition of Ulster' (Allen and Wilcox 1989: 86–102),[18] first presented
at the fifth Triennial Conference of the International Association of Anglo-Irish
Literature in Belfast, attempted a desperate accommodation of the structuralist
and post-structuralist agendas then dividing many English Departments in
Britain, while prefiguring the sea-change of the Anglo-Irish Agreement signed
on 15 November of that year. The one organisation which could reasonably
be viewed in the light of both these cultural events, Field Day, was the
paper's object of study, and it stands as a fascinating example of the critical
act as written to the moment;[19] a reading which forgives the slightly dated
air it now exudes:

> The critical condition of Ireland at the present time seems undivorceable
> from the condition of criticism in Ireland. The failure of Irish society is the
> failure of criticism. First of all, the failure of objectivity, of the generosity that
> permits objectivity, of the sympathetic faculty that impels generosity.
> Secondly, the failure of reflection and self-examination. Thirdly, the failure of

an intelligent assertion of legitimate sectarian interest, heritage and identity
possible only when objectivity has been striven for.
(Allen and Wilcox 1989: 86)

Remembering that Deane's Field Day pamphlet, according to Longley, 'rules
out any objective language of fact or value', Foster's strategic liberal humanist
reading of the Company's work has to labour with some urgency to find an
accommodating framework capable of bringing the structuralist agenda of
'competing discourses' into the pale of civilised generosity. In this way 'The
Critical Condition of Ulster' seeks ways of reconciling the theoretical drive
of Field Day to Foster's own critical instincts while actually addressing the
irreconcilability of nationalist and unionist agendas. To enable this Foster
establishes a linkage between liberal humanism and the liberal unionism he
locates in Robert McCartney's Field Day pamphlet that he was also to
continue in his consideration of the later Field Day pamphlets published as
'News from Orchard Street' (1987). However, although McCartney's pamphlet
is seen as problematic in that while 'the aspiration towards a united Ireland
might be granted to northern nationalists as a civil and individual right, that
aspiration, if it is pursued too actively or successfully, will be opposed and the
right rescinded' (Allen and Wilcox 1989: 98), Foster can only state as his
own credo that 'Mine is, unashamedly, the old liberal humanism (Arnold's
disinterestedness, even, but strategically courted) co-opting the methods of
structuralism and post-structuralism, but prepared to entertain, though not
permit, its own supersession' (Allen and Wilcox 1989: 101).

Foster, in seeking the limits of 'critical generosity and 'disinterestedness'
continually runs up against the barrier between the personal critical act and
the socially expedient gesture which, as I have demonstrated, also troubles
Longley's much more strategic (and therefore transformable) unionism. For
Foster, however, it is around the notional 'intelligent assertion of legitimate
sectarian self-interest' (an example of 'competing discourses' in itself) that
this difficulty crystallises as, although it represents a state of being that has yet
to come into existence in that it follows from the critical recognition of
objectivity, it is through such a strategy that the activities of counter-
hegemonic intellectuals can be circumscribed within the grounds of expediency. Significantly it would not be until Foster's response to the Downing
Street Declaration, written nearly ten years after 'The Critical Condition of
Ulster', that this 'legitimate sectarian self-interest' would reassert itself in a
new and less pluralist guise:

> The stern task facing those who believe they are British, and wish to remain
> so, is to display to England and the world the benign, rational, positive,
> engaging face of unionism. It will require effort and courage, and in the
> vanguard should be those best equipped to perform the task – academics and
> professionals who believe in the union, who have been educated courtesy of

the union, and who now slumber over their subsidies and grants and salaries without saying a word in public in its defence.

(Foster 1994: 37)

In its insistence on the economic basis of intellectual activity Foster suggests the limits of the 'generosity' that he had previously felt able to invoke without definition. With this the ghost of the Butler Education Act returns to haunt the argument as, so the subtext might read, those dissident Northern intellectuals who seek to destabilise Northern Ireland are also beneficiaries of an education 'courtesy of the union'. Clearly in times of insecurity the actual 'disinterestedness' of Arnold, with all its ultimate ironies, foreclosures and exclusions, is fully revealed. A prefigurement of this inflexibility can be located in 'The Critical Condition of Ulster' when it considers Field Day's pamphlets and plays as distinct counter-hegemonic activity. To leave his own unionism intact Foster turns to a slightly crude historically determined model designed to guarantee the continued validity of his political position (specifically liberal unionist dissent) within contexts that would deny it the potential of the desired objectivity:

> The Free State came about only after forty years of cultural preparation. By 1920 Ireland had asserted a sufficiently different culture, according, that is, to the people who turned out to be the ones who mattered – including, let us take note, the Anglo-Irish who studied well (if not too wisely) a culture not their own. Consider the contrasting case in Ulster. There has been no cultural preparation for a united Ireland WHATSOEVER. That being the case, it is an impossibility outside its military imposition.
>
> (Allen and Wilcox 1989: 94)

The paper is deliberately vague on who, other than the Anglo-Irish, actually did matter, but were such a scenario to be transposed to modern Ireland forty years hence it would be reasonable to assume that Foster would be one of them. However, as Foster's rhetoric becomes increasingly bullish through the course of the paper the awareness develops that he is writing his own disinterestedness out of the argument he has established; structuralism, Longley's enemy that thrives on the binary oppositional in the same way as the 'old' Orange/Green, Catholic/Protestant monolith, becomes associated with nationalism in that both are 'anti-individualist', or rather both threaten Foster's liberal humanism/unionism. Faced with this prospect, Foster creates a false opposition, invoking post-structuralism as a way of deconstructing the old polarities despite its perceived anti-humanist drive. Once deconstruction is countenanced, Foster then notes, by way of quoting one of David Lodge's bourgeois realist novels, that death (which 'a critical programme for Ireland' has to 'accommodate') is beyond deconstruction, thus leaving the reader back at the notion of the autonomous individual. Although this continues Foster's role in the scheme of things, it does entail that his final conclusion, again borrowed from Arnold, to 'follow the existing order of things till right is ready', contrasts uncomfortably with his opening statement detailing Irish society's current 'failure'. This, perhaps, is due to the fact that 'The Critical Condition of Ulster' actually accepts that Arnold's own prescriptives were 'disinterested' and not, as Eagleton has insisted, part of an ongoing process of marginalisation (Eagleton 1988: 13).

VERSIONS OF INTERVENTION

There are then certain correspondences between Longley's liberal humanism and Foster's. Both wish to maintain Northern Ireland's links with Great Britain in some form while attaching a certain disinterestedness to their own critical positions. Similarly they uphold the notion of a non-negotiable critical truth yet feel the need to defend this absolute with polemics. In opposition to this ideal is placed a conflation of structuralism and nationalism[20] which respects the fine print of neither; the former being merely a new reading of the old monoliths incapable of achieving anything other than reinforcing the established polarities. At the centre of such an interpretation remains the constitutional position of Northern Ireland and its incidental links with British Leavisite rationality. In this structuralism, and indeed post-structuralism, is forced into a rapport with Irish nationalism, and yet, as McCormack wittily points out, Deane 'is a weekend deconstructionist who would not get a union card from Paul de Man or Harold Bloom' (McCormack 1986: 63). Rather, such forces are banished from the recognisable context of Northern Ireland as object of rational enquiry because they represent destabilising points of otherness within the known certainties of the empirically real: after all, a border artificially created has to be constantly policed.

Luke Gibbons in a perceptive introduction to these arguments for *The Field Day Anthology of Irish Writing* has acknowledged the essential contradiction inherent in this position and suggested the reasons for the containing strategies it requires:

> The revisionist enterprise in Ireland, based as it is on a liberal humanist ethic, was faced with an intractable dilemma as it gradually became apparent that a belief in a human condition, transcending all historical and political divisions, belonged to the kind of cultural fantasy that Seán O'Faoláin associated with nationalism, except that it was now a humanist rather than a Gaelic mystique.
> (Deane ed. 1991, vol. III: 567)

It is because of this difficulty that the concept of Irish revisionism has been seen to harden into a distinct oppositional and insurgent stance, finding in historiography what is assumed to be lacking in literary or cultural theory.

Indeed, it is ironic that any conflation of unionism with literary critical unity across the United Kingdom had, by the mid-eighties, long since been dissipated, due to the overturning of established Leavisite paradigms and the concomitant rise in structuralist thinking in British University and Polytechnic English departments – a development which left Longley declaring a unilateral independence for the Northern Irish poetic aesthetic as she accused the (in all ways typical) British post-structuralist Antony Easthope (here viewed paradigmatically) of 'throwing rocks of jargon' (Longley 1986: 170) at the pentameter.

Interestingly, it is on this issue that opposing voices can be reconciled. Tom Paulin, who as I have previously demonstrated Longley sees as a major poetic heretic, attacked Easthope's contribution to the infamous revisionist text of British materialism *Re-Reading English* (Widdowson 1982) in the *London Review of Books*; a review which provoked one of the most sustained and passionate exchange of letters the journal has witnessed:

> The contributors are collectively of the opinion that English literature is a dying subject and they argue that it can be revived by adopting a 'socialist pedagogy' and introducing into the syllabus 'other forms of writing and cultural production than the canon of Literature'. . . . In what is perhaps the dimmest essay in this collection, Antony Easthope argues that traditional literary criticism encourages the reader to identify with the poet and that this is a 'narcissistic and elitist identification (you too can *be* Sir Philip Sidney)'. . . . Like many of his fellow contributors, Easthope has a Stalinist preference for mechanistic labour and he is able to make the experience of reading a sonnet by Sidney sound like a spell in a forced labour camp.
>
> (Paulin 1982)[21]

In retrospect, neither Easthope's contribution – which was at worst naive and at best a reasoned summary of a particular (if widely held) position – nor *Re-Reading English* as a whole was an especially subversive or revolutionary text. Widdowson's collection summarised much of the research that had taken place in Britain and elsewhere over the previous decade; it helped establish positions which now underpin commonly held procedures of materialist criticism which, moreover, now have an institutional existence in relative harmony with what Paulin termed 'traditional literary criticism'.[22] Indeed, taken in its entirety, the debate which Paulin initiated managed to address few of the issues originally raised by *Re-Reading English*. Rather it focused on the twin insecurities of both the liberal intelligentsia and what Paulin termed the 'dissident intelligentsia' in relation to the institutions they served. As other articles and letters in the *London Review of Books* of the period suggest, perhaps the real issue being debated, albeit covertly, was the role of liberal third-level English in a nation which had only a few months previously seen the triumph of Thatcherite nationalism in public reaction to the Falklands war. Maybe for this reason Paulin, it seems, profoundly misread the egalitarian drive of *Re-Reading English*, and was in turn, misunderstood by the subsequent letters his review engendered which accused him of being, variously, a 'philistine' (Nicholas Spice), 'tired' (Jonathon Dollimore), a critic lacking attention to principle (Stephen Logan) and exhibiting 'misinformed eccentricities' (Joseph Bristow), 'paranoid' (Easthope), 'disgraceful', 'laughable' and 'hapless' (Michal Egan), 'absurd', 'silly' and 'swaggering' (Terence Hawkes) and 'severely deficient in politics' (Widdowson).

In other words, although there was much anger, within a British context no one was entirely sure what Paulin represented. In the same review Paulin also considered Iain McGilchrist's *Against Criticism*, a conservative, slightly reactionary text which carries its Arnoldian agenda heavily, and dismissed it in one paragraph:

> Another morbid symptom is Iain McGilchrist's meandering and infinitely tedious non-argument that 'the only genuine critical theory is that of no theory'. Mr McGilchrist is a fellow of All Souls and an upholder of the elitist culture which so angers Widdowson's contributors. . . . He is, alas, fatally dull: 'One could say of art what Lewis said of the *Faerie Queen*, that it is life itself in another mode.' One could indeed, but one could, on the other hand, feel that those who want to re-read English are justified in their angry alienation from the vacuous and unintelligent attitudes which McGilchrist holds.
>
> (Paulin 1982)

With this comparison it can be argued that Paulin's verdict on *Re-Reading English* remained ultimately indefinite and it was this unwillingness to orient a critical strategy along left/right lines which led to the wooliness of the debate. Counter-polemic followed polemic and perhaps the only result was to establish Paulin's reputation as a dissident voice within the corridors of the British institution: an achievement perhaps consistent with Paulin's original aim as his comment that 'this new way of thinking . . . is a phenomenon which anyone acquainted with less peaceful cultures than the English is bound to recognise' suggests. Unwilling to be located solely within a British tradition of criticism, Paulin ignored his own prescription[23] and refused to state a personal credo, leaving him in absolute opposition: a metaphor of resistance both to the English institution and to the theoretical vision found therein. Paul de Man's late contemporaneous essay *The Resistance to Theory*[24] crystallises this point and allows a reading of Paulin's position as being, at some point, paradigmatic within the concerns of the institution:

> If there is indeed something about literature, as such, which allows for a discrepancy between truth and method, between *Wahrheit* and *Methode*, then scholarship and theory are no longer necessarily compatible; as a first casualty of this complication, the notion of 'literature as such' as well as the clear distinction between history and interpretation can no longer be taken for granted. For a method that cannot be made to suit the 'truth' of its object

can only teach delusion. . . . These uncertainties are manifest in the hostility directed at theory in the name of ethical and aesthetic values, as well as in the recuperative attempts of theoreticians to reassert their own subservience to these values. The most effective of these attacks will denounce theory as an obstacle to scholarship and, consequently, to teaching.

(Lodge 1988: 356)

Within the British context of Paulin's polemic, there is something prophetic in de Man's careful and tolerant reading of the seismic historical instabilities engendered by theory in western liberal institutions as well as, of course, something now irredeemably ironic: the 'ethical values' counter to theory being those which would reassert themselves in condemnation of his collaboration with the Nazis during the Second World War (an irony that Paulin would later recognise).[25] That said, it is as a threat to scholarship and teaching that Paulin condemns Re-Reading English, the other 'New Accents' volumes published by Methuen, and indeed Leavis who 'helped to discredit formal academic procedures – textual scholarship, the compilation of reference works, footnotes, indexes, bibliographies and the writing of scholarly articles and "standard" works'. In return Paulin's ideal English was defined as 'a rigorous and much drier discipline, like history' (Paulin 1982a).

In this sense Paulin's resistance, like de Man's conceptual entity, defines itself in straightforward adversarial terms invoking polemic as a self-conscious trope of despair and desperation and, in turn, reading theory (while not reading theory) as alien to a procedure at least recognisable if not ideal. In line with such an interpretation was Widdowson's eventual response to Paulin's attacks (1982a) which accused Paulin of wanting to be a 'man of letters', hence the initial review's hostility to Leavis, Lodge and Re-Reading English itself, since all of these question 'the naturalised subject of "English" and its canon' and thereby destabilise the unconscious flow of tradition in which the man of letters has his part. It is with this accusation, which unfortunately came at the end of the exchange of letters, that the misrecognition inherent in the entire argument becomes evident. Both de Man's conceptual embodiment of resistance and Widdowson's assumption of Paulin's 'man of letters' status are predicated on the figure in question not just belonging to the institution but being of the institution in a way which renders him (appropriately) as an essential force of formless reaction writing from securely within a culture. Rather, I would wish to argue, it was Paulin's interest in and tentative affiliation to, an unformed Irish culture which led to his polemic against Re-Reading English and Against Criticism, and it was the correspondents' inability to recognise this fact which suggests their own failure to accept cultural difference. The mode of response employed and, indeed, de Man's formulations of the same period, could not allow any diversion from the binary opposition of resistant/dissident as located solely within the institution: a breadth of vision which has since widened with the subsequent development of cultural studies in British institutions. This goes some way to explaining why the attacks on Paulin were so vague and inappropriate and why the defenders of, and contributors to, *Re-Reading English* were happier when addressing the comments of correspondents who, while not entirely in agreement with Paulin, at least wrote with the full force of the institution behind them (Nicholas Spice, Joseph Bristow, Peter Barry, Gabriel Josipovici).

For these reasons Paulin was perhaps not the adversary *Re-Reading English* needed, for while his attacks bore decided venom, his own agenda, in which isolationist individualism gestured towards a state of private and notional affiliation, prevented the kind of analysis the British departments of English badly required. This is illustrated by the poem 'Oxford v. Cambridge v. Birmingham etc.' which Paulin published in the *London Review of Books* (Paulin 1982b) during the exchange and which formed part of his eventual definition of dissent:

> Under a stony sun, a slabbed fate,
> there is a paved land
> called *nothing-original*
> which is the home – the near-buried home –
> of scholarship and humility; (. . .)
> But who can tell the puritan
> or the man who fucks texts
> that the green sappiness of life
> has no more to do
> with art, style, or a formal joy,
> than the warty skin a kid rips
> from a smelly, smashed elder-branch?
> Now that the academies are switching
> into self-disgust and gibberwick
> I've fallen in love again
> with a rich old library
> and those darkblue bindings;
> I'm bending the knee now
> to letter and copy-text,
> the fine print of the spirit.

By writing a response in poetry (although not, it is helpful to note, a poetry Edna Longley would recognise) Paulin can be seen as insisting on the uniqueness of both the aesthetic artefact and his own role as a producer of 'primary' texts, thus aligning himself against the 'frustrated sociologist who believes that sonnets and beer mats ought to be treated on an equal footing' (Paulin 1982). That said, 'Oxford v. Cambridge v. Birmingham etc.' is clearly a form of writing to the moment, and was not a poem which would appear in any later collection – certainly not having 'finally settled' in any recognisable way. The significance of the poem to these issues hinges on the 'etc.' of the title. In one reading it is an acknowledgement of the boredom in the provincial imagination; the Birmingham of David Lodge and the Centre for Contemporary Cultural Studies invading the versus of the traditional Oxbridge opposition (this is the reading concordant with Paulin as man of letters); in another reading it becomes a means of escape which gestures to all the locations physical and imaginative beyond the awareness and remit of the 'puritan' (Leavis at Cambridge) or 'the man who fucks texts' (a loose embodiment of the structuralist/post-structuralist agenda).[26] With such a development the poem gestures both thematically and stylistically towards Paulin's 'To the Linen Hall', later to be collected in *Liberty Tree* (Paulin 1983: 77–8), which culminates with a similar image of 'fretting scholars/who pray, invisibly,/to taste the true vine/and hum gently/in holy sweetness'. If, as it therefore seems likely, the 'rich old library' of 'Oxford v. Cambridge v. Birmingham etc.' is the Linen Hall Library, Belfast, of 'To the Linen Hall' then the poem ends formally in a location where the traditional practices of academia need not, and traditionally have not, been yoked to the prescriptions of the state. A location which, in turn, allows for the imagined 'sweet equal republic' of 'The Book of Juniper' from the same collection.[27]

If such a reading is accepted, 'Oxford v. Cambridge v. Birmingham etc.' removes Paulin from the debate he initiated and returns him both to poetry and his imaginative hinterland of Northern Ireland. Turning in disgust from the English institution of which he is part, he seeks, in a way not dissimilar to Longley and Foster, to find protected territory for the aesthetic within Ulster, although it should be noted that Paulin's aesthetic republicanism would not protect strategic partition in a similar manner. *Ireland and the English Crisis*, while including 'Faculty at War', develops this idea in a more knockabout way:

> Although the debate about what constitutes the 'canon' of English literature challenges the view that art is sacred and supranational, the argument's more extreme lunacies remind me of that sinister phrase, 'England's difficulty is Ireland's opportunity.' In moments of aggravation it seems to me that if England no longer wants both the canon of English literature *and* the desperate, wrecked state of Northern Ireland, then perhaps something could be created out of this double rejection? A united Irish Arts Council could buy up all those remaindered copies of *Hamlet* and *Macbeth* and use them to construct a new culture. MacMorris in *Henry V* could ask 'what ish my nation?' and his *auteur* could reply, 'same as mine ould boy'.
>
> (Paulin 1984: 15)

Although light-hearted, such an idea suggests the methods by which Paulin, by 1984, was establishing a critical position located in Ireland from which he could mount guerrilla-style assaults on the English canon (for instance 'Lawrence after Fifty Years', 'W.H. Auden: Disaffection and Defection' (Paulin 1984: 85–91, 106–17) and, most infamously, his polemic broadcast against Virginia

Woolf).[28] Usually in the form of brief articles or reviews and not afraid of the power of polemic (gestured by his 'moments of aggravation'), they subtend the accusation of belle-lettrism by their insistence on difference, by the constant acknowledgement that this is a culture the reviewer does not share. Certainly there is something slightly disingenuous about this. Paulin, with an English father, a primary degree from Hull and subsequent academic posts at Nottingham and Oxford, may be more deeply implicated in the processes of Englishness than he would have cared to admit at this stage of his thinking, but the strategic relocation of a critical identity in the future tense of an 'identity which has as yet no formal or institutional existence' (Paulin 1984: 17) allowed, and continues to allow, a method of avoiding recognition within internal British cultural dispute while still suggesting the possibility of intervention.

As a final comment on this rejection it is interesting to consider the opinions forwarded by Anthony Cronin, a novelist and commentator from the Republic, on Paulin's defence of the Faber anthology *Hard Lines* (a collection of poems by urban, often unemployed, young British people), a piece first published in 1986:

> Not long ago I saw Mr Tom Paulin on television. Since I had never seen him before, in the flesh, the spirit or the image, I was interested. He was discussing a recent anthology, published by Messrs Faber and Faber, called *Hard Lines*. (For those who do not know anything at all about him, Mr Paulin is a poet, what in some quarters is called 'a northern poet'). . . . Mr Paulin, being on the left, defended the publication hotly. A number of the pieces included, he said, were far more interesting as poetry than much that got into print through the normal cultural conduits of the society in which he lived.
>
> (Bolger 1991: 181)

It should be noted that Cronin's traditionalist (as opposed to traditional) mode of reaction does not pretend to speak from a consensus opinion (despite his strong links with Fianna Fail as a one-time adviser on cultural affairs to Charles Haughey), and it is fair to point out that the article was collected as part of an attempt to 'initiate a discourse about the rapidly changing society which is Ireland today' (Bolger 1991: 8), being seen by the editor as 'original and controversial'. Significantly, however, it is revealing to note that Cronin reads Paulin as Paulin read *Re-Reading English*: as a world-weary, slightly sarcastic outsider forced to engage with topics which only disgust him. Paulin, in turn, is exoticised both as a poet, and more importantly as 'a Northern poet', praising the aesthetic values of the poems anthologised in *Hard Lines* not for any actual merit but because of the circumstances of their production. Paulin has commented that in Ireland 'there is no ratified idea of culture which literary theorists could begin to undermine' (Paulin 1984: 15) and indeed Cronin is no McGilchrist but it is part of Paulin's dilemma that even on withdrawal from the British institutional arena he may find that his image of Irish citizenship, in actuality, has a culture less unformed than he would like.

I have demonstrated how, during the eighties, Edna Longley, John Wilson Foster and Tom Paulin all realised that Ireland's literary-critical links with Great Britain were seriously problematised. All made some critical gesture towards structuralist-generated theory, and, having realised the potential consequences of such an agenda on their own practices, subsequently retreated back to a humanism located in the North of Ireland where certain values could be protected and others rendered irreducibly alien. From that point onwards Britishness could only be contemplated as it was recognisable through the valorised techniques of the aesthetic artefact. 'Theory', which now constitutes a coherent embodiment of otherness inimical to the particular deformations of Northern Irish culture and society, forced this withdrawal and by so doing was considered in terms, outlined by de Man, which typify the strategies of the resistant: 'It is a recurrent strategy of any anxiety to defuse what it considers threatening by magnification or minimisation, by attributing to it claims to power of which it is bound to fall short. If a cat is called a tiger it can be easily be dismissed as a paper tiger; the question remains however why one was so scared of the cat in the first place' (Lodge 1988: 357).

Why indeed. The failure of critics concerned with Northern Irish culture to address or, more properly, to *use* the models suggested by structuralist/post-structuralist research has been, as Robin Wilson has noted, a severely disabling factor in the search for social and cultural models appropriate to the situation, and it can be argued that symptoms of its absence are now clearly discernible. In 1991, the respected Belfast-born poet and critic Gerald Dawe published a collection of essays, *How's the Poetry Going?: Literature and Politics and Ireland Today*,[29] which, as its subtitle suggests, is a serious intervention into a cultural debate on behalf of aesthetic values. Dawe's methodology throughout the work is to locate the fixed essence of the empirically real and then to test the effect of poetry as a positive or malign presence on that reality:

> What I am saying will hardly come as a surprise to many hundreds of thousands of people who read poetry (or novels, magazines, watch television, go to the theatre) and are sick, sore and tired of having their 'Identity Crisis', 'Loss of Language' and 'Cultural Legacies' endlessly talked about. Yet these are the issues that drift around like radioactive dust in the literary atmosphere. They animate, on this general level, the best of minds, but I wonder, when we boil it all down, what residue of relevance is left and how many people are affected by all this talk? . . . I think it is time we questioned these assumptions and started again from the facts and the actual setting of Ireland as we know them to be.

> (Dawe 1991: 13)

Having established this reality as a physical entity and concomitantly dismissed cultural difference as an ideological pastime of the intelligentsia – this from a joint-editor of *Across a Roaring Hill: The Protestant Imagination in Modern Ireland* – Dawe is free to extend his humanism towards the actual role of the aesthetic within such a community, and by so doing achieves all seven of the principle rhetorical figures which Barthes suggested 'outline the general prospect of this (bourgeois) *pseudo-physis*' (Barthes 1987: 150–5).[30] As Dawe states previously in his argument:

> I think, though, it is true to say that the greatest influence on a writer is the past. *Its* relevance is pervasive and often it is only when the past is unearthed beneath the rubble of today, that a poet begins to make sense of his or her own imaginings. Somehow the recovery of the world of the past not only helps a poet show what makes up the world but also helps make it a more 'livable' place *now*. In this sense, a poet is strictly 'anti-nostalgic'. . . .
> Williams' poem is the best of antidotes – direct and poetic, it brings out the difficult truth of writing poetry, the knowledge and beauty it can discover and the strange relentless power it has to show us what we are or think we are.
>
> (Dawe 1991: 10–11)

It is instructive to note the different strategies Dawe adopts in order to protect the essences of his original argument. Judgements that veer towards truism ('the greatest influence on a writer is the past') are couched in constructions expressing doubt as if to to suggest a note of both qualified inspiration and scepticism, while more problematic statements ('helps a poet show what makes up the world') appear mid-sentence with no qualification. When the critical parameters are too narrow to allow a coherent escape from a particular blind alley, Dawe has recourse either to the ineffable ('Somehow . . .'), or to the tautological utterance (number four on Barthes's list) which can insist that the 'best' of poems are also the most 'poetic'. The final result of this methodology is that the concept of the writer as Dawe envisages it remains trapped in a deterministic social framework consisting of fully individuated subjects who, nevertheless, all recognise and respond to social forces in an identical manner. The physical existence of the past, of community, of the 'actual setting of Ireland', of the good poem, are never in doubt; as Barthes has it, 'one no longer needs to choose, but only to endorse' (number five, 'Neither-Norism'). However, despite such passivity, this stance constitutes a mode of resistance which, as with Longley's criticism, reaffirms Irish cultural activity as defined by lived experience rather than method, and as such returns us to de Man's distinction between *Wahrheit* and *Methode* drawn by the resistant. However, that there are certain methodological questions surrounding *How's the Poetry Going?* is ultimately of little significance. What *is* significant is that the intellectual climate which produced it also sustained its pronouncements: not one review challenged the scope of its vision nor questioned the seamless parameters on which it was based.

However, this particular application of empiricist literary-critical methodology in Irish culture tells only half the story. Although Dawe's criticism pushes the Irish liberal humanist ideology of letters towards a linguistic terminus by suggesting the limits of its possibilities, it is in a similar, albeit potentially more successful, application of literary critical paradigms to social usage that resolution is still sought. Although I have traced congruences in Longley, Foster and Paulin, these writers, in themselves, do not suggest a distinct Northern Irish critical practice. Indeed the possibility, or even desirability, of such a critical movement can only be tentatively forwarded, as many critics would be hostile to such an identity. Rather the fragmentation of Northern Irish society, a fragmentation found at every socio-economic level, is mirrored in the critical activity of writers from the province, the vast majority of whom have had to (or wanted to) find work elsewhere. Moreover, while one would never expect nor desire consensus, the frameworks of interpretation are often so disparate as to make comparative analysis all but impossible.

For instance, Longley and Deane will, seemingly, always misrecognise and misrepresent one another's positions as they acknowledge neither a shared canon, tradition, geography nor practice; the only point of convergence is the occasional 'primary' text that is unfortunate enough to be caught in the crossfire. Indeed at times one can only agree with O'Seaghdha who has noted despairingly of this process: 'When it becomes obvious that two people supposed to be engaged in a public debate are in fact delivering parallel monologues, it may be time for members of the audience to question the terms of the debate' (O'Seaghdha 1989–90: 19). This does not mean that concurrences cannot be found but is instead to note that seeking such linkages is often to write, not just against the wishes of the critics concerned, but against coherency and tradition and for the (genuinely Irish) experience of heterogeneity and breakdown. It is for these reasons that McCormack can pay tribute to the 'robust good humour' (McCormack 1986: 60) of Irish criticism as it searches the partitioned sensibility for moments of self-recognition; there may never be common ground but there is the possibility of tolerance.

Perhaps this in part suggests why Edna Longley, for one, has espoused an interpretation of Northern Ireland as a 'cultural corridor' in the essay 'Opening Up: A New Pluralism' (1987). Informed by the practice of close reading, the concept reorientates the New-Critical paradigm in seeking heterogeneity in the aesthetic artefact. In turn, the critical evaluations thereby produced can be applied to the social whole:

> The literature produced by Ulster people suggests that, instead of brooding
> on Celtic and Orange dawns, its inhabitants might accept this

province-in-two-contexts as a cultural corridor. Unionists want to block the
corridor at one end, republicans at the other. Culture, like common sense,
insists it can't be done. Ulster Irishness and Ulster Britishness are bound to
each other and to Britain and Ireland. And the Republic will have to come
cleaner about its own *de facto* connections with Britain. Only by promoting
circulation within and through Ulster will the place ever be part of a healthy
system.

(Longley 1987: 24–5)

Although this protects partition in the strategic short term (echoing Foster's
'till right is ready') it also, seemingly, allows for the possibility of any future
occurrence as long as it is remains within the remit of 'common sense'.
'Opening Up: A New Pluralism' deploys its rhetoric in the hope of
compromising the definitional aspects of the Field Day anthology then in
preparation yet, at the same time, it seeks the critical generosity to which
Foster aspires in 'The Critical Condition of Ulster': a shift in sensibility
perhaps best illustrated by the difference between Paulin's call to cultural
and political affiliation in *Ireland and the English Crisis* (Paulin 1984: 16) and
the historian Roy Foster's comment that 'if a "solution" is a political mirage,
we should turn to irrigating the cultural and social desert' (Crozier 1989:
22). Foster's comments were made during the Cultural Traditions Group
Conference in 1989, an organisation drawn together by the Central Community
Relations Unit in Belfast in 1988 and consisting mostly of prominent figures
from local arts administration, education, publishing and broadcasting. With
a starting budget of £3,000,000 over three years and funded initially as a
sub-committee of the CCRU and then as a sub-committee of the autonomous
Community Relations Council,[31] it forms part of a wider hegemonic process
including Education For Mutual Understanding, and is based on the premise
that 'community relations and cultural diversity cannot be separated. While
the first is a problem, the second is surely an asset, provided its richness can
be celebrated in non-threatening ways' (Crozier 1989: vii). Of this process
Michael Longley, one of the group's first members, has suggested: 'we expect
no quick returns. This is a waiting game' (M. Longley 1994: 70). Again, the
success of Northern culture (particularly in regional literature) is assumed to
disfigure the binary mentalities which structure the political and social framework
of Northern Ireland, and in so doing can be made to work to the referential
end of greater harmony within the boundary of partition.[32]

This becomes problematic in that at times it conflates liberal humanism
and liberal unionism in precisely the same way as John Wilson Foster's
oppositional reading of Field Day: indeed the concept of the cultural corridor
enables the celebration of all aspects of nationalist culture except the aspiration
itself. As Steve Bruce has recently noted: 'The wonder of the cultural-traditions
school is that it fails to appreciate that the relativism which can be permitted

in thinking about religious divisions or dress styles cannot work in the obdurate world of constitutional politics' (Bruce 1994: 139). Moreover, it is not unfair to note that, for Edna Longley at least, such an aspiration if located within a poem would immediately negate its status as poetry and, therefore, its use-value. Instead, the artefact would become propaganda and, with such a reading, part of the problem rather than a possible answer. Maurice Hayes, the Chairman of the Group, has illustrated this difficulty in his pamphlet, *Whither Cultural Diversity* (1991), which reads the poetry of Louis MacNeice, Heaney and Hewitt as authentic expressions of binary thinking. In opposition to this he posits the sense of identity as distinctive and yet permeable to outside influences and as such brings 'culture' – perceived as a lived system of values – into unwitting collision with 'tradition' as ratification:[33]

> Then there is the Cultural Traditions Group – where the main object was to promote discussion, debate about the validity of the various cultural traditions in Northern Ireland in a constructive and non-confrontational atmosphere. One shorthand was to help Protestants to contemplate the Irish language without necessarily feeling offended by it, or for Catholics to look on Orange processions without feeling intimidated. Of course this rather begs the question that some Orange processions are indeed intended to assert a claim to territory, or to superiority, and sometimes to intimidate.
>
> (Hayes 1991: 18)

The gentility of the phrase 'this rather begs the question' disguises the more obvious negotiations of power implicit to tradition as a ratifying force, and although the question is begged, it is not one that Hayes answers. Instead the 'debate about the validity of various cultural traditions' is resolved within two paragraphs when we read that 'the Group's philosophy involves a general acceptance of the validity of all cultural traditions' (Hayes 1991: 19). By expressing such timidity the philosophy of the Group tends to suggest that underlying traditional forms of communal identification is a natural state of *cultural* expression that is not only recoverable but which also has only recently been tainted by the deforming effects of socio-sectarianism. That a cultural artefact may have had such sectarianism needled into its very fabric is an issue that the Group has yet to engage with.

Transformed into the present social reality this reading can be expressed, in a term used by Richard English, as 'the equal legitimacy thesis'.[34] In this concept the different traditions of the province are granted equal validity regardless of the hierarchy of power validated by partition that supports, amongst much else, the Cultural Traditions Group itself. In this way the limits of liberalism are revealed and it becomes clear why the initially appealing reading of Northern Ireland as culturally heterogeneous has not led to any substantive body of critical work.[35] Pushed to extreme limits such a position requires little more than the celebration of each individual's own cultural position and a willingness to celebrate that of one's fully individuated neighbour – not so much cultural understanding, one might be tempted to argue, as interpellation into the practices of the bourgeois state.[36]

However, these recent developments in the tentative analysis of tradition as a cultural determinant and the wider projects of community reconciliation groups in the province have tended to emphasise the role and importance of this perceived individuation as a means of achieving social stability. Again the materials suited to the task have been found in the cultural diversity of Northern Irish aesthetic artefacts. Most startling amongst this overall movement is the report of the Opsahl Commission on Northern Ireland (Pollak 1993), the centrepiece to the *Initiative '92* programme. Attempting to draw the people of the province and elsewhere into a dialogue which, whether intended or not, reveals the democratic shortfall endured by the citizens of Northern Ireland, the project attempts to achieve at the level of the individual what has been foreclosed through the ballot box.[37]

Collating 554 written and taped submissions, the Opsahl Commission's attempt to create a ' "shared space" for discussion and debate' (Pollak 1993: x) represents the fullest manifestation so far of Edna Longley's ideal reading of the North as a cultural corridor, and suggests a method whereby the intellectual middle class could have some input into a future constitutional settlement. Concomitantly, poetry, or rather the individual poem as an artefact marked by plurality, becomes a form of secular theology appropriate to the contingent pluralities of northern society and thus it is fitting that *A Citizen's Enquiry* is blessed not by a bishop but by Michael Longley:

> *A Blessing*

> Initiative Ninety-
> Two (-three, -four, -five . . .)
> Offers space, a clearing
> In the jungle for me
> And you to stay alive
> By sharing thought and word.
> Are *you* within hearing?
> Am *I* being heard?

Perhaps uncertain of the ideal tone required for such a gesture, Longley has recourse to the homiletic style of Paul Durcan[38] and in so doing conflates the space cleared by *Initiative '92* with the space created by the poetic artefact. If the Northern Irish poem is indeed paradigmatic then Longley's blessing invites the Opsahl Report to aspire to its possibilities.

Ultimately, any account of criticism in Northern Ireland will labour to find totalised or even cohesive ideological patterns of behaviour if only because the generation of critics I have concentrated on in this chapter constitute their identities, as all individuals do, from cultural determinants and influences that cut across and subtend the foreclosed binarisms that currently dominate the debate.[39] In this regard it would be incorrect to perceive Northern Ireland as having a deforming effect on cultural identity, as such heterogeneity places it within the very paradigm of modern society from which it is often excluded. Indeed, it is possible that in a reading of the contradictions and misunderstandings that prevent the reconciliation of often similar critical positions (for instance Edna Longley and Paulin) we can find an example of the cultural excess that overloads the containing discourses of opposition. 'Unconscious Partitionism' (1987), an account of the 1986 Kavanagh's Yearly weekend by Michael Foley (who as I have demonstrated in a previous chapter is a satirist of some skill), celebrates this breakdown[40] and finds in the manoeuvres of the Irish academics and writers gathered at this heterogeneous annual literary conference moments of potential value. Regarded as a celebration of Patrick Kavanagh's life and work, and located in Ulster though not in Northern Ireland, it is at events such as this that the personal codes which constitute a Northern critical aesthetic, and indeed a concomitant Southern critical aesthetic, are revealed. However, as Foley satirically points out, such possibilities are easily threatened:

> Dismissiveness is often automatic and operates on a North-South basis – what Tarpaulin ['Tom Paulin], in a rare articulation of a useful thought, called 'unconscious partitionism'. For instance, one has the feeling that, whatever Edna Longley said, she would still be a 'fuckin' unionist'. Any suggestion that her presence showed nerve or at least the noticing so craved by the south is met with howls of laughter and ridicule. Those eejits from London who understand nothing! Doesn't everyone know she does it for the glory?
>
> (Foley 1987: 25)

It is appropriate to end a consideration of these issues, through Kavanagh's Yearly, with Kavanagh himself who, living along the fault-lines of partition, railed against the disabling effects of marginality yet out of that anger created a poetry of inclusivity and generosity, the legacy of which is still to be inherited. Similarly, to be of and concerned with the culture of Northern Ireland is to feel the weight of difference in all ideological gestures. Denials have to be conscious and allegiances always declared. For this reason, the timid 'I' that can enter any debate or text will often be read as 'we', as individuated definitions of dissent are relocated within groupings far from the discourse of liberal humanism. That connections between these liberal strands of thought are not made has often more to do with the shifting dominant hegemonic positions within Northern Ireland itself than it has with the more intransigent issues surrounding border politics. For instance, Edna Longley's belief in the province as a cultural corridor and the work of the Cultural Traditions Group as a whole can now be seen appropriately as an expression of the post-Stormont dominant hegemony in that they seek to rectify rather than transform the binary formations of social relations inherited from the residual hegemonic position (defined by Longley in terms of monolithic and strictly non-pluralist unionism). As David Lloyd has argued in relation to the nineteenth-century Irish novel: 'the significance of movements in which moral economies are articulated lies not merely in what they advocate but in the fact that they emerge as organised social formations at a moment when economic and social transitions are in the process of dissolving an old order of domination' (Lloyd 1993: 145).

As the next chapter will argue, through this model the activities of Field Day (and with these, Paulin's political aesthetic) become in turn a series of negotiations between the company's current status as counter-hegemonic and its transformative interpretation of Irish social relations coherent with the sense of a possible emergent hegemony. For the dominant hegemonic positions, the insistent role of culture as rectification has had a deforming effect on the practices of New Criticism within the literary institution, suggesting, to return to Eamonn Hughes's argument with which I began this chapter, that perhaps Leavis was never an option for Northern Ireland in any case. The actuality of partition has, in this way, made as explicit the strained intellectual links Northern Ireland has with Great Britain as it has those with the Republic, for even to declare for a monologic tradition is to render conscious the essentially unconscious delights of Leavis's homogeneous culture. Pushed to something near its extremity, the manoeuvres of Longley, Foster and Dawe demonstrate how much of the liberal humanist agenda has to be compromised to exist in an actively heterogeneous society, and it is to their credit that they do not refocus their beliefs to the notionally Leavisite concept of a minority reading elite. To be of a partitionist mentality is neither to accept nor oppose the present constitutional position of Northern Ireland, but to recognise that all beliefs must be exposed and that all positions are formally learned. Paradoxically, to exist in a zone of cultural confluence is to be unable to take anything for granted.

NOTES

1. For a stimulating reading of the lure of provincialism within the modernist aesthetic see Robert Crawford, *Devolving English Literature* (1992)
2. Anne Samson's book *F.R. Leavis* (1992: 172), comments on Leavis's immense popularity in the United States, Australia and India.
3. It is of interest to note that these critics are culturally all from the Irish Protestant community.

4. For instance Edna Longley, *From Cathleen to Anorexia: The Breakdown of Irelands* (1990:3).
5. It is worth stressing that while much of Longley's work intersects the categories of social and literary criticism her belief in the autonomy of poetic voice requires their continued individuation.
6. See (Leavis 1948: 135–6): '. . . the governing ideal here is to attain some sense of the "mind of Europe", that whole order referred to by Mr Eliot, the order *within which English literature has its place*' (emphasis added).
7. One of the epigraphs to 'Poetry and Politics in Northern Ireland' is Derek Mahon's maxim: 'A good poem is a paradigm of good politics' – a curious statement if one considers the theological and absolutist stance Mahon's aesthetic requires.
8. In the introduction to *Poetry in the Wars* Longley also attacks the 'pseudo-democracy of "text" and "discourse". It is a ludicrous equation of art with society to assume that if we distinguish a poem on merit, it will instantly seize power' (Longley 1986: 14).
9. In this instance *Inviolable Voice: History and Twentieth-Century Poetry* (1982).
10. While this is an isolationist position it is not in fact isolated. Critics such as Geoffrey Thurley (*Counter-Modernism in Current Critical Theory*), Laurence Lerner (ed. *Reconstructing Literature*) and Peter Washington (*Fraud: Literary Theory and the End of English*) write from similar theoretical if not political beginnings.
11. For instance structuralism, Marxism, post-structuralism: specifically the critics Antony Easthope, Seamus Deane, Declan Kiberd, Terry Eagleton, Tom Paulin, Donald Davie and anything by Field Day, nearly all modernist and postmodernist poetry, specifically T.S. Eliot, Thomas Kinsella, Tom Paulin and Seamus Deane (again).
12. Where Longley and Hughes teach.
13. Wellek, 'Literary Criticism and Philosophy' (1937); Leavis, 'Literary Criticism and Philosophy: A Reply' (1937); Wellek, 'Letter' (1937a).
14. For instance Seamus Deane, Declan Kiberd, David Lloyd, Fredric Jameson.
15. Originally from Mahon's 'The Last of the Fire Kings', this sentiment is a pervasive ideal in much of Longley's work.
16. Tom Paulin 'A new look at the language question'; Seamus Heaney 'An open letter'; Seamus Deane 'Civilians and barbarians' (1983); Seamus Deane 'Heroic stylers: the tradition of an idea'; Richard Kearney 'Myth and motherland'; Declan Kiberd 'Anglo-Irish attitudes' (1984); Terence Brown 'The whole Protestant community; the making of a historical myth'; Marianne Elliot 'Watchmen in Sion: the Protestant idea of liberty', R.L. McCartney 'Liberty and authority in Ireland' (1985); Eanna Mulloy 'Dynasties of coercion'; Michael Farrell 'The apparatus of repression'; Patrick J. McGrory 'Law and the constitution: present discontents' (1986); Terry Eagleton 'Nationalism: irony and commitment'; Fredric Jameson 'Modernism and imperialism'; Edward W. Said 'Yeats and decolonization' (1988).
17. W.A. Maguire in his study, *Belfast* (1993) notes that one of the particular modifications of the act for Northern Ireland was the raising of the capital grant to voluntary (in reality Catholic) schools from 50 per cent to 65 per cent (172).
18. Page references will be for this volume. The paper also appeared in *The Honest Ulsterman*, 79 (1985): 33–55 and, more recently, *Colonial Consequences*, 215–33, a sign, perhaps, of the importance Foster ascribes to it.
19. The moment in question, the Belfast IASAIL conference of 1985, seems to me to be of significance. The academics there gathered, including Foster, Longley,

Paulin, Deane and Hughes, contributed to a literary conference at which both post-structuralist and National questions were foregrounded, perhaps for the first time in Ireland. Edna Longley, in a review of *Colonial Consequences* (Longley 1992a) writes of Foster as having 'locked horns with the Field Day stags'; a suitably combative metaphor for a combative conference, the issues raised at which are still current.

20. 'Deane's own atavised rationalism betrays more clearly than usual the strains of reconciling Derry with Derrida' (Longley 1986: 195).

21. Later republished in Paulin's *Ireland and the English Crisis* as 'English Now' (1984: 148–54).

22. For a persuasive account of this development see Evans 1993: 129–58.

23. 'Although most radical critics and educationalists are more interested in texts which enforce a type of class-consciousness, it seems to me that it is the term "English" which needs to be first deconstructed and then redefined. This involves arguing from and for a specifically post-colonial or post-imperial idea – it means that the critic must come out into the open and say "*credo*" ' (Paulin 1984: 15–16).

24. 1982. Collected in *The Resistance to Theory* (1986) and *Modern Criticism and Theory: A Reader*, ed. David Lodge (1988).

25. There is a sense in which Paulin read the revelations about de Man's wartime past as a symptom of the ethical bankruptcy inherent in all post-structuralism. See *Minotaur* (1992: 13).

26.   One of the major symptoms of the present crisis is the manner in which the word 'reading' has become a self-conscious term – critics like Widdowson now observe themselves reading in a curiously onanistic manner and they appear to derive a sexual excitement from the mysterious act of 'decoding' signs. . . . Textual criticism becomes a peculiarly masculine species of pornography in which the 'professional' critic is the lonely voyeur of his own sensations. Such critics – men who fuck texts – believe that literary works ought to be given an egalitarian treatment and this means that any text is as 'interesting' as the next.

(Paulin 1983a)

27. Although this is Paulin's interpretation of the symbolic importance of the Linen Hall, the fact that the IRA firebombed the building on 1 January 1994 suggests that this insurgent reading does not as yet constitute a consensual opinion within Ireland.

28. 'J'accuse', *Without Walls*, broadcast Channel Four (9 June 1991).

29. The volume's subtitle is variously conceived as 'Literary Politics and Ireland Today' (cover) and 'Literature and Politics in Ireland Today' (title page – by 'Dawe, Gerlad'): an interesting, albeit unconscious, acknowledgement of the meaningless qualities these words can have when overused for book titles.

30. The quotation cited above provides a useful illustration of Barthes's rhetorical figures six and seven: 'The Quantification of Quality' and 'The Statement of Fact': '*common sense*, that is, truth when it stops on the arbitrary order of him who speaks it'.

31. Although correct at the time of writing, the imminent restructuring of the Arts Council by central government will almost certainly change the Cultural Traditions Group funding position, resulting in a clearer division between practical projects

(EMU and primary and second level cultural exchange between and within communities) and the more theorised work of Cultural Traditions.

32. The nature of the various bodies indirectly funding the Cultural Traditions Group prevent it from engaging in cross-border dialogue. It is therefore appropriate to see it as concerned purely with the internal relationships of the communities within Northern Ireland. The Cultures of Ireland Group, which has no formal, but many informal, links with Cultural Traditions, continues this work in an island context. It receives some funding from the CCRU and the CRU, but mostly is supported by the privately funded Co-Operation North body.

33. 'Tradition' by this reading concurs with Raymond Williams's definition in *Keywords* (Williams 1983: 319): 'Considering only how much has been handed down to us, and how various it actually is, this, in its own way, is both a betrayal and a surrender.'

34. This controversial paper argues persuasively that the activities of the Cultural Traditions Group may have increased the incidences of sectarian violence: 'It appears to take the ground from underneath unionist (and, more crucially, loyalist) feet and it undoubtably sustains the nationalist (and, more crucially, republican) illusion that British withdrawal/Irish unity are not only feasible, but have a certain measure of support within British governmental circles' (English 1994: 100).

35. The nearest, although not exact, example of such a work is, perhaps, *Culture and Politics in Northern Ireland*, ed. Eamonn Hughes (1991) which, in its introduction (p. 10) celebrates the desire of Heaney, Muldoon and Paulin to cross borders, commenting in relation to Heaney's 'is it any wonder when I thought/I would have second thoughts?': 'This is no longer a statement of reticence, shyness or indecision in the face of the "other", but a richly ambiguous statement of the always-at-least-dual nature of the Northern Irish and their cultures, which is made possible by the recognition that borders can be crossed.'

36. The appearance in *The Honest Ulsterman* ('Conference Abstract: Light Verse', pp. 95, 21) of a cutting satire by Longley on the effectiveness of the many conferences engendered by the Cultural Traditions philosophy suggests some of these problems have yet to be worked through by the Cultural Traditions Group itself: 'How many Irish Studies academics does it take to change a light-bulb?/None of them actually *changes* the light-bulb/Because half of them don't want it to change/And the other half think it will change anyway/But/They hold eighteen extremely successful conferences/(With NIE and ESB sponsorship). . . .'

37. Despite this, it is salutary to note Bruce's comments on the Opsahl enquiry: 'Its report frequently refers to the dangers of stereotyping Northern Ireland people as being simply Catholic or Protestant, nationalist or unionist, but then recommends that "each community has an equal voice in making and executing the laws or a veto on their execution and equally shares administrative authority". This, of course, requires that all people identify themselves with an ethnic group and act on the basis of ethnic self-interest' (Bruce 1994: 144).

38. Compare '*A Blessing*' with Durcan's 'Ireland 1977' (Durcan 1982: 81).

39. Hughes develops this point interestingly in his introduction to *Culture and Politics in Northern Ireland* (Hughes 1991: 1–12).

40. Foley 1987: 24.

Noticing Edna and Tarpaulin [Paulin] on a sofa in the hotel foyer, I move
to record what could be another key confrontation.
'Michael,' Tarpaulin says in what, naïve as ever, I take to be affability.
'Will you take a message to Jimmy Simmons?'
'Certainly,' I agree, gratified to be noticed, even as a messenger boy.
'Tell him this,' he says, suddenly rising up on the sofa, an ominous sign
given his chronic weariness. 'Tell him he's a fucking broken-down, clapped
out spavined, retarded . . .'
'*Retarded?*' I cry, looking about wildly for corroboration. Jimmy is no French
intellectual but 'retarded' seems a bit strong.
'Not retarded, *retired*,' says a helpful American academic, rising hurriedly to
leave.
'. . . stupid, vain, childish, hairy-chested, macho,' roars Tarpaulin, dangerously
close to core meltdown, 'Those fucking stupid photographs on his books . . .
doesn't he wear a fucking *medallion . . . fuck.*'

CHAPTER FIVE

'Nothing Left but the Sense of Exhaustion': Field Day and Counter-hegemony

THE DEVELOPMENT OF A NORTHERN INTELLIGENTSIA

The Field Day theatre company, which has not presented a stage production since 1991, has made its administrator redundant and its board of directors is taking a six-month 'sabbatical' before deciding on its future, the company has confirmed.

Mr Gary McKeone, Field Day's administrator for the past three years, told *The Irish Times* yesterday that, following a decision by the company's board of directors, he would be out of a job from this Friday....

Yesterday's developments seem to have been in the offing for some time, because at the end of last year Field Day did not apply to the arts councils in either Northern Ireland or the Republic for funding, as would have been expected if further theatrical productions were planned. Last year, Field Day was refused a £65,000 grant by the organisers of the year-long Impact '92 festival in Derry, which it had understood it was to be offered to stage Mr Friel's *The Freedom of the City*. The production was subsequently cancelled.

(Moriarty 1993: 1)

Making the front page of the *Irish Times* on a slow news day in April 1993, it was difficult not to read the story of Field Day's voluntary mothballing symbolically. In its thirteen-year life until that point the company's work had often been structured around binary oppositions, the polemic form, and as such it was hard to imagine it merely fading away to a more passive and occasional existence beyond the image of itself as a news event. However, the implications were unsettling. The essentially quotidian nature of the difficulties highlighted by the newspaper report (the unavailability of funding which it had previously attracted with a degree of regularity if not comfort) resonated against a sense of theoretical exhaustion engendered by the final completion of the company's major achievement, the first edition of *The Field Day Anthology of Irish Writing* (Deane ed. 1991) and the subsequent, often damning, critical response it received. In this way, although the temporary decision to suspend activities was only financially based it played against the image Field Day has fostered of itself as a team of tightly knit counter-hegemonists involved in an inexorable transformative programme and could only rewrite the statements of credo often detailed by the company in a politically harmful light. If, in 1985, 'the political crisis in the North and its reverberations in the Republic had made the necessity of a reappraisal of Ireland's political and cultural situation explicit and urgent' (Deane ed. 1985: vii), should one assume that by 1993 Ireland's situation was less urgent? If so what happened in the meantime? Field Day has long perceived itself as operating within a society in crisis,[1] and indeed it is as a considered response to a notional crisis rather than a particular societal grouping that the company has defined itself. However, the company's disinclination to examine this sense of crisis and the concomitant acute linguistic pressure placed on the concept has often threatened to unbalance the whole project. If, then, Field Day desired to remove themselves from the equation in 1993 can it be inferred that its other half, the crisis, had therefore been cancelled out? The idea remains too Utopian; while, as I have outlined in the previous chapter, there are those Irish critics such as Edna Longley who would not lament Field Day's passing, the particular rhetorical strategies in which the company are involved seem as urgent now as in 1980, and it is certainly too premature for an obituary: at this point in time any hint of Field Day's eventual dissolution would not suggest supersession but rather a vacuum.

Perhaps such a judgement grants too much credence to Field Day's own carefully promulgated self-image. Since its foundation Field Day has constantly revised its own history and its teleological vision. It has forged its own sense of macro-narrative, and with the publication of the anthology, established a tradition which culminates with the editors' own work. Beyond this achievement lies the empty homogeneous time of continued political deadlock. The event of rhetoric is, therefore, more than self-publicity and can be seen as an attempt to rebegin history and to awaken from the somnambulism of empty time. It is this reading, derived from the Frankfurt School's theoreticisation of historiography, which suggests some of the problems now afflicting Field Day. As Horkheimer noted, critical theory 'constructs the unfolding picture of the whole, the existential judgement contained in history'.[2] With such a belief in progress the theorist can be defined as 'the theoretician whose only concern is to accelerate a development which should lead to a society without exploitation'. This Hegelian model (about which Walter Benjamin remained sceptical) forces the cultural manifestation to act, in Michael W. Jennings's phrase, as the 'motor of historical change' (Jennings 1987: 43), and this, in turn, suggests the possibility of a distinct counter-hegemonic practice. It is here that Field Day's notional sense of crisis as event becomes significant.

While drawing on the Hegelian sense of the intellectual which looks for the 'unfolding picture of the whole' there is in Field Day's post-colonial vision a scepticism which emphasises the empirical event (Field Day itself)[3] as distinct from the time of history which surrounds it. The teleological drive implicit in a Hegelian model of history and development must be retained so as to protect from outright collapse Seamus Deane's assertion in the General Introduction to the anthology that 'there *is* a story here, a meta-narrative, which is we believe, hospitable to all the micro-narratives' (Deane ed. 1991: xix). However, such an assertion must also stress its difference from previous meta-narratives of possession. To enable this, Field Day's philosophy, while retaining the teleological, progressivist instinct, seeks a historical materialism closer to Benjamin's definition in the 'Theses on the Philosophy of History': 'A historical materialist approaches a historical subject only where he encounters it as a monad. In this structure he recognises the sign of a Messianic cessation of happening, or, to put it differently, a revolutionary chance in the fight for the oppressed past. He takes cognizance of it in order to blast a specific era out of the homogeneous course of history . . .' (Benjamin 1973: 254).

This corresponds, I believe, not only to Field Day's own sense of itself but to the historically determined model which underwrites it. In this way the hunger strikes of the early eighties, which are contemporaneous with Field Day's initial activity, were read by Deane in the Field Day pamphlet *Civilians and Barbarians* as just such a 'revolutionary chance in the fight for the oppressed past':

> But it was an important success. For it changed nothing. Therefore it was a success for the State. It merely confirmed and spread the demonising mythology. Later, the dirty protest at the Maze was to supply it with the most horrific imagery of degradation. . . . That changed nothing either. Nor did the hunger strikes, although for a time it seemed as though they might change everything. The point of crisis was passed without anyone seeming to know why the explosion did not come. Perhaps the truth is that both sides had played out their self-appointed roles to such a literal end, that there was nothing left but the sense of exhaustion.
>
> (Deane ed. 1985: 42)

The issue which troubles Deane, that the point of crisis was passed with no discernible change in the existing course of the dominant discourse of history, is the point at which the recognition of the cessation of happening contradicts the teleological position a counter-hegemonic organisation must maintain. It is for this reason that Field Day has had to insist on the concept of crisis (read as revolutionary chance) to justify its own intervention while acknowledging (by April 1993) that the historically determined vision of the anthology had rendered such a position slightly anomalous. As Benjamin notes in the *Theses*: 'A historical materialist cannot do without the notion of

123

a present which is not in transition, but in which time stands still and has come to a stop' (Benjamin 1973: 254).

It is by turning to Gramsci that this contradiction can be, to some extent, reimagined. Gramsci's emphasis on the role of the counter-hegemonic within and towards class liberation can be extended to a consideration of the relationship between the coloniser and the colonised. Within both, Gramsci foresaw the organic intelligentsia (a possible way of reading the post-1947 generation of academics allied to Field Day) as essential creators of the counter-hegemony, with liberation being gained by way of, in a phrase reinvented by Fredric Jameson, the 'long march through the institutions' (Jameson 1988: 48). The organic intelligentsia, by confronting the traditional intellectual who has survived from a previous position of social dominance, both assimilates[4] and conquers that previous position, and by so doing achieves a new form of hegemonic dominance distinguished by the 'sentimental connection between intellectuals and people-nation' (Gramsci 1971: 418). In Gramsci's terms, the particular possibility of liberation occurs when there is an intersection of two political states. Firstly the existence of established counter-hegemonic activity as created by the expansive organic intelligentsia and, secondly, the moment of vulnerability when the ruling (colonial) power's own hegemonic practice has failed at some strategic and significant moment, thus revealing the forces of physical coercion to the oppressed. Gramsci makes clear that the two factors must be present simultaneously if the oppressed are to be able to advance their own interests and reach towards a new consciousness. The former prerequisite, that of the revolutionary moment, is one which is readily amenable to an interpretation of Northern Ireland since the late sixties, where the working classes of both communities of the province have often seen the coercive physical force of the ruling state as its hegemonic framework has gradually evolved/eroded. Similarly, the enforced shift in governmental policy in Northern Ireland from an emphasis on the Ideological State Apparatus to hybrid forms of Repressive and Ideological State Apparatus (in Gramsci's terms the shift from ' "spontaneous" consent' to 'state coercive power';[5] 1971: 12) has occurred concomitantly with the development of an intelligentsia capable of envisioning the choices such a situation could offer. It is as this point of focus that Field Day has offered itself while reading the sense of crisis as fundamentally one within the sphere of authority.

The twin issues of concern then are whether Field Day can extend the perception of state weakness by continuing to focus on the possibility of crisis as it exists in both Northern Ireland and the Republic, and in so doing can develop a counter-hegemonic framework capable of responding to the problem with alternatives. In all ways this becomes a matter of finding (and prolonging) the revolutionary chance, the interval in the meta-narrative of state historical discourse, and blasting 'the era out of the homogeneous course of history'.

To return to Benjamin, this search engenders a shift in the methodology of the perceptual rather than of the actual as, 'the tradition of the oppressed teaches us that the "state of emergency" in which we live is not the exception but the rule. . . . Then we shall clearly realise that it is our task to bring about a real state of emergency' (Benjamin 1973: 248). Unfortunately, in testing the validity of this model we have to rely on the kind of linear time-scales inimical to Benjamin's own philosophy, although by invoking these we can gain an awareness of Field Day's perception of its own success and the overall significance of their sabbatical of the early to mid nineties (hard though it is to imagine a revolutionary intelligentsia taking a sabbatical). As I have considered in a previous chapter, this issue of hegemonic time is one which has concerned John Wilson Foster, a critic who would be suspicious of if not hostile to the kind of models I am employing, when he has considered the likely success of Field Day within an all-Ireland context:

> The Free State came about only after forty years of cultural preparation. By 1920 Ireland had asserted a sufficiently different culture, according, that is, to the people who turned out to be the ones who mattered. . . . Consider the contrasting case in Ulster. There has been no preparation for a united Ireland WHATSOEVER. That being the case it is an impossibility outside its military imposition.
>
> (Allen and Wilcox 1989: 94)

There is no need to cover old ground here nor to consider the actual ideology from which such a statement could emanate, but it is worthwhile to note that Foster does not use the term hegemony in his analysis, preferring the slightly more coy 'cultural preparation'. This is perhaps because a model of development based on material class interests, although remaining organic, tends to unsettle the more commonly found organicism of regionalism. That said, as David Cairns and Shaun Richards have demonstrated in an Irish context (Cairns and Richards 1988: 15), it is in culture where hegemony has its very being. Indeed Foster's sense of cultural assertion within the Free State is close to Gramsci's concept of 'cultural-social unity' where 'dispersed wills, with heterogeneous aims (would be) welded together with a single aim, on the basis of an equal and common conception of the world' (Gramsci 1971: 349). However, it is Foster's insistence on forty years as the length of time necessary to inculcate cultural difference during the Revival period which is of interest as it maintains a sub-text (considering the overall paper's subject) which suggests that not only is Field Day's approach failing ('no preparation . . . WHATSOEVER') even if it were not, there would still be another thirty-five years to go[6] before actual change could occur peacefully and successfully.

If this sounds too prescriptive it is not, we should note, too far from Deane's own envisioning of Field Day's development as he perceived it in

1990: 'The enterprise is threefold. It comprises theater, the Field Day pamphlets, and *The Field Day Anthology*. By 1990, Field Day will have completed the first phase of its operations' (Deane ed. 1990: 14). In this way it can be seen that Field Day too have an established programme of counter-hegemonic practice which involves reading backwards to 1980 (when Deane's involvement was less pronounced)[7] and forwards to areas still undefined. It has taken a decade for Field Day to complete the first phase of their operations so, while Deane does not suggest how many further stages are to come or how long they will last, a time-scale similar to Foster's does not seem inappropriate.

The second issue of importance in Field Day's attempts to establish a counter-hegemony is whether the directors of the board can be seen as fulfilling adequately the position of organic intellectuals within Gramsci's schemata. I have already outlined the role of the organic intelligentsia as one which seeks to vanquish the established traditional intellectual positions of the state, but it is at this point of conquest that the distinction between expansive and transformist hegemony becomes important. While it is in the maintenance and expansion of Gramsci's 'sentimental connection' that a truly expansionist hegemonic practice can be recognised, the alternative, 'transformist hegemony', is more clearly marked by the process of assimilation into the ruling ideology of potentially resistant intellectual forces. This has been concisely defined by Cairns and Richards as a process which 'does not advance the interests of the whole class-alliance functioning, instead, by incorporating subordinate groups (or significant individuals from those groups) into the ranks of the leading group with the effect of neutralizing potential challengers to the leading group by depriving them of their intellectuals' (Cairns and Richards 1988: 14). To read Field Day in and against these terms it is again necessary to note the importance of the Butler Education Act of 1947 (for Northern Ireland) which, in its extension of educational funds to a greater proportion of the society, had made possible the existence of an organic intelligentsia sharing the aspirations of the class to which it belonged, and yet concomitantly aware of both the temptation of assimilation and the importance of resistance.

Such issues are raised in Heaney's poem 'The Ministry of Fear' (Heaney 1975: 63–5), part of the larger sequence 'Singing School', which in its dedication and address to Deane foregrounds the role of an expansionist hegemony while prefiguring the later alliance the two intellectuals would form under the Field Day name:

> Then Belfast, and then Berkeley.
> Here's two on's are sophisticated,
> Dabbling in verses till they have become
> A life: from bulky envelopes arriving
> In vacation time to slim volumes

Despatched 'with the author's compliments'.
Those poems in longhand, ripped from the wire spine
Of your exercise book, bewildered me –
Vowels and ideas bandied free
As the seed-pods blowing off our sycamores.
I tried to write about the sycamores
And innovated a South Derry rhyme
With *hushed* and *lulled* full chimes for *pushed* and *pulled*.
Those hobnailed boots from beyond the mountain
Were walking, by God, all over the fine
Lawns of elocution.
                              Have our accents
Changed? 'Catholics, in general, don't speak
As well as students from Protestant schools.'
Remember that stuff? Inferiority
Complexes, stuff that dreams were made on.
                    . . .
Ulster was British, but with no rights on
The English lyric: all around us, though
We hadn't named it, the ministry of fear.

It is of relevance to note that during the period in which this poem is located Heaney considered Deane as a poet and himself as an academic (Parker 1993: 147), thereby reinforcing an overall reading of their position as intellectuals defined only in relation (or sentimental connection) to their communal Derry origins. The poem pulls towards the practices of the traditional academic intelligentsia while insisting on difference even within the text's own exoticisation of its author and subject as coming from 'beyond the mountain'; the traditional home of the barbarian. With this Ireland is recognised as divided along both east-west and north-south axes. The national territory is only signified by its internal stresses and the marginal spaces thereby created.[8] For this reason, it is not adequate to consider 'The Ministry of Fear' simply as Heaney's response to poetic forms gestated in England nor as a reading of the Irish subject confronting that which constitutes an alien culture. Rather, the poem is deeply rooted in the dilemma of the colonial subject as intellectual and addresses both the desire and the resistance towards the culture of the coloniser implicit in that condition ('Have our accents changed?'). The poem first recognises its producer as a member of the intelligentsia, offers the temptation of assimilation while acknowledging the impossibility of such a condition, before finally coming to a conditional rest at the point of irreducible difference: the final stanza recognising both the weakness in the state's hegemonic structure (in that the coercive force of the coloniser and its literary culture are now clearly distinguishable) and the possibility of a future counter-hegemony.

It is this insistence on difference within the projected assimilation of the colonised intellectual into the established culture which David Lloyd locates as the essential form of emergent nationalism. This is important to a reading of Field Day as an organic *expansivist* intellectual movement in that it predicates such a position on the necessary contact with the traditional intelligentsia and the lure of transformist hegemony thereby offered:

> Nationalism is generated as an oppositional discourse by intellectuals who appear, by virtue of their formation in imperial state institutions, as in the first place subjected to rather than subjects of assimilation. . . . Simultaneously, the logic of assimilation resists its own ideal model: since the process is legitimated by the judgement of the essential inferiority of the colonized, its very rationale would be negated in the case of a perfect assimilation of colonized subjects without remainder. Therefore it is at once both the power and weakness of assimilation as the cultural arm of hegemonic imperialism that a total integration of the colonized into the imperial state is necessarily foreclosed. Recognition of this inescapable relegation to hybrid status among 'native' intellectuals formed by the premise of an ever-withheld subjecthood is a principal impulse to nationalism at the same time as it determines the monologic mode of nationalist ideology.
>
> (Lloyd 1993: 112–13)

The contradictory nature of assimilation as Lloyd defines it asserts that transformist hegemony is not only undesirable but impossible within colonial discourse, an awareness that 'The Ministry of Fear' also makes explicit in its recognition of the ever-withheld nature of English poetic subjecthood to the colonial.[9] In these terms, by rejecting assimilation Field Day's strategy must develop the organic hegemonic formation by reinforcing the 'sentimental connection' between classes. This will ultimately lead to a synthesis of broad class interests while maintaining the insurgent notion of nationhood. Certainly this is no easy task in a culture in which the bourgeois populist interpretation of the intellectual is one distanced from the activity of labour. In an important early essay which prefigures fundamentally the Field Day enterprise, 'An Irish Intelligentsia: Reflections on its Desirability' (Deane 1975), Deane remarks on this difficulty that 'no division is more loaded with contradiction than that between the intellectual and the worker. One is set apart in a world of eternal verities; the other is steeped in a world of eternal underprivilege.' In this, it seems that Deane is establishing a form of organic intellectualism which is overwhelmingly expansive in its orientation and is doing so in a society in which there is no such previous tradition. He goes on:

> They are not merely classes, these two, they are sects. In the Irish situation, the worker has never had an intelligentsia to give him his counter-image. Had there been one, he might never have found it in his religious opposite and his economic equal; had there been one, he and the intelligentsia might have learned the nature of a dialogue between the two sects which, in their antithetical ways, expose to each other the means by which that entity called society distributes certain kinds of energy and rewards for the sake of its own security.
>
> (Deane 1975: 29)

In a full analysis of 'An Irish Intelligentsia: Reflections on its Desirability' the importance Deane attaches to the development of an intelligentsia in Irish cultural life is revealed as properly transformative of social relations and not another form of rectification. Moreover, in the formal modes and constraints of the essay is a structure of opposition which will resurface in Deane's 1983 pamphlet *Civilians and Barbarians*. Clearly, five years before the foundation of Field Day, Deane was thinking of the possibilities open to an established and tightly organised team of polemicists operating under Gramscian principles in Ireland.[10] Indeed, even in 1975, Deane was aware of the particular literary orientation such a movement should have; the reasons for this being 'the prestige of literature in a country undistinguished in the other arts' and the separation of the humanities from 'the world of business, commerce and government' – a contradiction that Gramsci also addresses (Gramsci 1971: 12).[11] Although the latter is considered as much of a problem as a benefit, it is as part of a strategy to forge a unity between the counter-hegemonic and the economic base that Deane largely circumnavigates both the issues of partition and sectarianism within the nation. More properly, the essay forms a definition of dissent predicated on difference which allows parallels to be drawn with the contemporaneous 'The Ministry of Fear'.

It would, however, be incorrect to suggest that Deane's movement towards the formation of an all-Irish intelligentsia was an isolated response. Instead 'An Irish Intelligentsia: Reflections on its Desirability' can be seen as simply the most comprehensive and programmatic statement of intent within an ongoing debate on the role of literature and culture within the nation. As with Deane's essay, the major argument is thus focused on a fundamental contradiction in Irish cultural life as being between the excellence of the national literary canon and the paucity of philosophical/literary critical traditions. This was foregrounded as a legacy of Ireland's colonial past (and present): the establishment of a critical tradition being heralded as a way of both defining difference *and* insisting on internationalism through that difference. Desmond Fennell, commenting in 1968, established criteria with which Deane would later work:

> The fact that the Republic of Ireland is an independent state and the product of a revolution makes us expect to find intellectual counterparts there in the various fields of humane endeavour. This expectation is nourished in respect of literary criticism by our awareness that the contribution of Irish writers and poets to contemporary literature has been considerable and distinctive. But just as the general expectation is disappointed by our continuing provincial mindedness in the intellectual terrain as a whole, the special expectation in regard to literary criticism is disappointed too. . . . Our cultural paralysis and mental abjectness are much too serious for us to permit ourselves the irresponsible luxury of those neo-Byzantine word-games which often pass for literary criticism today. Irresponsible, because literary criticism

should be fighting humanity's battle against the dehumanising status quo, not
supporting the status quo by aesthetic abstention.

(Fennell 1968: 12)

Fennell's journalistic criticism of this period is important to a consideration
of the forces which led to Field Day's formation as his work accepts both
the necessity and the possibility of an intelligentsia in Ireland and, therefore,
the existence of the nation-people as a readily definable concept. Of course,
care needs to be exercised at this point as Fennell's envisioning of an intelligentsia
in this instance probably owes more to de Valera's paternalistic sense of the
Irish fireside as a 'forum for the wisdom of serene old age'[12] than it does to
Gramsci, but (as Lloyd has pointed out), the monologic nature of nationalism
allows the tension between these two forces to have a dialectic result. This
can happen by subtending the contradiction in opposition to, what Fennell
terms, the 'Anglo-Saxon establishment': a strategy also familiar to the early
Field Day pamphlets as they sought to overturn British liberal empiricist
paradigms by relativist oppositional structures.

It is in this framework that a notional 'sentimental connection' between
the intelligentsia and what is considered the nation-people becomes an essential
prerequisite to national liberation. In Ireland, this can gain definition through
a wide variety of ideological positions as the varieties of these connections
are ultimately perceived to be unified through the discourse of homogeneous
nationalism. To some extent this can be seen as anomalous to Ireland as the
apparent triumph of Irish nationalism in 1922 only institutionalised, in Lloyd's
term, 'certain racial and sectarian divisions' (Lloyd 1993: 18) in the establishment
of partition. This is crucial as it is only through recourse to a fragile sense of
a nation-people that the discontinuities inherent in partition can be overcome.
Oppression, while readily definable in Northern Ireland, becomes less so in
the Republic if de Valera's appeal to the people-nation is accepted as a
successful attempt to redraw the nation in terms of the state. Fennell's 'Irish
Literary Criticism', seemingly, has little interest in Northern Ireland and
considers the Republic as exemplifying the triumph of Irish nationalism,
hence his belief that it is the product of a revolution. Deane in 'An Irish
Intelligentsia: Reflections on its Desirability' forthrightly challenges this view,
and by so doing not only reinvigorates the issue of partition but expresses
the division there illustrated as analogous to the division between the intelligentsia
and the people: 'Ireland has its intellectuals, but has never had an intelligentsia,
just as it has had its rebellions but never a revolution. An intellectual is not,
by any definition, a necessarily political individual; an intelligentsia, on the
other hand, is necessarily a politicised grouping.'

A direct line, then, can be traced between the aspiration towards the national
territory, expressed through its people, and the sundering of those people by

the lack of a sentimental connection between the organic intellectual and the worker. This is central to Field Day's task as Deane's programme notes to Field Day's production of Chekov's *Three Sisters* (1981) demonstrates: 'Field Day goes to the people, not for their sake but for its own . . . but in the conviction that it will eventually be for their benefit if they are sufficiently to its benefit.' Paul Hadfield and Lynda Henderson, in the otherwise stimulating essay, 'Field Day: The Magical Mystery', I think misread this announcement as an 'echo of the imperial stance so resoundingly dismissed by the company in their production of Friel's *Translations* the previous year'. Rather, in line with the reading I am proposing, it can be seen as the classic definition of an expansive hegemony as mediated through an aspirationally organic intelligentsia. This is clear if it is read in line with contemporaneous statements made by Friel in interview which suggested that Field Day's activity 'should lead to a cultural state, not a political state. And I think that out of that cultural state, a possibility of a political state follows' (O'Toole 1982). Friel, at best, makes an unwilling hegemonist, but it is with him that overall authority lies within the company. Despite occasional contradictions, Field Day operates as a politicised grouping, and the overall coherency of intent displayed by the individual board members when operating under the Field Day name is striking.[13]

By interpreting Field Day with this methodology the theoretical development of the company becomes more sharply defined. Centrally placed in this is the sense of division; between the intellectual and the worker, the North and South of the island, the contradiction inherent in the colonial subject's own self-perception. Similarly, the pamphlets the company have produced in the first phase of their existence[14] image that division in their own, often starkly rooted, binary oppositions, yet with such a form is the concomitant desire for wholeness and unity. The 'ever-withheld nature' of citizenship, the impossibility of assimilation, gesture both to rhetorical procedure and the oppositional form as the only method suitable to assess the predicament. This in turn suggests the possibility of a future dialectical criticism: the appropriate development for a movement based on hegemonic principles and one which ultimately allows a moment of fusion. For Field Day, this embryonic desire is actualised in two significant ways: through a reading of Derry as the company's spiritual and physical home and through the concept of the fifth province. Both have been widely criticised as mythologisations of the contemporary situation of Ireland,[15] yet to do so does not fully account for the scepticism towards history evinced by the company as it reaches towards an Irish materialist historiography yet unformed. To illustrate this dilemma it is necessary to consider Benjamin's famous conception of the 'Angel of History' and the sense that 'where we perceive a chain of events, he sees one single catastrophe which keeps piling wreckage upon wreckage and hurls it in front of his feet' (Benjamin 1973: 247).

It is in this maelstrom of history that Field Day locates itself. The desire to find tradition or continuity, as with the tentative explorations undertaken by the anthology (which, in this context, celebrates discontinuity as fully as it acknowledges continuity), contrasts with the resistance towards a historicism which denies the possibility of a revolutionary moment. Following this, Field Day's adaptation of the concept of the fifth province, which I will return to later, suggests aspects of Benjamin's ultimate messianism, while their reading of Derry in its physicality owes much to Benjamin's angel. In returning to the city as a point of departure into the future tense, Field Day find, not a continuous narrative, but the wreckage from 'the often violent collision of a past that has been recuperated in bits and pieces and a present badly in need of insight into what has been' (Jennings 1987: 50–1). Such an interpretation functions as a necessary internal resistance to the paradigms of history offered by the pamphlets,[16] as it emphasises in the contradictory iconography of the city a freedom from the meta-narrative while allowing the eternally transitory notion of the present to establish a dialogue with the past. This explains why, for Deane, Derry is not only 'a symbolic city in the minds of the unionist and nationalist people', it is also 'possibly the most sensitive city in Ireland and the site where both cultures meet and collide' (MacDermott 1985). Such a collision does not privilege, or recognise, either culture as the dominant narrative, but instead offers the possibility of a reading of the past as fragment which allows understanding to 'leap like a spark between the various elements in the larger pattern' (Jennings 1987: 50).[17] The centrality of this progression to Field Day's operations since *Translations* is reinforced by Deane's awareness in the programme notes to *Three Sisters* that 'The company has already, with *Translations*, created a consciousness of itself as a force involved with history. . . . But it needs a dialectic.'

This interpretation of Derry as a place of conflict, a city in which the meta-narratives of loyalist and nationalist historicism are rendered subjective (and therefore inert) by the fragmentation of the present is not one unique to Field Day's own ideological vision. Rather, Field Day's practices, which make use of the anomalies inherent to the city, are coherent with readings of the city common since partition. The relentless urge towards mythologisation which is the shared trait of these readings does not therefore suggest the triumph of one historical narrative over another, but rather details the failure of those narratives to gain and establish dominance. This has rendered Derry as an isolated city within a Northern Irish context while partition has prevented its assimilation into the Republic (which contains most of its natural hinterland). There is, then a formative tradition to its otherness which speaks of its location as a place apart:

> For the past 45 years Derry has been a city apart. There has always been this open-sore in the body politic of Northern Ireland. Derry is a city with a

legitimate grievance. When Ireland was partitioned it was Derry's terrible
misfortune to lose a great part of her hinterland and especially the Inishowen
Peninsula in East Donegal. . . . She never recovered from this disastrous blow.
When times are bad Derry suffers most and unfortunately times have very
often been bad for the city. Recently she had been dealt another blow by the
decision of the Government to deprive her of one of her transport links with
a very wide area. It is not surprising that she considers herself the forgotten
city. There is ample justification for the feeling. The Government's decision
to reject her claims to the university is the last straw.

(Warnock 1965)

This agonised statement from a letter published in the *Derry Journal* in 1965,
reads the city in terms similar to Benjamin's 'one single catastrophe' from
which there is not a causal chain of events but a simple accumulation of
'wreckage upon wreckage' (Benjamin 1973: 247). Resulting from such an
event is Derry as both 'forgotten' and 'apart'; forced to repeat the terms of
its own abandonment in each new humiliation, it is denied a place within a
linear developmental historiography. Deane too has considered Derry in these
terms, finding its people 'locked into the city and its history' by 'the oppressive
sense of siege' (Deane 1983). Central to both these readings is the crepuscular
situation of Derry in the mid sixties and, most importantly, the decision in
1965 to grant the new University of Ulster to the small, unionist, town of
Coleraine rather than to Northern Ireland's second city.[18] The sense of
bewilderment engendered by this decision was considerable and reinforced
the perception of the city as extraneous to the Union yet unable to enter
into any new relationship.

A more recent essay by Seamus Deane, 'Political Football' (1991), focused
on Derry City's removal from the Irish League[19] in 1972 and, as he comments,
'It is hard to resist the emblematic appeal of some features of this story':

Its (Derry City's) presence in the League of Ireland is as significant or
insignificant as is the Irish government presence at Maryfield. It does not
represent something that is going to happen; it represents something that
might have happened. It is politics in the past subjunctive, which is about as
close to the future as we can get at the moment. Still, I remember the Derry
centre-forward, Cliff Forsythe, blundering his way over the Linfield line with
a ball laid on for him by Delaney, one Saturday afternoon. We saluted him
with 'A Nation Once Again' while the Linfield supporters roared abuse at
his 'Fenian' origins. Clifford is now a unionist MP, of the right-wing, not the
centre-forward, persuasion. But he did smile and wave at us as we roared for
the once-again nation, the nation that had never been, but was spectrally
present that Saturday in 1954, as an Irish unionist and protestant converted a
Glasgow Celtic pass into a goal against the Orange team to the delight of the
nationalist supporters of Derry, while the RUC glowered.
Maybe that's what sport is – a ridiculous hallucination with moments of
sublime possibility. Or is that politics?

In this extended metaphor we can see Deane moving towards a dialectical criticism by locating the political moment, the revolutionary moment, within an allegorical rather than temporal landscape. By so doing Deane's nationalism is both expressed and frustrated through his urge towards narrative simultaneity. His acknowledgement of a wider community (the Derry City supporters), of which he is indivisibly a part, gestures towards an individualistic imagining of the subject as part of a wider human activity moving *through* history. The teleological drive to this impels a displacement of the subject within a narrative defined by a sense of, in Benedict Anderson's terms, 'transverse, cross-time, marked not by prefiguring and fulfilment, but by temporal coincidence, and measured by clock and calendar' (Anderson 1991: 24). However, while this is in process it is simultaneously denied by the allegorical method which rewrites the specific moment of possible liberation as paradigmatic by extending the meaning across homogeneous time. Rather than allowing the possibility of a unique fulfilment, liberation becomes a moment of frustrated possibility eternally present yet eternally withheld in the allegory. In the absence of political process, the allegory 'represents something that might have happened'. For these reasons 'Political Football' is part of the tradition of imagining Derry as beyond the liberation of history, and explains why the urge to mythologise the city is a concomitant response. The 'moments of sublime possibility' allowed by Deane, can be visualised only as retrospective glimpses for the 'one single catastrophe' envisaged by Benjamin has effectively destroyed the possibility of awakening into narrative. Although not written as part of the Field Day agenda, 'Political Football' allows us to understand the company's attitudes both to Derry and to its own self-perception in two significant ways. Firstly, it suggests the opposition by which the Hegelian aspects implicit to Field Day's manoeuvres gain meaning in relation to the established hegemonic structure: the imposed subjective recourse to myth enforced by the absence of history as opposed to the liberation into teleology proposed through the counter-hegemonic process. Secondly, Deane's alignment with (and submersion into) the homogeneous 'nationalist supporters of Derry' and statements such as 'we threw a few experimental stones in their (Linfield supporters) direction after the match' have little to do with the sociology of football violence but a lot to do with a deep engagement with the power of coterie as a means of expressing rebellion. Which, in another discourse, would point to Field Day itself.

DERRY AND THE ANGEL OF HISTORY

By approaching Field Day's treatment of Derry as a mythologised entity from this angle I am suggesting that, rather than offering a pre-lapsarian vision of the city based on Republican pieties, it is acknowledging the current political and cultural stasis and offering methods of understanding how that condition can hint at a future state beyond the mythological. Paulin's programme notes for Friel's play *The Communication Cord* (1982) comments on the city's current 'Hobbesian civic wilderness', but notes: 'Nevertheless, they can also perceive that there is in Derry an effort at civil definition which appears to be absent, or less keenly felt, in Belfast and Dublin. Imaginatively, Derry is the most advanced city in Ireland and the Guildhall is a temple which joins the stained, bright images of empire to the idea of a new *res publica*.' Edna Longley has commented on Paulin's vision of Derry that, 'The projection on to "history" of contemporary aspirations accords with the Republican viewpoint from which history stands still: an attitude that refuses to accept the internal Northern vendetta as at least a variation on the old colonial theme' (Longley 1986: 192). This is a criticism that needs to be engaged with, as does her later comment that Field Day's 'locus is a visionary Derry awaiting Jacobite restoration' (Longley 1992: 21), yet such an interpretation also has to be seen to reflect, to some measure, the ongoing homogenisation of the diverse strands of republicanism necessitated by partition to which I have made earlier reference. Field Day certainly do have a grievance against history, although it is not the empirically underwritten history Longley would recognise, but rather than perceiving it as static it is contested as a form of endlessly cyclical and endlessly displaced subjection. For this reason, Paulin finds in the Guildhall not a repository of history but a physical symbol of eternally present possibility which links the homogeneous past dialectically to an *idea* of the future.

Field Day's use of the Guildhall in Derry to première their new dramatic productions has lent itself irresistibly to this kind of symbolism on many levels. For Stephen Rea it is 'a huge symbol of Empire, of the Union, of some kind of adherence to English principles',[20] while Shaun Richards has noted dramatically:

Derry is the unhappy home of significant events whose anniversaries have resounded bloodily across centuries of the city's history; most recently the infamous 'Bloody Sunday', but most notably, and notoriously, the annual 12 August parade of the Apprentice Boys who beat their way around the city walls to celebrate the lifting of the siege in 1689 and simultaneously declare the contemporary protestant refusal to surrender. Since 1980 another date has entered the Derry calendar: the third Wednesday of September on which the Field Day Theatre Company premieres its annual production prior to a tour of venues in Northern Ireland and the Republic. It is the choice of Derry's Guildhall as the location of the premieres, however, which strikes the symbolic note. Not only has the seat of administrative power been entered by art, albeit temporarily, but this stark Victorian edifice stands outside the city walls on the banks of the Foyle and so looks out to a wider world than that admitted by the beleagured insularity which those walls have historically expressed.

(Richards 1988: 52)

It is interesting to note the ways in which Richards, a critic who has expressed reservations about the Field Day project, writes Derry and the Guildhall into a historical framework amenable to the company's own practices. The history of the city is read not as a narrative but as a compression into a series of anniversaries subject only to the logic of the calendar year. These events, in turn, can be said to be significant only in their function as physical fragments of the past, so that the annual parade of the Apprentice Boys does not so much actually displace the original lifting of the siege 300 years previously as enact it within simultaneous time. In this sense Field Day's establishment of a new date in the Derry calendar becomes precisely as significant as any other ritual: the progression being not a displacement of archaic ceremonial by the contemporary happening, as a linear reading would stress, but an arbitrary massing of data which can link symbolically but not causally. By locating Derry in homogeneous, empty time, the only aspects of its past which become significant are those which can exist in the dimensions of the present as physical, tactile artifacts. This, however, does not provide a stable framework of referents in itself. The Guildhall, central to Field Day's own symbolic structure, can be read as a monolithic and unyielding relic of an imperial past (Rea), a point of possibility and plurality located beyond the city walls (Richards), or both (Paulin). Parochial in a province-wide context yet central to the city itself, it embodies the contradictions implicit in defining the politics of identity as it operates both as physical desire (for the area) and resistance (to the unionist hegemony).

While Field Day have largely accepted this plurality as amenable to a reading of the company as barbarians within the citadel, it should be acknowledged that the primary political moment which allows this reading (the première of *Translations* in 1980) provided other symbols for the Guildhall's more permanent occupants which accord with Richards's notion of art entering the seat of administrative power. Perhaps unaware that Friel's earlier play *The Freedom of the City* was located in the Guildhall, and included the character Skinner (played by Rea) telling his fellow captives that 'this is theirs, boys and your presence here is a sacrilege' (Friel 1988: 140), *Translations*' première was seen to offer 'a unique occasion, with loyalists and nationalists, Unionists and SDLP, Northerners and Southerners laying aside their differences to join together in applauding a play by a fellow Derryman' (Editorial *Irish Press* 1980). It is difficult to assess the extent to which Field Day acquiesced with this neo-Arnoldian interpretation of their venture – the City Council were, after all, heavily funding the project – but it represents another point of opportunity which, if taken, would have led Field Day on a very different path. What *Translations* was actually saying in its absolute condemnation of territorial appropriation rarely impinged on the euphoric reception the play received in Derry: swept along on a tide of reconciliatory impulses which sought unity within the remit of culture, Field Day's own ideological position was ironically displaced within a framework the later pamphlets would harshly dismiss.

Perhaps because of this difficulty the directors of Field Day have been careful in offering versions of their own past which foreground the sense of the political moment as paradigmatic to their own concerns. Paulin's poem 'S/He', part of the collection *Liberty Tree* (Paulin 1983: 70–3), offered an early example of this contextualisation:

> Yesterday I stared
> at this girl with cropped hair –
> a grandpa shirt on her
> and lovebites on her neck,
> little pinky bruises
> like a rope had snagged there.
> Ah shite, the bitter joy
> as the plunged head gets born! –
> a March wind
> hits the main street
> of a village called Convoy
> and I'm starved
> by the first screech that's torn
> from the guts of the blind poet.
>
> Something in the air,
> too-quiet-altogether
> on the back road that slips
> down into Derry.
> Where that open pasture
> slopes from a close wood
> to a file of chestnuts
> there's a counterfeit sense
> that unsettles me just now.
> It might be the landlord's absence
> from a version of pastoral,
> or the hidden scanner
> that has to be somewhere. . . .
>
> 'Would you give us a lift, love?
> it's that late n'scary . . . .'
> I was only half there
> like a girl after a dance,
> wary, on the road to Muff.
> We might've been out after curfew

in the buzzy *deux-chevaux*,
slipping past the chestnuts
on a street in provincial France.

It stuck close to me, though,
how all through the last half
a helicopter held itself
above the Guildhall –
Vershinin's lines were slewed
by the blind chopping blades,
though Olga looked chuffed
when she sighed, 'Won't it be odd
with no soldiers on the streets?'

Paulin's technique of collage and fracture denies the possibility of a linearly narrated poetic strategy while searching for, and eventually finding, the political moment in the reception of Field Day's *Three Sisters* in Derry 1981. Through this search the poem inhabits a number of theoretical locations, both cultural and geographic, which are both rejected and assimilated in the final image. Micro-narratives are found and simultaneously dismissed ('a village called Convoy') as inadequate points of transition rendered stationary; a legacy of the frozen displaced moment both desired by the poem and indicative of the political stalemate imposed by partition. With this the poem becomes a baedeker of Irish poetic forms, gesturing towards John Montague's *The Rough Field* and, more significantly, Heaney's 'Punishment' and 'Strange Fruit' (Heaney 1975: 37–9). Invoking the latter, the poem can stare voyeuristically at 'this girl with cropped hair', finding on her the marks of tribal vengeance but recognising these as marks of affection. Remembering that this is yesterday's event and that the metaphor does not carry, the poem dismisses it as alien to its own procedures while still looking for the signifying framework which will allow its own teleological fulfilment. This is found, albeit with qualifications, on the descent into Derry. The poem, unable to make its own significance, 'slips down' into the pastiche and forgery of a landscape underwritten by the totalitarian and corrupt before coming to the 'hereness' of Derry: the   :
crystallisation of the eternally transitory moment.

In the Guildhall performance of *Three Sisters*, a play set in a provincial military garrison, the poem seeks closure and, through that, a mode of rebeginning beyond the endless circling of images and previous frustrations. This urge to reawaken into narrative is prevented by the presence of the British Army helicopter which 'held itself above' the performance as it simultaneously holds back the fruition of the moment leaving little but the possibility of a veiled irony in a subversive gesture. It is at this point, it seems to me, that Richards misreads 'S/He' and its relationship to *Three Sisters*:

'While the sense of Chekov's play is that the sisters feel deserted and desolate as a result of the garrison's departure, the preferred reading – in Paulin's poem – is that Olga should look "chuffed" by the troops' withdrawal' (Hughes 1991: 141). Rather than Olga's gesture being seen as a distinctly predetermined rewrite of Chekov's original play as Richards suggests, Paulin's reading in 'S/He' is beholden to the chance collision of indeterminates mediated through the original moment of the play's cultural existence. This is not the 'preferred reading' as intended by the overall production of the play but an attempt to consider as paradigmatic the resistant strategies of art as they exist at any one moment.

Ultimately, 'S/He' cannot find a point of fixity but it does allow us to read Field Day in terms of the relationships and incongruities it establishes.[21] Alienated from the now tired concept of the meta-narrative, any authority found in the poem acknowledges its primary debt to Zbigniew Herbert's poetic device 'Mr Cogito': the metaphysical principle of logic set loose in the totalitarian framework of historiography and defined by Paulin as 'a Cartesian spectre . . . whose thought processes never lead to the consoling infinite I AM. To call Mr Cogito Herbert's poetic persona is to clothe him in the myth of the individual; instead, Cogito is the poet as non-person speaking invisibly and silently in the empty daylight. He is the voice of an underground or naturally mobile nation' (Paulin 1992: 204–5). It is this denial of subjecthood under the sign of totalitarian erasure that links Herbert, 'S/He' and Field Day, and allows, as Field Day's dramatic material and the locations inhabited in 'S/He' suggest, a pan-European reading of the company's work. In 'S/He', 'the road to Muff' across the border (and to Friel's home at the time) could be a 'street in provincial France' after the curfew or indeed any place within the 'dank mitteleuropa' which haunts Paulin's poetry. Locations only gain significance in relation to locations elsewhere and within Field Day's anxiety to present Chekov in Ireland is Friel's awareness of the dilemma of the Irish actor 'pretending to be an Englishman, pretending you're a Russian'.

There are then strategic reasons for the European orientation the company has taken, not least in the rejection of what Edna Longley has termed the 'cultural cringe' often denounced in the triangular relationship of Belfast, Dublin and London. This is given a voice in Translations through the character of Hugh: 'Wordsworth? . . . no. I'm afraid we're not familiar with your literature, Lieutenant. We feel closer to the warm Mediterranean. We tend to overlook your island' (Friel 1981: 41). In Field Day's pamphlets this rejection takes a more specific form in the desire to escape from British empirical paradigms and to present Irish nationalism as part of a larger and more inclusive debate designed to deny a reading of it as anomalous. This progression culminated in 1988 with Field Day's publication of three pamphlets offering an international Marxist perspective on Ireland.[22] While these essays were widely criticised for, amongst other things, their application of what was seen as an inappropriate terminology to the subtlety of Anglo-Irish relations (Hughes 1991: 146–7), they largely succeeded in bringing Field Day more conclusively into the wider nationalist debate.

Eamonn Hughes has also identified the broader perspective Field Day are seeking to bring to Irish cultural examination, and has located this within the turn the pamphlets have taken towards structuralism and post-structuralism. Seeing in this a response to the wider institutional 'crisis of the subject' particularised by Field Day's own concern with Ireland as a area of displacement, he writes:

> The separation of these coinciding bases is almost impossible even though it is difficult to trace in the pamphlets anything other than the most general acknowledgement of the wider intellectual context. This does not stop the arguments around Field Day being complicated by the overlay of the wider upon the narrower moment and has led to a sense on the part of some critics that the project of Field Day is a very much more doctrinaire, or at least developed, affair than it actually is. What the identification of Field Day as a project informed by structuralist and post-structuralist theories allows us to do is, however, to recognise it *not* as a doctrinaire enterprise but as an enterprise which is alert to the world beyond the constrictions of Irish cultural debate.
>
> (Hughes 1990: 69)

Hughes is, I feel, right to perceive Field Day as only *informed* by structuralism. To mistake the early pamphlets for a fully realised structuralist practice would be to confuse the desire for a dialectic with the actuality which is yet unformed. That said, the pamphleteers have, in the main, been liberated by the wider perspective to which Hughes refers and have demonstrated a greater freedom of critical interpretation than those critics of Field Day (especially Longley and Foster but also Eavan Boland) who perhaps, as my previous chapter demonstrates, *are* trapped in a doctrinaire project which forbids the analysis of certain given prerequisites.

It was with the eventual publication of *The Field Day Anthology of Irish Writing* (Deane ed. 1991) that the discussion of these issues became most heated. Criticised in nearly every aspect, the anthology's textual life has been one of upheaval, planned revision and (often) absolute condemnation. Rather than helping to 'produce analyses of the established myths and stereotypes' it has sharply revealed the disparities inherent in many aspects of Irish cultural expression. This has worrying implications for a reading of Field Day as a counter-hegemonic project. While, with its emphasis on the counter-hegemonic, it *is* to some extent right to consider Field Day's operations as a doctrinaire agenda,[23] the perceived monolithic nature of that term – and with it 'tradition' and 'identity' – allows, seemingly, no possibility for appropriation and reapplication. Edna Longley, in a hostile review of the work for the *London Review of Books* (Longley 1990), saw the project as a 'newsletter from a section of the Irish Intelligentsia' and noted: 'The conflict in, and about, Northern Ireland has renewed a struggle for cultural hegemony that took various forms in 19th- and early 20th-century Ireland. The anthology rehearses those earlier debates and is itself a hegemonic attempt: a heavy-gun emplacement on a *Kulturkampf* which has engaged Irish literary critics, historians and some writers during the past decade.'[24]

In this 'struggle' for hegemony there remains a reading of the process that does not acknowledge the dominant hegemonic positions that more or less remained in place during the periods Longley considers; a strategy typical of revisionist historiography in its Irish manifestation (see Whelan 1991: 23–6). Any sense of hegemonic activity as dialectic, as transformative of lived social relations, is denied; rather it becomes a form of appropriation divorced from the conditions of the present and limited to a reading of the intelligentsia in its most dismissive form. Not that Longley's review was anything other than typical; the condemnation the anthology received tended to speak more loudly about the suspicion Field Day's overall manoeuvres have engendered rather than the text itself. Relatively, this is no bad thing, but it does suggest that Field Day's self-image as an organic intelligentsia is still an isolated position, and that Field Day, as Deane has it, is still not free 'from the accusation that it is taking one snap-shot of a permanently mobile field and claiming that this single frame is the picture that represents the poetry-in-motion of the whole' (Deane ed. 1990). This is unfortunate in that a counter-hegemonic process, if it is to be receptive to the movement in the dominant hegemony, has to be by definition, fluid and polymorphous. As David Lloyd has persuasively argued in relation to Gramsci:

> Suspicion of much contemporary 'post-colonial theory' has been justly grounded in the criticism of the easy transferability which, like metaphor itself, risks discovering identity at the expense of significant difference. Gramsci, on the contrary, offers a model in which a given conceptual apparatus gains in complexity according to the levels of specificity at which it is applied. At the same time, he recognises in what he terms the 'ethical state' the expression of the finally universal claims of hegemonic institutions within which conflicting and contradictory interests are negotiated.
>
> (Lloyd 1993: 9)

Apart from Hughes's 'To Define your Dissent', there has been no widespread recognition of this potential in any of the analyses of the company so far undertaken. Rather, the disparity of definition revealed by the reviews of the anthology, which at times seemed to be speaking a different language altogether, have led to a bizarre realignment of responses in opposition to Field Day which has, in turn, rendered the anthology as representative of the reactionary, the traditional and the monolithic. In this sense a consensus *has* been created by the anthology but it is one which suggests the overall strength and triumph of revisionism within Irish historiography. In opposition to this, Field Day are seen to have a ·'Totalising Imperative' – the title of perhaps the most condemnatory review of the work written by Damian Smyth:

> Whatever about the lure of capitalism or the rhetoric of 'freedom', it is ultimately the old myth that all ills – economic, social and political – can be cured by a magic formula of national coherence, and the elimination of difference, within the single monotonous discourse of 'nationalism', which is the real issue at the cutting edge of European affairs. . . . In this context, the *Field Day Anthology of Irish Writing*, published last year, appears as the most arrogant and challenging example of such a neo-Romantic, totalising vision to be produced in Europe. There is a fundamental absurdity to the project: in spite of the language of 'discontinuity' and 'rupture' displayed as fashion accessories in the critical framing, there seems to be something primordially continuous about 'Ireland' and 'being Irish' over a 1500–year period. A kind of absolute history is asserted.
>
> (Smyth 1992: 26)

Aware of what Field Day are up to, Smyth is having none of it. Although, in many ways, this is perhaps the most astute (*and* polemic) review of the anthology available, Smyth's reluctance to address the existing dominant cultural detritus leads him to a position whereby Field Day become upholders of the 'status quo'; a reading which confuses textual strategies of representation with the actual hierarchies of power needled through the province. Moreover, his refusal to take seriously Field Day's theoretical agenda – they deploy 'rhetoric', use language as 'fashion accessories' and 'buzz-terms', and speak 'gibberish' – aligns him with critics such as Longley who can only see the usage of such vocabulary as an imposition onto the recognised literary-empirical fabric of Ireland.[25] This alienation of another discourse brings to mind Raymond Williams's definition of 'jargon' in *Keywords,* in that its usage as a dismissive term 'could as readily be seen as a fact about the person who calls this "jargon", in an overbearing qualitative judgement of its presumed object' (Williams 1983: 174). Ultimately, in identifying Field Day's totalising imperative and accusing them of 'intellectual ethnic cleansing', Smyth mistakes an imagined sense of nation for its actuality and confuses 'the dominant ideology on the island' (by his reading, monolithic nationalism) with that ideology's ultimate (and unrealised) triumph. An interpretation which actually succeeds in erasing from his own version of Irish history the institutionalised divisions and oppressions implicit in partition itself.

This is not to suggest, however, that Smyth's review was anomalous. By invoking the definitive aspects appropriate to an anthology of such size, Field Day's own oppositional position has been inverted due to the textual and formal properties of its ultimate manifestation. One could argue that the transition from drama to pamphlet form to three-volume anthology made such a transformation inevitable and certainly Deane prefigured this line of criticism through comments he made in his 1984 Field Day pamphlet *Heroic Styles: The Tradition of an Idea*:

> The dissolution of that mystique is an urgent necessity if any lasting solution to the North is to be found. One step towards that dissolution would be the revision of our prevailing idea of what it is that constitutes the Irish reality. In literature that could take the form of a definition, in the form of a comprehensive anthology, of what writing in this country has been for the last 300–500 years and, through that, an exposure of the fact that the myth of Irishness, the notion of Irish unreality, the notions surrounding Irish eloquence, are all political themes upon which literature has battened to an extreme degree . . . .
>
> (Deane ed. 1985: 58)

It is actually unclear whether *The Field Day Anthology of Irish Writing* is the intended product of this desire, certainly Deane was careful to distance himself from ideas of comprehensiveness in his role as General Editor,[26] but there is an unavoidable irony in the fact that it was those who held to the 'prevailing idea' of Irish reality who so roundly turned on the anthology when it appeared. However, it should be recognised that even at his most polemic, Deane's ambitions for the anthology can be seen as strictly limited. Rather than attempting a 'definitive action' the introduction emphasises that the text is an 'act of definition', rather than ratifying the triumph of a particular tradition of writing it hopes to aid the process whereby such concepts take a 'long-delayed and much-deserved hammering' (Deane 1990a). Within the parameters of the counter-hegemonic it could hardly be otherwise. Envisaged by its opponents as a culminative act (a reading reinforced by the decision of the Field Day directors to take a sabbatical soon afterwards) its publication was, in fact, in all ways strategic. Produced to the moment for the moment, it becomes a 'kind of work-in-progress, an invention of the present moment and thereby a reinvention of the past'. It is with this that the anthology defines its own sense of tradition, a reading which accords with Paulin's sense of the project as one which does not 'present an ideology, but ideologies' and thereby says to the reader 'make what you want of them' (Hughes 1991: 146).

It is only in the form of the anthology as definitional statement, then, that a sense of a totalising imperative can hold. While the Field Day Anthology can be seen as a strategic gesture designed to shape the empty, homogeneous time, it also simultaneously gestures to the metaphysical dimension within nationalism which seeks to realise what Deane terms its 'intrinsic essence' (Deane ed. 1990: 8) in a tangible form. For the sake of my argument care needs to be exercised here. While the transient nature of the anthology is readily identifiable, not only theoretically but also practically (as the near immediate decision to add a further volume to the collection to address the overall marginalisation of writing by women in the initial work suggests),[27] it also operates as a physical metaphor for a future state of being in which Field Day would be superfluous. The anthology itself does not achieve this – *cannot* achieve this – but within the micro-moment of a text's production is a paradigmatic factor which seeks eventual closure. Optimistically, this becomes a mode of ironic resistance, a trope identified in Eagleton's pamphlet *Nationalism: Irony and Commitment*:

> A utopian thought which does not risk simply making us ill is one able to trace within the present that secret lack of identity with itself which is the spot where a feasible future might germinate – the place where the future overshadows and hollows out the present's spurious repleteness. To 'know the future' can only mean to grasp the present under the sign of its internal contradictions, in the alienations of its desire, in its persistent inability ever quite to coincide with itself.
>
> (Eagleton 1988: 7)

For Eagleton, this awareness is only possible under the sign of irony as it is predicated on a sense that all oppositional politics are 'ineluctably parasitic on their antagonists'. With this, the oppositional, binary nature of the antagonism cannot be prematurely foreclosed but must, as Deane suggests, 'be lived through in the present' (Deane ed. 1990: 4). Irony is necessary to this condition in order to ensure that the oppressive conditions of the moment are engaged with yet not reproduced. Importantly, Deane has invoked 'a degree of ironic self-consciousness' (Deane ed. 1990: 15) as an integral factor in the compilation of the anthology. With this the anthology adopts a canonical form which can both image and reject the process of canonisation in its awareness of the present 'internal contradictions':

> The point is not to establish a canon as such; it is to engage in the action of establishing a system that has an enabling, a mobilizing energy, the energy of assertion and difference, while remaining aware that all such systems – like anthologies of other national literatures – are fictions that have inscribed within them principles of hierarchy and of exclusion, as well as inclusion.

Read in such a way the inversion of Field Day's position within the dominant matrices of Irish culture to which I have made previous reference is precisely the result of the absolute dependence of oppositional politics on the established hegemony. Similar in its intentional forms, it can only insist on difference by conscious self-proclamation and the ultimate desire for its own elimination. A recognition of the contradictions engendered by this is part of the process by which those in opposition can live dialectically, by which a cultural materialist practice can begin. However, this only partly disguises the aspects to the process which can lead only to pessimism. Present within the dimensions of the dialectic moment is, what Deane terms, 'the inevitable monotony', the 'endless search for a lost communal or even personal identity' (Deane ed. 1990: 11), within which the constant acknowledgement of the artificial strategic gesture denies any sense of culture as redemption or teleological fulfilment. As he notes: 'Just naming it indicates that it is lost; once named it can never be unnamed. In the second place, such an identity is wholly unreal. It can be made manifest only by pretending that it is the conclusion to a search of which it was the origin.' In the desire to render conscious the interiorised aspects of an imposed identity then is the concomitant danger that in so doing nothing can be left as naturalised. The compilation of the anthology, in this framework, does not represent a premature homogenisation of a tradition yet unformed but rather draws attention to the fact of absolute fragmentation and breakdown through a moment of ironic resistance akin to Olga's gesture at the end of 'S/He'.

This can return us to the philosophy of Benjamin. Seeing the major communities in the North compelled to 'rehearse positions from which there is no exit' (Deane ed. 1990: 15) while attempting to begin a narrative through a dialectical practice which involves the acknowledgement of absolute loss, Field Day has had recourse in the past to the concept of the fifth province as 'the secret centre ... the place where all oppositions were resolved' (Hederman 1985: 110).[28] In this is an image of unity and wholeness beyond both the geographical four provinces and the temporal competing narratives: 'a transcendent location' as Friel has defined it. Although such a desire does not operate teleologically, in Field Day's notional fifth province are traces of Benjamin's messianism: a means of reconciling the permanent catastrophe of history to the Hegelian ideal of progress implicit to both philosophies. While Benjamin's longing for the messianic moment involves a concomitant desire for the apocalyptic end to history, it also allows the perfection of the moment in the idea, an idea which only has existence and meaning outside history itself. Field Day, taking a gamble on the future, have needed just such an escape in their own practices. Finding themselves, like the angel of history, irresistibly thrown forwards by a force they cannot as yet control, their ultimate failure is, in many ways, both assured and inevitable. However, as Deane makes clear, this does not belittle the worth of the attempt:

A commitment towards comprehending the system is what Field Day is about and, what's more, I recognise our failures. In fact, we could not *but* fail, given all the limitations of the situation with which we started, given the limitations of the individuals in Field Day. But Field Day is trying to say to people in Ireland not to sell their soul to an idea of Irishness, or to anything other than an attempt to analyse and understand what is. Of course, it can only be an attempt at any given stage, and every attempt, like the Field Day

145

attempt, is culture-bound and time-bound, and therefore subject to the same limitations other subjects have been.

(Lundy and MacPóilin 1992: 25–6)

As there are strategic reasons for Field Day's operations there are also strategic reasons for wishing to defend the validity of the project at this point in time. The emphasis on the company's counter-hegemonic designs, a reading problematised by the publication of the anthology, needs to be stressed in a critical climate where Field Day can be seen as upholding the 'status quo' – if only because such a reading can remind us that the status quo, in actuality, has been a twenty-five-year-long crisis during which thousands of people have lost their lives. If the Field Day project has so far failed, it is as much a failure on the part of the Irish intellectual community as a whole to extend the critical vocabulary used in the discussion of culture to a location which would allow at least the recognition of Field Day's terminology. It is this lack, more than any other, which Field Day's reception as a politicised phenomenon has highlighted.

NOTES

1. There are at least nine references to 'crisis' in Deane's introduction to *Nationalism, Colonialism and Literature* (Deane ed. 1990).
2. Here as elsewhere I am indebted to Michael W. Jennings's *Dialectical Images: Walter Benjamin's Theory of Literary Criticism* (Jennings 1987: 38).
3. The programme notes for Field Day's first dramatic production *Translations* (1980) define the company's name as 'a day on which troops are drawn up for exercise in field evolution, a military review, a day occupied with brilliant or exciting events'. The emphasis on the transitory moment in time as empirical event is clear.
4. As I will demonstrate, within post-colonial models of analysis this assimilation into the strategies of the dominant (coloniser) is considered ever withheld.
5. The latter is 'constituted for the whole of society in anticipation of moments of crisis of command and direction when spontaneous consent has failed' (Gramsci 1971: 12).
6. A matter of arithmetic; the paper was presented in 1985, Field Day was formed in 1980.
7. There are interesting issues of authority within the Field Day committee itself which question Deane's position as the major ideological instigant. Originally founded around the Brian Friel and Stephen Rea (Field Day's name is in part based on the names 'Friel' and 'Rea'), the company's need for charitable status required an increase in the membership of the board. Seamus Heaney, Seamus Deane, Tom Paulin and David Hammond were appointed as directors. Of these, only Deane and Hammond also became members of the company being granted

one share each; Friel and Rea each have six. According to the Articles of Association *'seniority shall be determined by the order in which the names stand in the register of members'*. The first name in the register is Friel's. For further analysis of the implications of this see Hadfield and Henderson 1983: 63–6.

8. As I will discuss, it is through Field Day's understanding of Derry as essentially marginal that it gains its particular resonances for the company's work.

9. Heaney's Field Day pamphlet, *An Open Letter* (Field Day Pamphlet 2) makes this point more saliently when considering the British Queen: 'Except that from the start her reign/of crown and rose/Defied, displaced, *would not combine*/what I'd espouse' (emphasis added).

10. It is worth noting that the magazines *Atlantis* (1970–74) and *The Crane Bag* (1977–85) attempted to form similar movements albeit without the specific agenda which so demarcates Field Day. Deane was closely involved in *Atlantis* (being on the editorial board), less so in *The Crane Bag*.

11. 'The relationship between the intellectuals and the mode of production is not as direct as it is with the fundamental social groups but is, in varying social degrees, "mediated" by the whole fabric of society and by the complex of superstructures, of which the intellectuals are, precisely, the "functionaries".'

12. St Patrick's Day Broadcast, 1943 (Deane ed. 1991, vol. III: 748).

13. The most interesting example of this is the report of a press conference held in New York in Spring 1987. Part of a fund-raising venture for the Field Day Foundation involving Friel, Deane, Heaney and Paulin, the nature of the event necessitated collective responsibility for any answer given. Geoffrey Stokes comments: 'All three (Heaney, Deane and Paulin), it should be said, were tired; Paulin was nursing a heavy cold, and Heaney spent much of the time stretched out on a hotel-room couch' (Stokes 1987: 29).

14. The pamphlet medium is in itself an indicator of the hegemonic designs the company have. By invoking the tradition of pamphleteering the company places itself in opposition to the standard volume of critical enquiry (written by intellectuals for intellectuals) and in support of the subterfugal gesture.

15. For instance Longley 1986: 191–2.

16. Perhaps the best example of these being Deane's observation in *Civilians and Barbarians* that 'Of all the blighting distinctions which govern our responses and limit our imaginations at the moment, none is more potent than this four hundred year-old distinction between barbarians and civilians' (Deane ed. 1985: 42).

17. This fragmentation is contained in the city's name. With neither 'Derry' nor 'Londonderry' being able to gain absolute dominance, the city is often represented as 'L'Derry'.

18. I owe this awareness to the extensive research carried out by Marilynn Richtarik in her invaluable study *Acting Between the Lines: The Field Day Theatre Company and Irish Cultural Politics, 1980–84* (Richtarik 1995).

19. For the uninitiated it should be noted that the Irish League is the representative body for Northern Irish football (not GAA), and is not to be confused with the League of Ireland (in which Derry City now play successfully) which represents teams from the Republic. Derry City's removal effectively confined any real interest in the Irish League to clubs based in the eastern part of the province.

20. 'History Boys on the Rampage', *Arena*, BBC2 programme (December 1988).

21. Although appropriate to this particular poem, it would be unwise to extend Field Day's totalising imperative to all aspects of the individual director's work. In the case of Paulin and Heaney (less so with Deane) the overall poetic strategy

of the writers prevents absolute subsumption into the mechanics of a coterie. As Heaney comments: 'The relationship between us is supportive and confirmatory and reinforcing at a level previous to and posthumous to the act of writing itself. The act of writing for each of us remains as solitary and impossible as it ever was' (Stokes 1987).

22. Respectively, *Nationalism: Irony and Commitment*, by Terry Eagleton (Field Day Pamphlet 13); *Modernism and Imperialism*, by Fredric Jameson (14); and *Yeats and Decolonisation*, by Edward W. Said (15).

23. Richtarik's detailed study (1995) of the first five years of the company argues convincingly that in its original manifestation it would be incorrect to perceive Field Day as having formulated a particular agenda. However, as she makes clear (p. 243), the gradual increase in Deane's involvement through this period also constituted the development of a stated ideological practice.

24. Longley's description of Field Day's manoeuvres as operating within a *Kulturkampf* has interesting implications, as it was the name given to Bismark's attacks on Catholic opposition to his own Prussian hegemony. As Hoare and Nowell Smith comment in a footnote to Gramsci's *Prison Notebooks* (p. 22), *Kulturkampf* can be seen as an aspect 'of the bourgeois-democratic struggle against the residues of reactionary social forces'.

25. See Edna Longley, 'Writing, Revisionism and Grass-seed: Literary Mythologies in Ireland' (Lundy and MacPóilin 1992: 18–19).

26. 'Obviously an anthology must be selective. Any claim to comprehensiveness would seem to be subverted by that simple necessity' (Deane 1990a).

27. See Katie Donovan, 'Absence stirs anger amongst women', *The Irish Times* (27 February 1992: 10) and Nuala O'Faolain, 'The voice that Field Day didn't record', *The Irish Times* (11 November 1991: 14). The overall under-representation of women's writing in the initial anthology has to be seen as Field Day's most blatant mistake to date.

28. Richards' 'Field Day's fifth province: avenue or impasse?' (Hughes 1991) further develops the company's use of this concept.

CHAPTER SIX

'Just Another Twist in the Plot': Seamus Heaney, Paul Muldoon and the Final Institution

PARADIGMS OF POSSIBILITY

So you drive on to the frontier of writing
where it happens again. The guns on tripods;
the sergeant with his off-on mike repeating

data about you, waiting for the squawk
of clearance; the marksman training down
out of the sun upon you like a hawk.

And suddenly you're through, arraigned yet freed,
as if you'd passed from behind a waterfall
on the black current of a tarmac road

past armour-plated vehicles, out between
the posted soldiers flowing and receding
like tree shadows into the polished windscreen.

(Heaney 1987: 6)

Seamus Heaney's journey through the check points of writing presents a readily identifiable parable of the literary self-conscious: a parable that poetry from Northern Ireland has had recourse to many times. In 'From the Frontier of Writing', the journey from doubt, through confrontation, to a visionary state of artistic confidence is one that offers a paradigm of poetic development which Heaney has located in the work of Patrick Kavanagh (Heaney 1988: 3–14) and which also, microcosmically, images Heaney's own poetic career from *North* (1975), through *Station Island* (1984), and into the future tense with *Seeing Things* (1991). The final state of achievement is one dependent on the 'squawk of clearance' granted by literary criticism, an examination which leaves him 'a little emptier' ('as always') but to which he is equal. While such a reading may seem to portray Heaney's poetic manoeuvres as slightly pat, I would rather emphasise the liberation through cynicism that 'From the Frontier of Writing' proffers simultaneously; an interpretation which allows the poem a prefigurative quality beyond the ineffable world of the transcendent or prophetic. Central to this is the intersection of the British military presence in Heaney's known landscape and the preponderance of literary critical terminology (not only the 'Frontier of Writing' itself, but the 'nilness round that space' and the 'pure interrogation' of the original encounter) that describes their operations within the parameters of the poetic artefact.

I have previously demonstrated how British empirical paradigms of criticism have been developed in Ireland and how these paradigms not only have had a prolonged existence that extended beyond British criticism but, in some instances, have been used to protect partition itself. 'From the Frontier of Writing' carries a similar awareness and, as such, is analogous to the dissection of British literary critical colonialism Heaney undertakes in his Field Day pamphlet 'An Open Letter' (Deane ed. 1985: 23–30). It is not that the forces of physical coercion and cultural interpellation are seen as equally oppressive or equally undesirable but rather that both require Heaney to submit to their strictures in order to gain poetic subjecthood. Significantly, the result of this process is to render the subject as typical in all aspects. To be 'arraigned yet freed' is to allow the poet something close to the status of the visionary or the prophet but only once that status has been valorised by the process of examination which renders the individual as exemplary.

David Lloyd, in an astute essay on Heaney, has codified this trope as one in which 'the identity of the individual, his integrity, is expressed by the degree to which that individual identifies himself with and integrates his difference in a national consciousness' (Lloyd 1993: 15). This goes some way towards depicting the central dilemma to which Heaney's poetry has continually addressed itself. While the binary oppositional nature of Northern Irish society makes such an integration unavoidable – as do, in a sense, the binary comparative methods of literary New Criticism (gestured by the 'on-off mike' of the sergeant) – Heaney's fundamentally bourgeois poetic has chosen to represent that integration as a constant crisis of interest between the urge to a full individuation and the desire for assimilation. As existing within the genre of the journey poem then, 'From the Frontier of Writing' is swept along 'the black current of a tarmac road' to a destination which is always in view and which is not to be evaded. It culminates with Heaney's knowledge of his assured canonical status within the institution, a status posthumously conferred on both Kavanagh and Yeats before him, and, in another sense, can be said to mark the transition from writing to poetry.

It is interesting to test this progression against the critical reception accorded to Heaney since the publication of his latest collection of poetry, *Seeing*

Things – a title which, if ironically, suggests the kind of visionary state which looks beyond the critical judgement in itself and on towards posterity. For John Carey, writing in the *Sunday Times* (Carey 1991), the experience was transcendent: 'Reading these and several other poems, you feel what the first readers of, say, Keats's odes or Milton's 1654 [*sic*] collection must have felt – the peculiar excitement of watching a new masterwork emerge and take its permanent place in our literature.' As an English critic (and one perhaps sensitive to Heaney's previous statements of dissent from British traditions), Carey can only adumbrate his praise in terms of the sensation of reading not criticism. This allows a form of appropriation to take place but only within the liberal framework of 'our literature': an absolute inversion of Barthes's famous statement that, 'to go from reading to criticism is to change desires; it is no longer to desire the work itself but to desire one's own language' (Barthes 1987a: 143).

Secure in his language, Carey desires *Seeing Things* as a readerly pleasure; it is presented as literally *beyond* criticism. Certainly, as Declan Kiberd pointed out in his own review of the collection, 'Greater love no English critic hath than to write such lines of an Irish poet' (Kiberd 1991), yet this only begins to tell part of the astonishing story of Heaney's rise. As now undoubtedly the most famous Irish poet since Yeats, Heaney is the physical embodiment of George Moore's belief that art 'must be parochial in the beginning to become cosmopolitan in the end' (Moore 1985: 56). To witness the unfolding of each stage of his mature aesthetic design is to become aware of the slightly anomalous position he now holds in relation to other contemporary Irish poets. While the rapid rise to institutional pre-eminence of Irish poetry in general and Northern Irish poetry in particular over the last twenty five years has been echoed by a developing interest in Irish literary and cultural criticism (of which Field Day is the clearest example), Heaney's work now places him fundamentally beyond the parameters of such interpretation.[1] Instead, his work often occupies a landscape of absolutes, a location in which language becomes only an unwarranted intrusion in the ongoing drive to present unity and reconciliation within the transcendent experience:

> I am trying to name and describe magic, the magic of a poetry deft, accurate and pure, but I might as well try to spear satellites with a pitchfork. There is a Sufi term, *baraka,* which connotes, among other things, blessedness, as in the unmediated blessedness of being. This is a book steeped in *baraka,* a pure poetry of what almost escapes us in this extraordinary world.
>
> (Dorgan 1991: 3)

Having invoked an absolute as a definitive term, Theo Dorgan is left with no other option but to invoke another. *Seeing Things* itself becomes an icon, a receptacle for all that is left perfect in a fallen world, and a text which forms its own community – beyond social fracture – of pure believers. With this awareness the collection becomes the Koran of modern poetry, while Heaney, appropriately, figures as the prophet raised up from the people. Sharing their difficulties yet simultaneously removed from them he is rendered exotic, displaced, within the quotidian actualities of everyday life:

> The problem with a conversation with Seamus Heaney is its range is so wide, its levels so various and its diversions so many that, unintentionally – he is the most courteous of men – questions become redundant. They assume an emaciated, tentative tone, as one becomes aware of the resonances of his talk, the mastery of his language and the searching restlessness of his mind.
>
> Not that he is ungenerous with his time, his ideas, and, above all, discussion of his craft. Sustained by coffee, digestive biscuits and the offer of malt whisky, I was gripped by the diversity of his phrases, the intricacy of his word relationships and the luminosity of his thought. He used no word that wouldn't be at home on his Derry farm or in a Belfast or Dublin pub. But the words and phrases were formed by a rare golden vision.
>
> I had asked him to talk about the difference between a playwright and a poet, and I was reminded of another poet as he answered. A poet is a human being speaking to others – albeit one endowed with more lively sensibility, more enthusiasm and tenderness, with greater knowledge of human nature and a more comprehensive soul than are supposed to be common among humankind. Wordsworth's words are not, I imagine, those that would be chosen by Heaney for himself. But they echoed in my mind as he spoke.
>
> (Keyes 1990)

It is in the reconciliation of the division between 'digestive biscuits and the offer of malt whisky' and the 'rare golden vision' that, for John Keyes, Heaney's success becomes explicit.[2] His example forges a unity between the present and the canonical ghosts of the past which transcend not only historical fracture, but the division between the quotidian, fallible, individual and the great work of art. A recent study of Heaney by Michael Parker (1993) extended this perception into a full poetic biography and was revealingly subtitled *The Making of the Poet*. Through the course of the book the narrative portrays Heaney as simultaneously typical of the south Derry community from which he comes while emphasising the paradigmatic nature of his life-work in the production of a universal poetry. With this, as with the Keyes article, the overall emphasis falls on the role of the poet as a mediator of experience: a central aspect of Romantic ideology as Keyes's quotation from the 'Preface' to *Lyrical Ballads*, wittingly or not, demonstrates.[3] Perhaps in this instance, Heaney is only the most successful embodiment of an idea of the poet in Ireland present, especially in the North, since the sixties; an idea that has been seen to fulfill a strategic contemporary need. Centrally placed within this ideal is a notional ideology of poetics predicated on the belief in an achievable perfection of the matured voice; a tendency first located in Heaney by Clive James in 1972: 'With Seamus Heaney, an already achieved, uniquely precocious maturity is being deepened into a tragic voice. He has already left the point at which his contemporaries are now arriving. Soon people are going to start comparing him with Yeats' (James 1972: 25).

James's early awareness of the analogous nature of Heaney's poetic persona (although, it should be noted, this is an awareness carefully expressed) is one which has become increasingly popular and further allows the tentative codification of a number of assumptions about the Northern Irish poet which can be organised for the purposes of this chapter as a general paradigm. In this it is appropriate to follow Antony Easthope's definition of the concept of the paradigm in *Literary Into Cultural Studies* (1991), as one amenable to my own methods in that it 'signals the dependence of understanding on discourse while including the idea of knowledge, and so, crucially, an epistemology involving a subject–object relation'. Moreover, while a paradigm does not expect nor desire to find any particular subject existing in perfect relation to the objective paradigm itself, it can in Easthope's terms, bring 'object and subject into a *relation* of knowledge' (Easthope 1991: 9). The particular paradigm of Northern Irish poetics I am attempting to outline necessarily involves a consideration of the subject as both the poem as text and the poet as creator and embodiment of those texts. This need not be contradictory or overtly problematic if the poet is approached textually within the framework of the object. There are then six features which can be said to constitute this paradigm. These are:

(1) a reading of the poet as rooted to a physical location and community;
(2) a sense of the poet as exemplifying the values of that community;
(3) an insistence that the poet can mediate the truths already inherent in the community to the community;
(4) a field of interpretation in which the poem does not so much represent truth as embody it in its actuality;
(5) the assumption that within the poet is the possibility of teleological perfection;
(6) a literary critical practice which recognises both the primacy of the poem and the limits of its own discursive empirical practices in relation to it.

It should be recognised that these features are not necessarily restricted to Northern Irish poetry. As Easthope points out (after Kuhn), 'paradigms are inter-paradigmatic, internalising for themselves features shared by other paradigms'. However, in this is the possibility of making explicit naturalised or traditional forms as well as a method of identifying the inevitable declensions from the paradigm as they are present in each particular example. Naturally,

as such codification can tend towards the stereotypical there are other ways of presenting this subject-object distinction.

In 1974, *Fortnight*, aware of the growing interest in Northern poetry as a recognisably distinct entity, carried a feature on 'The Ulster Poets' by Harry Chambers. To illustrate this article on the front cover of the magazine was a cartoon by Martyn Turner[4] – perhaps the most incisive of Irish political caricaturists – which presented the stereotypical Ulster poet (with 'Ulster' probably taking a wry look back at Kavanagh) and his environment. Perhaps the intention was to play this stereotyped image against the specific differences Chambers encountered in his consideration of particular poets: an aim frustrated by Chambers' own reluctance to dispense with that homogeneous model. However, Turner's cartoon provides a visual representation of most of the features of the paradigm I have previously outlined. In the foreground is the figure of the poet sporting clipped beard, checked shirt and ill-fitting jacket. His right hand clutches a loose-leafed manuscript, his left is upraised in a gesture of enunciation. In the background is a divided landscape sundered (or linked) by the figure of the poet. To the right is an image of a rural agrarian location, to the left, the barbed wire, burning houses and broken glass of a riot-torn Belfast, Derry, Portadown, or wherever. The foregrounded figure of the poet mediates our reading of the background; Northern Ireland is not encountered through the poetry in his hand but through the values embodied in the stance he adopts. Moreover, it is only the poet figure who can link the two disparate landscapes in continuity. The urban-rural divide signals one form of fracture while gesturing both to a temporal discontinuity (past/present) and a conflict, understood empirically, between reality and image. It is only possible to quantify these juxtapositions by recourse to the central figure who can embody, reconcile and represent the oppositions within his own example. A critical practice which destabilises this centre cannot, therefore, hope to access the privileged continuities it offers.

This paradigm was most fully tested by the publication, one year later, of Heaney's *North*, a collection which relied heavily on the mediating figure of the poet to reconcile the mythological elements of the work to the political actuality which became its insistent function. While there is a danger of overstressing Heaney's reliance on this model within an argument ill-equipped to analyse its complications, it is fair comment to note that Heaney's agonisings though *North* about the role of the poet within society are best understood as a series of abdications and reaffirmations from and to the paradigm as I have previously outlined it. Moreover, in interview, Heaney could comment:

> The Tollund Man seemed to me like an ancestor almost, one of my old uncles, one of those moustached archaic faces you used to meet all over the Irish countryside. I felt very close to this. And the sacrificial element, the territorial religious element, the whole mythological field surrounding these images was very potent. So I tried, not explicitly, to make a connection between the sacrificial, ritual, religious element in the violence of contemporary Ireland and this terrible sacrificial religious thing in *The Bog People*. This wasn't thought out. It began with a genuinely magnetic, almost entranced relationship with those heads. . . . And when I wrote that poem ('The Tollund Man') I had a sense of crossing a line really, that my whole being was involved in the sense of − the root sense − of religion, being bonded to something, being bound to do something. I felt it a vow; I felt my whole being caught in this. . . . I'm very angry with a couple of snotty remarks by people who don't know what they are talking about and speak as if the bog images were picked up for convenience instead of being a deeply felt part of my own life.
>
> (Randall 1979: 18–19)

This necessary emphasis on intuition stresses a framework of interpretation absolutely beholden to the figure of the poet as a mediating presence. With this the possibility of theorising the relationship between present-day violence and ritual sacrifice, even if it were possible, is significant only in that it would challenge the position of Heaney as the central function of the myth; it has to be accepted on his terms or cannot be understood at all. Read in this way, the 'snotty remarks by people who don't know what they are talking about' can be seen as the frustrated aspiration of certain aspects of literary criticism to overthrow the primacy of poetry as a privileged discourse within Irish culture. Heaney's connections to the original myth, both familial ('like an ancestor almost') and ineffable, prevent any sympathetic consideration of the effectiveness of his parallels which do not first acknowledge an implicit trust in his instinctive judgement.

Edna Longley, not usually the sort of critic inclined to trust the opinion of the poet over the content of the poem, recognises this in her own consideration of *North* and begins her analysis with the admission that 'His reaction to the Man's photograph deserves the much abused term "epiphany", with its full Joycean connotations: a revelation of personal and artistic destiny expressed in religious language' (Longley 1986: 140). As further on in the essay Longley can comment that 'Heaney may have mistaken his initial epiphany for a literal signpost, when it was really a destination', this becomes a mode of criticism aware of the fact that to challenge the initial validity of Heaney's vision would be to render the complete volume as synthetic and open to theoretical procedure, its primary structural principle being one which revolves around the mysteries of Heaney himself. Similarly, Conor Cruise O'Brien, in an influential and now famous review of *North*, commented:

> I had the uncanny feeling, reading these poems, of listening to the thing itself, the actual substance of historical agony and dissolution, the tragedy of people in a place: the Catholics of Northern Ireland. Yes, the Catholics: there is no equivalent Protestant voice. Poetry is as unfair as history, though in a different way. Seamus Heaney takes his distances – archaeology, Berkeley, love-hate of the English language, Spain, County Wicklow (not the least distant) – but his Derry is always with him, the ash somehow, now standing out even more on the forehead.
>
> (O'Brien 1975: 23–4)

Again, it is in the realm of the mysterious, 'the uncanny', that Heaney's work transubstantiates into 'the thing itself'. Beyond representation, the poetry becomes an embodiment of the real angst of the community and its place, while Heaney is absolutely assimilated into its people. As always, the more Heaney's achievement becomes remarkable, the more typical he is rendered.

Inevitably the result of such procedures deeply underplays the complex relationship of the contemporary political situation in Northern Ireland to the ongoing violence. As Lloyd has noted, by basing his poetic in the concept of identity Heaney is 'unable ever to address the relation between politics and writing more than superficially, in terms of thematic concerns, or superstitiously in terms of a vision of the poet as a diviner of the hypothetical pre-political consciousness of his race' (Lloyd 1993: 14). Ciaran Carson, in a perceptive review of *North* (1975), was one of the first critics to identify this tendency. Observing that Edward McGuire's recent portrait of Heaney allowed the poet the 'status of myth, of institution' while 'forestall(ing) criticism', he comments: 'One can hardly resist the suspicion that *North* itself, as a work of art, has succumbed to this notion; Heaney seems to have moved – unwillingly perhaps – from being a writer with the gift of precision, to become the laureate of violence – a mythmaker, an anthropologist of ritual killing, an apologist for "the situation", in the last resort, a mystifier' (Carson 1975: 186).

Ultimately Carson's most vivid comments on the difficulties of this aesthetic were not found in prose but in the relentless probing of identity which constituted his collection *The Irish For No* (1987), yet his preliminary accusations were well aimed. Unwilling or unable to reconcile liberal individuation to social assimilation, much of Heaney's poetry can only find resolution of the contradiction within the notional closure offered by the well-made poem. A technique informed by practical criticism, Heaney's predominantly lyrical style allows a notional poetic voice to achieve a reconciliation of issues – a perfection of form – which addresses the contradictions inherent in his commitment to the paradigm. Such an interpretation, ironically if one considers 'From the Frontier of Writing', takes its methodology and example from within the institution and conforms to what Easthope (after Jane Tompkins) refers to as 'the Modernist reading' (Easthope 1991: 16–17). Within this, the text is intransitive, is presumed to be significant in the interaction of all possible meanings, yet simultaneously is restrictive of those meanings in the overall unity of the text. This often contradictory process is reliant on the transformative power of the ineffable statement; an absence which Roland Barthes identified in *Writing Degree Zero* as one located within the poetic word itself which: 'prepares to radiate towards innumerable uncertain and possible connections' (Barthes 1968: 47).

Able to reconcile all difference, the modernist reading's central emphasis on the poetic word not only encourages the play of meaning within the artefact but requires such play as a crucial factor in its overall efficacy. This has been necessarily important to the assimilation of Northern Irish poetry into an English interpretative framework. The specificities of difference, expressed as the strange or the dissenting ambiguity, can be welcomed in so far as they contribute to the overall richness of the poem's textual fabric – a progression which places the textual manifestation of the paradigm of Northern Irish poetics as I have previously outlined it within an institutional context. Heaney has written of his induction into this process with mixed feelings. At one level he maintains his insistence on the connection between 'the core of a poet's speaking voice and the core of his poetic voice', on another he recognises the benefits which can accrue through the modernist reading:

> I couldn't say, of course, that I had found a voice but I had found a game. I knew the thing was only word-play, and I hadn't even the guts to put my

name to it. I called myself *Incertus*, uncertain, a shy soul fretting and all that. I was in love with words themselves, but had no sense of a poem as a whole structure and no experience of how the successful achievement of a poem could be a stepping stone in your life. Those verses were what we might call 'trial-pieces', little stiff inept designs in imitation of the master's fluent interlacing patterns, heavy-handed clues to the whole craft.

(Heaney 1980: 45)

It is difficult to assess the significance of this apprenticeship to Heaney's later work, if only because his sense of the process as 'a game' – an artificial impediment to his primary and natural love of words – conflicts with his later awareness of the transformative possibilities of the lyric form to the lifework. As with the critical-thought militia of 'From the Frontier of Writing', Heaney's poetic undergoes an examination which leaves him 'arraigned yet freed'. He is granted a certain liberty yet remains absolutely implicated in the machinations of the literary critical institution. Indeed this conflict is reinforced by the Foreword to *Preoccupations* (Heaney 1980: 13), which deems it necessary to highlight those prose pieces which bear the hallmark of 'the slightly constricted utterance of somebody who underwent his academic rite of passage when practical criticism held great sway in the academy'. Heaney's 'slightly constricted utterance' has been well documented and criticised,[5] but its root cause has rarely been located as part of a specific critical practice. However, if this argument is accepted it can be seen that it is solely within the modernist reading that Heaney's expression of dissent has its being: an awareness which gives credence to Lloyd's contentious accusation that 'almost without exception, the poems respond compliantly to analysis based on assumptions about the nature of the well-made lyric poem' (Lloyd 1993: 35).

Desmond Fennell, coming from an entirely different tradition of criticism to Lloyd's, has similarly noted the welcome afforded to Heaney's work by academics (whom he places in opposition to 'Ordinary Readers'; Fennell 1991: 21), while Heaney, in interview with Randall, has commented that many of his poems are 'usually pulled tight at the end with little drawstrings in the last line or two' (Randall 1979: 18). Perhaps this tendency is most clearly expressed by reference to the lyric poem 'Making Strange'. Part of the 1984 collection *Station Island* – a volume often considered as undertaking the sternest form of self-analysis within Heaney's canon – it subtends its nominal consideration of identity as expressed in relation to geography under a desire to achieve a satisfactory form of coherent closure within its own formal limits:

> I stood between them,
> the one with his travelled intelligence
> and tawny containment,
> his speech like the twang of a bowstring,

and another, unshorn and bewildered
in the tubs of his wellingtons,
smiling at me for help,
faced with this stranger I'd brought him.

Then a cunning middle voice
came out of the field across the road
saying, 'Be adept and be dialect,
tell of this wind coming past the zinc hut,

call me sweetbriar after the rain
or snowberries cooled in the fog.
But love the cut of this travelled one
and call me also the cornfield of Boaz.

Go beyond what's reliable
in all that keeps pleading and pleading,
these eyes and puddles and stones,
and recollect how bold you were

when I visited you first
with departures you cannot go back on.'
A chaffinch flicked from an ash and next thing
I found myself driving the stranger

through my own country, adept
at dialect, reciting my pride
in all that I knew, that began to make strange
at that same recitation.

Michael Parker has helpfully noted that this poem has its genesis in a guided tour of South Derry undertaken by Heaney for the benefit of the Jamaican poet Louis Simpson (Parker 1993: 189). Encountering a childhood acquaintance, Heaney is cast as a mediator between the two men, who concomitantly embody aspects of his own lyric persona. It is in this mediation that a reconciliation of the parochial with the universal is made possible. Heaney, as the articulate expression of his community, is asked 'for help' by its voiceless, 'bewildered' aspects. Embodying the location through the relationship of dialect to territory, Heaney's strategy is, at first, 'cunning': a mode of evading the awkward confrontation. This is eased by the shift the poem takes towards formal closure through its emphasis on the poetic voice – a transformation which Parker notes approvingly: 'As a result of the stranger's presence, and because of the increased sophistication of his technique, he is able to recover his country, rediscover its familiar features and figures by means of metaphor and allusion that "make strange".'

While this reading of the process delimits the full range of *poetic* coherencies available it should be noted that it allows Heaney a closure which would be unobtainable in any other form. Rather than suggesting a rediscovery of the location, the pressure implicit to the concept of 'making strange' formalises Heaney's initial impressions of the country, rendering the absolute fracture between the community and the individual gestured by 'I stood between them' as little more than an ironic aftertouch by a poet securely in command of his craft. In this sense, while Heaney acknowledges the difference engendered by his induction into 'the game' he remains satisfied with the ultimate forms of closure it offers. 'Making Strange' can be seen as asking sterner questions of Heaney's relationship with his poetic than the longer title poem 'Station Island', yet those questions are not so much left unanswered as evaded through its insistence on being judged as a well-made poem. In other words, the aspects of Heaney's work which conform to the paradigm can only remain unproblematic if approached via the intransitive self-contained modernist reading.

CONCLUSION: *MADOC* AND THE INSTITUTION

DEANE: Do you think that if some political stance is not adopted by you and
the Northern poets at large, this refusal might lead to a dangerous
strengthening of earlier notions of the autonomy of poetry and
corroborate the recent English notion of the happy limitations of a
'well-made poem'? And furthermore, do you feel that this disdain of
poetry for all that would break its own autonomy could lead to the
sponsoring of a literature which would be almost deliberately
minor?

HEANEY: I think it could. . . .

DEANE: Do you think it has?

HEANEY: Most poetry is inevitably so. . . .

DEANE: But not deliberately so!

(Deane 1982: 67)

There are times when language breaks down. Part of an interview in *The Crane Bag* in which Seamus Deane, according to Edna Longley, 'tries to lick (Heaney) into political shape' (Longley 1986: 196), the exchange in one sense forms another critique of the New-Critical paradigm as one unsuitable for Ireland. Indeed in his homogenisation of the 'Northern poets', the idea of commitment Deane wishes them to espouse is one which does not find its oppositional image in the English tradition of New Criticism. This is important if we understand New Criticism not as an epistemology as such but rather as a pedagogy that has its ultimate home in the practices of the educational institution. In this the 'happy limitations' that Deane attacks are those confined to English institutional locations: the destination that Heaney's poetry 'inevitably' reaches. However Heaney's work is not isolated in this tendency. If such passive inevitability runs close to a symbiotic complicity with the interpellative reading practices of New Criticism within the institution, it is a complicity shared, most fascinatingly, by the poetry of Paul Muldoon.

As I will argue, Muldoon's long poem 'Madoc: A Mystery' (1990) can be read as an extended negotiation with the assimilating forces of the institution. The modernist readings that accrue from such forces are at once both satirised by the text and yet recognised as necessary to the poem's overall reading strategy. By placing New-Critical discourses within a pedagogical paradigm the developmental, almost teleological, drive to its methodology is rendered explicit. As 'Madoc' dramatises the attempted assimilation of colonial subjects within the imperial project, so its emphasis on riddles, word-games, and inter textual references gestures to a New-Critical reading which is similarly interpellative.[6] While the poem, to some extent, is reliant on the efficacy of these games for its success, the final institutional location that the poem inhabits – the Orwellian 'Unitel' – implies the actual limits of the plurality that New-Critical reading strategies are seen to offer. In this, the poem abandons us at the final end of all possibilities: the over-arching institution in which insurgent forces are effortlessly and endlessly contained. As we shall realise, the one voice of 'Unitel' becomes also the expression of a single and unitary telos. This is the point at which, in Gramsci's terms, a new 'arrangement' is reached within hegemony out of 'widespread scepticism' (Gramsci 1971: 276): an arrangement which marks the end of the interregnum and a return to the cyclical, homogeneous, parade of history.

It is through a consideration of the treatment of 'Madoc' in review that the implications of this awareness can be illustrated. Within the foreclosed system of interpretation offered by the text, the emphasis on linguistic and structural puns delimited the extent of a New-Critical interpretive elite[7] as one in harmony with Muldoon's complex juxtapositions. In this the possibility of dissident readings was severely restricted; as Longley noted in her own review of the work: '"Madoc" will tease academics and appeal to lovers of detective-stories, crosswords, riddles, codes, signs and portents, teeny-weeny keys' (Longley 1991a). If, as I have demonstrated, Heaney's *Seeing Things* was encountered within a paradigm of readerly pleasure untainted by the process of criticism, so the roughly contemporaneous 'Madoc' was seen to depend on a critical methodology of some sophistication and rigour: 'the wrestle with interpretation is so intense the poor reader suffers from continuous free-floating anxiety, desperately needing to locate meaning beneath the infinite conflicts and ambiguities generated by the poem' (O'Brien 1991: 29–30).

It is worth noting in Peggy O'Brien's analysis of the work that this labour does not deny the pleasure the poem can afford. Rather such pleasure is perceived as in direct relation to the amount of critical labour expended on its 'infinite conflicts'. With this, few reviewers felt willing or able to read the poem beyond or against its own insistent parameters. The complexity of the allusive totality established by 'Madoc' – encapsulated by Lucy McDiarmid's understanding of it as *'sui generis'* – was such that other contexts could not impinge on its linguistic integrity. The irony of this phenomenon is unavoidable. As the perception of the poem as richly allusive and open to pluralistic instabilities became greater, so the interpretive strategies suitable to the object of study were restricted. It is in this way that a reading of 'Unitel' as New-Critical institution becomes apposite, for it is from that location that, 'though it may seem improbable,/all that follows/flickers and flows/from the back of his right eyeball' (Muldoon 1990: 20). The extent to which Muldoon desired this framework of interpretation is unknowable, although worth considering if only because of his comment in interview that 'there will be a few suicides after this book comes out – all the academic fraternity. I can't wait. And sorority' (Noble 1990: 65). Muldoon's apparent dislike of these academic formations, however humorously expressed, should not disguise the fact that his work and reputation exist almost solely within their parameters; outside 'Unitel' 'Madoc', like its narrative, does not exist.

If this reading suggests a certain ambivalence on the part of Muldoon towards the institution his work is complicit with, it further develops the sense of marginality he has long been anxious to hold as his own. While 'Madoc' represents a working through of these issues to a pessimistic and foreclosed end, in his earlier long poem '7, Middagh Street' (Muldoon 1987: 36–60) there is a practice more alive to the possibilities inherent to an ideal of creative autonomy. Finding a reconciliation of the aesthetic and the political polarities by a conscious displacement through exile, as Longley has demonstrated in a perceptive essay, it becomes a form of *Immram* in its 'rowing' around the locus of activity – a perception heightened by the circularity of the corona form it employs (Longley 1988: 77).[8] Seemingly rooted, unlike *Madoc*, to a reading of the historical moment and the spatial location, events are happening elsewhere: Spain, the blitz in London and Belfast, and the beginnings of a protracted world war. In October 1940 W.H. Auden had moved into Middagh Street in Brooklyn Heights, New York: a residence owned by George Davis, the fiction editor for *Harper's Bazaar*, and housing, among others, the novelist Carson McCullers, Benjamin Britten, Peter Pears, the strip-tease artist Gypsy Rose Lee and (significantly briefly) Louis MacNeice.

It is this bohemian moment – one which Pears would later consider 'sordid beyond belief' (Carpenter 1981: 304) – which Muldoon makes use of as part of an extended meditation on the importance of marginality within the moment of political and institutional totality. The artists who shelter at the address are inheritors of no stable tradition; hiding from the events which suggest artistic involvement, their monologues establish interior narratives which are not linked in a linear formation which gestures towards closure but by the poem's overall circularity.

Analogies with Muldoon's own relationship to modern Northern Ireland are hard to avoid but should be undertaken with care. Rather than suggesting, along with Eamonn Hughes, that '7, Middagh Street' is primarily an 'intertextual debate on whether poetry can make things happen' (Hill and Barber 1990: 55) – although that is clearly part of its purpose – or that the poem accords entirely with Deane's perception of Muldoon's 'denial' (Deane 1986: 244), it speaks of his desire to be 'out on the edge', and the concomitant awareness of the dilemma a Northern Irish poet must address when attempting to write in relation to social violence. As Muldoon has remarked in interview: 'the trouble with this place is that if you don't engage in it, you're an ostrich (whatever "engage in it" means). If you do engage in it, you're using the situation as a kind of . . . you're on the make, almost, cashing in' (Longley 1986: 12–13).

This is a pressure engendered in the main by readings of Northern culture based on the idea of centrality: the kind of assumption crystalised in the conclusion to Adrian Frazier's comparative essay 'Juniper, Otherwise Known: Poems by Paulin and Muldoon' which finally suggests: 'What pulls these poets together is the very large audience that awaits them all, asking for news of the Troubles' (Frazier 1984: 133). '7, Middagh Street', as with much of Muldoon's work, brings news of the Troubles to an audience, but does so deliberately at a spatial and geographic remove from the locus of activity. Obsessively questioning the primacy of historical narrative it subtends its initial debate about the role of poetry as a motor of history under the wider knowledge that the fictionalising of the historical moment is in itself a happening, an awareness counter to the homogeneity of the cyclical historiography of 'Madoc'. This moment is in itself ironically part of an intertextual reading of Humphrey Carpenter's biography of Auden (1981), to the extent that a reading of '7, Middagh Street' without recourse to *W.H. Auden: A Biography* is almost impossible:

> I had just left Reeves
> and needed a place to stay. As must Wynstan,
>
> dear Wynnie-Pooh, who's given to caution
> the rest of us every
> time we sit down, be it to jerky
> or this afternoon's Thanksgiving dinner, every
> blessed time, 'We'll have crawfish, turkey,
> salad and savoury,
> and no political discussion' –

> (Muldoon 1987: 52)

163

'He would preface a meal', recalls Paul Bowles, 'by announcing: "We've got a roast and two veg, salad and savoury, and there will be no political discussion." '

(Carpenter 1981: 305)

Interestingly, Carpenter's biography is one that Tom Paulin too has encountered in review (Paulin 1984: 85–91), and he places it in 'the little-England tradition of literary biography' with its passing of 'the first test of bad biography on page 131 when Mr Carpenter informs us that Auden once ate six eggs for supper'. In this way Paulin's main reservation about the work is its concentration on 'foibles and personal habits' at the expense of a thorough analysis of the ideological vision of Auden's life and work: a perception which is mediated through the biography directly into '7, Middagh Street'. By consciously using Carpenter's version of Auden, Muldoon foregrounds the quotidian over the direct ideological determinant in his desire to stress Auden's political disaffection, and in so doing sees in the foibles of individual identity part of the excess that ultimately cannot be restrained within the institution.

'7, Middagh Street' ends, as so often in Muldoon's work, with a return to the thought of MacNeice. After the surrealistic linkages forged by Dali in 'SALVADOR', and the painful reminiscences of McCullers, MacNeice returns the reader briefly to a scene of absolute political polarity: the sectarian world of the Belfast shipyards (although should this seem too much of a transition, Muldoon typically frames it in the form of a hallucination). MacNeice is not a resident at the address but, as Carpenter reveals, merely a guest, and the naturally symbolic nature of this in relation to MacNeice's own poetic preoccupations is one which suits Muldoon's purpose. His culminating presence in the poem complicates the debate undertaken and is a reminder that the efficacy of aesthetic internationalism is predicated on the parochial sensibility. He is not a permanent fixture in the otherness of Middagh Street yet his intrusion is entirely inevitable, unfreezing with his essentially pluralistic concerns the iced-up polarities of art and politics symbolised by the frozen-stiff marital figures of Auden and Isherwood at the start of the poem (a process which 'SALVADOR' had already begun):

> In dreams begin responsibilities;
> it was on account of just such an allegory
> that Lorca
> was riddled with bullets
>
> and lay mouth-down
> in the fickle shadow of his own blood.
> As the drunken soldiers of the *Gypsy Ballads*
> started back for town

they heard him calling through the mist,
'When I die leave the balcony shutters open.'
For poetry *can* make things happen –
not only can, but *must* –

and the very painting of that oyster
is in itself a political gesture.

By taking the poem to Harland and Wolff, MacNeice is forced to confront hostile otherness as it can exist in the parochial – a self-imposed decision which forces a division between himself and Auden. His attempt to enter the shipyard, to work on the 'quinquereme of Nineveh', and therefore to complete the cohesion of the corona, is frustrated by sectarian prejudice and the inconclusiveness of identity. If the self is as uncertain as the foreman's accusation suggests, the context of the question Auden and MacNeice ponder begins to look quite unstable. MacNeice cannot or will not protest his Protestantism to attain the formal textual closure, and the reconciliation that he nominally represented is frustrated by a tribal hatred 'out of Homer'.[9] The corona is ultimately achieved but it is muted and inconclusive, attained only through the rhetoric of political intransigence. As with Muldoon's earlier quest poems such as 'Immrama' (Muldoon 1980: 23), the form of the text is restrictive of its aspirational ambitions. Deadlock is reasserted and we are returned to the mallemaroking of Isherwood and Auden on the decks of the ice-bound *Champlain*:

> After drinking all night in a Sands Street shebeen
> where a sailor played a melodeon
> made from a merman's spine
> I left by the back door of Muldoon's
>
> (it might have been the Rotterdam)
> on a Monday morning, falling in with
> the thousands of shipyardmen who tramped
> towards the front gates of Harland and Wolff.
>
> The one-eyed foreman had strayed out of Homer;
> 'MacNeice? That's a Fenian name.'
> As if to say, 'None of your sort, none of you
>
> will as much as go for a rubber hammer
> never mind chalk a rivet, never mind caulk a seam
> on the quinquereme of Nineveh.'

Such frustration, however, should be seen as the direct result of MacNeice's essentially aesthetic denial of assimilating forces. As such the socio-sectarian cycle of historical oppression that ends the poem exists and gains strength only in relation to those individual human determinants it cannot subtend.

In this remains the possibility of a dialectic poetic practice in which pluralism has its necessary place. If a sense of autonomy only gains resonance in relation to the social and institutional forces that seek to constrain it, so it is through a reading of the specific historical moment that contingent and resistant pluralities gain their full expression.

While this, in part, suggests '7, Middagh Street' as a poem reflective of the condition of interregnum in that its oppositions do not constitute a new 'arrangement', 'Madoc' more forthrightly insists on a 'post' state of existence in that it inhabits a theoretical location close to that which Lloyd refers to as 'the finally universal claims of the hegemonic institutions within which conflicting and contradictory interests are negotiated' (Lloyd 1993: 9). In turn those characters or events that cannot be assimilated into the institutional forms of representation that obsess the poem become purely unrepresentable and entirely without agency; the narratives they enact no longer enter into a dialectical relationship with the now dominant arrangement. The paradigmatic nature of the pre-colonial–colonial–post-colonial narrative in 'Madoc' makes such a reading unavoidable and yet troubling. We may find in this (as do Longley and O'Brien in review) an implicit warning about the dangers of totalising epistemological or political systems, yet this in turn may be to avoid the totalising agenda that is, in itself, implicit to a reading of the poem as subversive within its own foreclosed linguistic riddling. Moreover, Muldoon's complex depiction of the fate of the Cayuga Indians, their transformation from the 'Geckoes' who capture South(ey) at the beginning of the poem to their final revenge on him in the section '[Putnam]' (Muldoon 1990: 254), suggests an awareness of a received alienation inherent to colonial subjection that goes beyond sceptical readings of meta-narration. For this reason the act of terrorism that destabilises the state-institution in the final section of the poem '[Hawking]' (Muldoon 1990: 261) is marked only by silence, an inarticulate *symptom* of insurgency:

> The Cayugas have shouldered their Lasabers
> And smoothed their scalp-locks.
>
> A scrap of paper in a valise
> now falls within the range
>
> of a sensor-tile. The corridor
> awash in slime. Trifoliate Chinese orange.
> One leg held on by a frivolous
> blood-garter.

As the final six lines of the poem make clear ('It will all be over, de dum,/in next to no time') this marks the end of all possibilities within the current hegemonic formation. It may be possible to send a 'shiver' through Unitel but without a counter-hegemonic practice on the part of the dispossessed no other change can occur beyond the 'arrangement' of the present. Muldoon's recurring use throughout the poem of the motif 'de dum, de dum' provides a relevant although subtle example of this tendency. At once both a marker of the passage of time – reminding us that the narrative is being remade for us from a point within the institution – and an echo of Native American drums,[10] as Jacqueline McCurry has pointed out in a perceptive essay (McCurry 1992: 103), its gradual transformation into 'Te Deum' (which we may also read as 'tedium') as the poem progresses 'enacts the gradual but relentless imperialism and eventual victory of Christianity'. Developing this idea, the eventual re-establishment of 'de dum' as the dominant motif of pure narration towards the end of the poem suggests that the hegemonic drive of 'Te Deum' has culminated in a new arrangement which now primarily gestures towards the endless spaces of homogeneous time:

> It will all be over, de dum,
> in next to no time –
>
> long before 'The fluted cypresses
> rear'd up their living obelisks'
>
> has sent a shiver, de dum, de dum,
> through Unitel, its iridescent dome.

(Muldoon 1990: 261)

In this state of historical quietude the manner in which 'Madoc' insists on the paradigmatic nature of the numerous colonial encounters that occur through the poem denies the possibility of a materialist historiography. Rather than gaining the existence of 'monad', in Walter Benjamin's definition 'a revolutionary chance in the fight for the oppressed past' (Benjamin 1973: 254), they function rather as the ever-growing 'pile of debris' that gathers at the feet of the Angel of History (Benjamin 1973: 249); a version of 'the illustrious dung-hill' that appears in '[Burnet]' (Muldoon 1990: 101). Interestingly this does not imply that the concept of the 'monad' is entirely discounted but rather that its existence in the text as a potential method of understanding the enveloping chaos is always placed out of reach and perceived as part of a tradition now shattered. As Bucephalus, the prophetic talking horse, notes in '[Leibniz]':

> 'Since we're now approaching the gates of Hell
> you should know that the "nock" in Mount Monad-
> nock
> is indeed the Gaelic word *cnoc*, a hill.'

(Muldoon 1990: 106)

Understood only as an archaism, the absence of such procedures within homogeneous time leaves the idea of narrative as a fragile and precious commodity – the only way of distinguishing between the different forms of arbitrary data. In this the retinagraph harnessed to South(ey)'s eye can only afford a strictly teleological vision as our own, ultimately institutional, position forecloses the various possibilities the poem raises. In place of this development all 'Madoc' can offer is 'just another twist in the plot' (Muldoon 1990: 16). This raises interesting questions of the structural methodology out of which the poem is constructed. In the section '[Lévi-Strauss]' Coleridge's appropriate attempts to impose a structure on the disparate experience he is presented with is interrupted by an intrusive narrative voice, ' "At any moment now, his retina will disintegrate" ' (Muldoon 1990: 241), a line echoed significantly in '[Derrida]', ' "At any moment now, the retina will be in smithereens" ' (Muldoon 1990: 257).[11] Any attempt to follow Lévi-Strauss's model of mythic formation as a phenomic structural pattern operating beyond narrative sequence is, and has to be, in this way frustrated. In turn, what Terry Eagleton refers to as 'the quasi-objective collective experience of myth' (Eagleton 1983: 104) in Lévi-Strauss's work is similarly undercut as the individual experience against which it gains its currency is revealed as fatally fractured and only coherent as it is voiced in and through Unitel.

However, while this sequential and linear development of narrative may be seen as a consciously inadequate expression of the colonial subject, the expectation that it *may* offer at least some passage out of the Pantisocratic nightmare remains and it is this desire that Muldoon will continually satirise. Our trail through the narrative is mirrored, in the section '[Maimonides]' through to '[Aquinas]' (Muldoon 1990: 60–4), by a Mohawk who 'goads and bullies' Coleridge 'up a spiral staircase with precisely two hundred and thirty-three steps' (the number of sections in the poem as a whole), 'through the hoopless hoop of a black rainbow', to the overwhelming and ironic question: 'Would you say you came here of your own free will?' As the options available to the major protagonists in the poem narrow increasingly in the consuming totality so the available strategies of reading become progressively foreclosed, progressively reliant on the thread of narrative intrusion. While this represents a restriction of moral agency it also constitutes another version of the search for the 'teeny-weeny key' (Muldoon 1990: 117) that is assumed will open the poem to theoretical procedure. Although the search for this key remains a necessary condition it simultaneously represents that which is forever lost, a return to pure beginnings unalloyed when language, as a transitive speech act, could effect change. As Muldoon expresses the issue in the poem, 'The Key', which opens the collection, it is the difficulty of 'matching sound to picture' (Muldoon 1990: 3).

The futility of this search through 'Madoc' should prompt us to ignore the promise of finding that which has been lost (it was never there in the first place) and instead to focus on the beginning of a historical method which does not merely replicate the institutions and forms of the colonisers. Taking cognisance of this, South(ey)'s narrative constitutes part of a discourse of post-colonialism which is also a discourse of failure; in the seamless replication of institutions no possibility of closure, or more importantly *beginning*, remains. This despair is voiced in one of the final sections of the poem, '[Harmon]', which ultimately settles one linguistic conundrum as 'Not "CROATAN", not "CROATOAN", but "CROTONA" ' (Muldoon 1990: 258). While, as Longley points out, a 'croton' is a 'drastic purgative' (Longley 1991a), 'Crotona' also refers, in Dillon Johnston's words, to 'Pythagoras' Utopian colony in Italy and . . . the site of his anti-imperialist speech in Ovid' (Johnston 1992: 213). In the insurgent possibilities of dissent this location promises one final significant connection can be drawn. While I have avoided a reading of the poem as a specific allegory of the Northern Irish cultural landscape, as Longley hints[12] certain one-for-one correspondences between the major characters and individual Northern writers and critics remain reasonably obvious. Rather than develop the inevitably contentious implications of this awareness it is perhaps enough to note the irony implicit to the section '[Nozick]': 'May, 1843. "Catlin's Indian Gallery" has now reached Ireland. Half-way between Belfast and Dublin, near the present site of Unitel West, the medicine-bag is either misplaced or stolen' (Muldoon 1990: 259).

'Catlin's Indian Gallery' was a European tour of paintings by the artist George Catlin of Native Americans (Catlin 1967). As these images of otherness represent within the poem a deliberation on the efficacy of representation they also gesture towards the possibility of a (albeit displaced) comparative method. In turn, the present site of 'Unitel West', 'half-way between Belfast and Dublin', may suggest Armagh, the location of many of Muldoon's poems and, more importantly, the site of Paulin's (who also appears in the poem) classically imagined post-colonial parliament, his own 'CROTONA':

> Will a shrunken, independent Northern Ireland barricade itself against an
> enlarged Republic? . . . Or will there be negotiation, argument, compromise,
> a new constitution, a parliament in Armagh and the beginnings of a new way
> of writing history that is neither Orange nor Green, but is instead as white as
> the middle band of the Irish tricolour? History, by its very nature, has no
> answers.
>
> (Paulin 1984: 173)

While in one sense this may conflate Muldoon's 'Unitel West' with Field Day, as the once emergent and now dominant hegemonic formation, it also hints at the ideal of 'arrangement' as one unable to contain all the insurgent elements that constitute it at any one time. As the end of the interregnum is signalled by the foreclosure of uncertainty within the institution so it is appropriate to conclude with Paulin's belief in a history without answers, for it is only in this way, as ultimately 'Madoc' too may hint, that readings of Northern Irish culture can understand Benjamin's exasperated awareness that: 'The current amazement that the things we are experiencing are "still" possible in the twentieth century is *not* philosophical. This amazement is not the beginning of knowledge – unless it is the knowledge that the view of history which gives rise to it is untenable' (Benjamin 1973: 249).

NOTES

1. It is an awareness of 'Heaney's quasi-institutional acceptance on both sides of the Atlantic as a major poet' which led to Lloyd's 'Pap for the Dispossessed' (Lloyd 1993).
2. For a similar early example of this tendency see Haffenden 1979 (pp. 5–28).
3. For a fuller, if contentious, reading of this phenomenon see Lloyd 1993 (pp. 14–18).
4. This cartoon was republished in *Troubled Times: Fortnight Magazine and the Troubles in Northern Ireland 1970–91* (Bell et al. 1991: 106). A later cartoon of Heaney by Peter Brookes used to illustrate Lachlan MacKinnon's review of *Seeing Things* (MacKinnon 1991: 28) presented Heaney's head as the contours of Ireland itself. Although it is unlikely that Brookes knew of Turner's earlier cartoon, questions of mediation and embodiment, this time to an all-Ireland state, are similarly represented.
5. Most infamously in Desmond Fennell's pamphlet, '*Whatever You Say, Say Nothing*': *Why Seamus Heaney is No. 1* (Fennell 1991). Fennell's work forms possibly the most sustained attack on Heaney's poetry, particularly from within Ireland itself.
6. As I note in Chapter 4, following Ashcroft, Griffiths and Tiffin it is in many ways appropriate to see New Criticism as a post-colonial phenomenon (Ashcroft et al. 1989: 160–1).
7. 'This conception of elite indicates a small effective group which remains an elite only by regular circulation and recruitment' (Williams 1983: 114).
8. In light of his later appearance in the poem MacNeice's lines from 'Letter to Graham and Anne Shepard' (Auden and MacNeice 1937: 33) are also of relevance to an understanding of '7, Middagh Street' as *Immram*:

> This complex word exacts
> Hard work of simplifying; to get its focus
> You have to stand outside the crowd and caucus.

9. A conscious echo of Patrick Kavanagh's sonnet 'Epic' (Kavanagh 1990: 238): 'I inclined/to lose my faith in Ballyrush and Gortin/Till Homer's ghost came whispering to my mind/He said: I made the Iliad from such/A local row. Gods make their own importance.' Muldoon has referred to the importance of these lines in interview: 'It was about the two guys fighting in the field over the right of way, and he says Homer made the *Iliad* from such a local row. I think it's all

part of the same thing. It's the way we invent our histories, I believe, private and public' (Noble 1990: 65).

10. This reading connects the poem with Heaney's 'Ocean's Love to Ireland' (Heaney 1975: 46–7): 'Iambic drums/of English beat the woods where her poets/Sink like Onan.' Similarly, Clair Wills notes the manner in which the poem revises Heaney's 'Act of Union' (Wills 1993: 224).

11. Derrida's critique of Lévi-Strauss's *The Raw and the Cooked* found in the text's analysis at the level of the sign the very metaphysical oppositions Lévi-Strauss was hoping to transcend. Muldoon's repeated emphasis on 'disintegration' alludes to this. See 'Structure, Sign and Play in the Discourse of the Human Sciences' (Derrida 1978: 280).

12. 'As for further contemporary parallels, to quote an earlier Muldoon poem: "I could name names. I could be indiscreet" ' (Longley 1991a).

Works Cited

Adams G 1982 *Falls Memories* Brandon Books, Dingle.

Allen M, Wilcox A (eds) 1989 *Critical Approaches to Anglo-Irish Literature* Colin Smythe, Gerrards Cross.

Althusser L 1977 *Lenin and Philosophy and Other Essays* trans. B Brewster, New Left Books, London.

Anderson B 1991 *Imagined Communities: Reflections on the Origin and Spread of Nationalism* rev. edn, Verso, London.

Arts Council of Northern Ireland 1964–79 *Annual Reports* 1964–1979, 22–35 Arts Council of Northern Ireland, Belfast.

Ascherson N 1993 (28 February) Great Brain Spotter *Independent on Sunday*: 30–1.

Ashcroft B, Griffiths G, Tiffin H 1989 *The Empire Writes Back: Theory and Practice in Post-Colonial Literatures* Routledge, London.

Auden WH, MacNeice L 1937 *Letters From Iceland* Faber, London.

Balibar E, Macherey P 1978 Literature as an Ideological Form *Oxford Literary Review* **3** (1): 2–22.

Barry P 1982 (19 August) 'Faculty at War' letter *London Review of Books* **4** (15): 4.

Barthes R 1968 *Writing Degree Zero* trans. A Lavers and C Smith, ed. S Sontag, Hill and Wang, New York.

— 1987 *Mythologies* trans. A Lavers, Grafton Books, London.

— 1987a *Criticism and Truth* trans. K Pilcher Keuneman, Basil Blackwell, Oxford.

— 1990 *S/Z* trans. R Miller, Basil Blackwell, Oxford.

Baudrillard J 1988 *Selected Writings* ed. M Poster, Polity Press, Cambridge.

Bell R, Johnstone R, Wilson R 1991 *Troubled Times: Fortnight Magazine and the Troubles in Northern Ireland 1970–91* Blackstaff Press, Belfast.

Benjamin W 1973 *Illuminations* trans. H Zohn, ed. H Arendt, Fontana/Collins, London.

— 1977 *The Origin of German Tragic Drama* trans. J Osborne, New Left Books, London.

— 1979 *One-Way Street and Other Writings* trans. E Jephcott and K Shorter, New Left Books, London.

Bew P, Gillespie G 1993 *Northern Ireland: A Chronology of the Troubles 1968–93* Gill & Macmillan, Dublin.

Bolger D (ed.) 1991 *Letters From the New Ireland* Raven Arts Press, Dublin.

Boyle P 1968 (July) Ulster Revisited *Hibernia* **32** (7): 11.

Bristow J 1982 (5 August) 'Faculty at War' letter *London Review of Books* **4** (14): 4.

Brown J 1988 (Spring/Summer) Interview with Padraic Fiacc *Gown Literary Supplement*: 13–15.

Brown T 1977 *Northern Voices: Poets from Ulster* Gill & Macmillan, Dublin.

Bruce S 1994 *The Edge of the Union: The Ulster Loyalist Political Vision* Oxford University Press, Oxford.

Cairns D, Richards S 1988 *Writing Ireland: Colonialism, Nationalism and Culture* Manchester University Press, Manchester.

Carey J 1991 (2 June) Review of *Seeing Things, Sunday Times*: 22.

Carpenter H 1981 *W.H. Auden: A Biography* Allen & Unwin, London.

Carson C 1975 Escaped from the Massacre? review of *North Honest Ulsterman* **50**: 183–6.

— 1987 *The Irish For No* Gallery Press, Oldcastle.

— 1989 *Belfast Confetti* Gallery Press, Oldcastle.

Catlin G 1967 *O-Kee-Pa: A Religious Ceremony and other Customs of the Mandans* ed. J C Ewers. Yale University Press, Yale.

Chambers H 1974 (5 April) The Ulster Poets *Fortnight* **81**: 12–13.

Corcoran N (ed.) 1992 *The Chosen Ground: Essays on the Contemporary Poetry of Northern Ireland* Seren Books, Bridgend.

Craig P (ed.) 1992 *The Rattle of the North: An Anthology of Ulster Prose* Blackstaff Press, Belfast.

Crawford R 1992 *Devolving English Literature* Clarendon Press, Oxford.

Crewe C 1992 (18 February) Belfast Slabbers Pave a Literary Way *Guardian*: 32.

Crozier M (ed.) 1989 *Cultural Traditions in Northern Ireland: Varieties of Irishness* Queen's University of Belfast, Belfast.

Dawe G 1991 *How's the Poetry Going?: Literature and Politics in Ireland Today* Lagan Press, Belfast.

Dawe G, Foster JW (eds) 1991 *The Poet's Place: Ulster Literature and Society. Essays in Honour of John Hewitt 1907–87* Institute of Irish Studies, Belfast.

Dawe G, Longley E (eds) 1985 *Across a Roaring Hill: The Protestant Imagination in Modern Ireland* Blackstaff Press, Belfast.

Deane S 1970 (October) Mugwumps and Reptiles *Atlantis* **2**: 3–10.

— 1971 (January/February) Why Bogside? *The Honest Ulsterman* **27**: 1–8.

— 1975 (February) An Irish Intelligentsia: Reflections on its Desirability *The Honest Ulsterman* **46/7**: 27–34.

— 1982 Unhappy and at Home, interview with Seamus Heaney *The Crane Bag Book of Irish Studies* 1982, ed. MP Hederman and R Kearney, Blackwater Press, Dublin: 66–72.

— 1983 (October) Derry: City Besieged Within the Siege *Fortnight* **198**: 18–9.
— 1983a Black Mountain Jacobin, review of *Liberty Tree, The Honest Ulsterman* **74**: 63–4.
— 1985 *Celtic Revivals* Faber & Faber, London.
— 1986 *A Short History of Irish Literature* Hutchinson, London.
— 1990a (Spring/Summer) Hothouse Flowers or Anthologica Hibernia *Gown Literary Supplement*: 19.
— 1991 (second quarter) Political Football *Irish Reporter* **2**: 12–13.
— (ed.) 1985 *Ireland's Field Day* Hutchinson, London.
— (ed.) 1990 *Nationalism, Colonialism and Literature* University of Minnesota Press, Minneapolis.
— (ed.) eds 1991 *The Field Day Anthology of Irish Writing* (3 vols) Field Day, Derry.
Derrida J 1978 *Writing and Difference* trans. A Bass, Routledge & Kegan Paul, London.
Dollimore J 1982 (15 July) 'Faculty at War' letter *London Review of Books* **4** (13): 4.
Donoghue D 1986 *We Irish: Irish Literature and Society*, University of California Press, Berkeley.
Donovan K 1992 (27 February) Absence Stirs Anger Amongst Women, review of *The Field Day Anthology of Irish Writing, The Irish Times*: 10.
Dorgan T 1991 (9 June) Heaney's Vision Throws Light on the Ordinary review of *Seeing Things, The Sunday Tribune*: 3.
Draper RP (ed.) 1989 *The Literature of Region and Nation* Macmillan, London.
Dugdale N et al. 1976 (November/December) The Belfast Group: A Symposium *Honest Ulsterman* **53**: 53–63.
— **et al.** 1994 (Spring) Special Feature: The Belfast Group *The Honest Ulsterman* **97**: 3–26.
Durcan P 1982 *Selected Paul Durcan* ed. E Longley, Blackstaff Press, Belfast.
Eagleton T 1983 *Literary Theory: An Introduction* Basil Blackwell, Oxford.
— 1988 *Nationalism: Irony and Commitment* Field Day Pamphlet 13, Derry.
Easthope A 1982 (5 August) 'Faculty at War' letter *London Review of Books* **4** (14): 4.
— 1991 *Literary into Cultural Studies* Routledge, London.
Editorial 26 September 1980 Friel's Winner *Irish Press*: 2.
Egan M 1982 (19 August) Faculty at War letter *London Review of Books* **4** (15): 4.
Eliot TS 1951 *Selected Essays* Faber & Faber, London.
— 1984 *Collected Poems 1909–62* 2nd edn, Faber & Faber, London.
English R 1994 Cultural Traditions and Political Ambiguity *Irish Review* **15**: 97–106.
Evans C 1993 *English People: The Experience of Teaching and Learning English in British Universities* Open University Press, Buckingham.
Fallon P, Mahon D (eds) 1990 *The Penguin Book of Contemporary Irish Poetry* Penguin, London.

Fennell D 1968 (April) Irish Literary Criticism *Hibernia* **32** (4): 12.
— 1991 *'Whatever You Say, Say Nothing': Why Seamus Heaney is No. 1* ELO Press, Dublin.
Fiacc P 1968 (May) 'Seamus Heaney' *Hibernia* **32** (5): 23.
— 1969 (14 February) Ulster Happening *Hibernia* **33** (4): 18.
— 1972 (20 October) The North's Younger Poets *Hibernia* **36** (20): 12.
— 1974 (6 December) Violence and the Ulster Poet *Hibernia* **38** (23): 19.
— (ed.) 1974a *The Wearing of the Black* Blackstaff Press, Belfast.
— 1994 *Ruined Pages: Selected Poems* ed. G Dawe, A MacPóilin, Blackstaff Press, Belfast.
Foley M 1970 (October) Ulster Diary *The Honest Ulsterman* **25**: 2–3.
— 1971 (September) This Thing could Rule the World *Fortnight* **23**: 20.
— 1987 (January) Unconscious Partitionism *Fortnight* **247**: 24–5.
Foster JW 1987 News from Orchard Street: The Latest From Field Day *Canadian Journal of Irish Studies* **12** (1): 59–66.
— 1991 *Colonial Consequences: Essays in Irish Literature and Culture* Lilliput Press, Dublin.
— 1994 (March) Processed Peace *Fortnight*, **326**: 35–7.
Foster RF 1989 *Modern Ireland: 1600–1972* Penguin, London.
Frazier A 1984 Juniper, Otherwise Known: Poems by Paulin and Muldoon *Eire-Ireland* **19** (1): 123–33.
Friel B 1981 *Translations* Faber & Faber, London.
— 1988 *Selected Plays* Faber & Faber, London.
Gailey A (ed.) 1988 *The Use of Tradition: Essays Presented to G.B. Thompson* Ulster Folk and Transport Museum, Cultra.
Goldring M 1991 *Belfast: From Loyalty to Rebellion* Lawrence and Wishart, London.
Gordimer N 1989 *The Essential Gesture: Writing, Politics and Places* Penguin, London.
Gramsci A 1971 *Selections From the Prison Notebooks*, trans. and ed. Q Hoare, G Nowell Smith, Lawrence & Wishart, London.
Greene B 1976 (July) Hadden Hands Over *Hibernia* **40** (12): 10.
Hadfield P, Henderson L 1983 (May) Field Day: The Magical Mystery Theatre *Ireland* **2**: 63–9.
Haffenden J 1979 (June) Meeting Seamus Heaney *London Magazine*: 5–28.
Harmon M (ed.) 1984 *The Irish Writer and the City* Colin Smythe, Gerrards Cross.
Hawkes T October 1982 'Faculty at War' letter *London Review of Books* **4** (18): 4.
Hayes M 1991 *Whither Cultural Diversity?* Community Relations Council, Belfast.
Heaney S 1972 *Wintering Out* Faber & Faber, London.
— 1975 *North* Faber & Faber, London.
— 1979 *Field Work* Faber & Faber, London.
— 1980 *Preoccupations: Selected Prose 1968–78* Faber & Faber, London.
— 1984 *Station Island* Faber & Faber, London.

— 1987 *The Haw Lantern* Faber & Faber, London.
— 1988 *The Government of the Tongue: The T.S. Eliot Memorial Lectures and Other Critical Writings* Faber & Faber, London.
— 1990 *New Selected Poems 1966–1987* Faber & Faber, London.
— 1991 *Seeing Things* Faber & Faber, London.
Hederman MP 1985 Poetry and the Fifth Province *The Crane Bag* **9** (1): 107–15.
Hewitt J 1987 *Ancestral Voices: The Selected Prose of John Hewitt* ed. T Clyde. Blackstaff Press, Belfast.
— 1991 *Collected Poems* ed. F Ormsby. Blackstaff Press, Belfast.
Hill M, Barber S (eds) 1990 *Aspects of Irish Studies* Queen's University of Belfast, Belfast.
Hobsbaum P 1970 *A Theory of Communication* Macmillan, London.
— et al. *Belfast Creative Writing Group Sheets 1963–6* unpublished manuscripts Queen's University of Belfast, Belfast.
Holland J 1975 (21 March) Broken Images *Hibernia* **39** (6): 19.
— 1976 (23 April) Broken Images *Hibernia* **40** (9): 24.
Hughes E 1988 (Autumn) Leavis and Ireland: An Adequate Criticism? *Text and Context*: 112–32.
— 1990 (Spring) To Define Your Dissent: The Plays and Polemics of the Field Day Theatre Company *Theatre Research International* **15** (1): 67–77.
— (ed.) 1991 *Culture and Politics in Northern Ireland 1960–90* Open University Press, Buckingham.
James C 1972 (26 November) Review of *Wintering Out*, *Observer*: 25.
Jameson F 1974 *Marxism and Form: Twentieth Century Dialectical Theories of Literature* Princeton University Press, Princeton.
— 1988 *The Ideologies of Theory: Essays 1971–1986, Volume 2: Syntax of History* Routledge, London.
— 1988a *Modernism and Imperialism* Field Day Pamphlet 14, Derry.
Jennings MW 1987 *Dialectical Images: Walter Benjamin's Theory of Literary Criticism* Cornell University Press, Ithaca.
Johnston D 1985 *Irish Poetry After Joyce* Notre Dame Press, Indiana.
— 1992 Poetic Discoveries and Inventions of America *Colby Quarterly* **28** (4): 202–15.
Johnstone R 1990 *Belfast: Portraits of a City* Barrie & Jenkins, London.
— , **Kirk B** 1983 *Images of Belfast* Blackstaff Press, Belfast.
Jordan J 1972 (23 June) Northern Lights *Hibernia* **36** (13): 10.
Josipovici G 1982 (September) 'Faculty at War' letter *London Review of Books* **4** (16): 4.
'Jude the Obscure' 1972 (February) *The Honest Ulsterman* **32**: 27–8.
Kavanagh PJ 1990 *The Complete Poems* Goldsmith Press, Newbridge.
Kersnowski F 1975 *The Outsiders: Poets of Contemporary Ireland* Texas Christian University Press, Fort Worth.
Keyes J 1990 (October) A Dramatic Conversation, interview with Seamus Heaney *Fortnight* **288**: 25.
Kiberd D 1991 (9 June) Heaney's Magic *Sunday Tribune*: 21.

Kinahan F 1982 (Spring) Interview with Seamus Heaney *Critical Inquiry*: 405–14.

Leavis FR 1937 (June) Literary Criticism and Philosophy: A Reply *Scrutiny* **6** (1): 59–71.

— 1948 *Education and the University: A Sketch for an 'English School'* Chatto & Windus, London.

Lloyd D 1993 *Anomalous States: Irish Writing and the Post-Colonial Moment* Lilliput Press, Dublin.

Lodge D (ed.) 1988 *Modern Criticism and Theory: A Reader* Longman, Harlow.

Logan S 1982 (August) 'Faculty at War' letter *London Review of Books* **4** (14): 4.

Longley E 1983 (August) Sweet Dreams or Rifles, review of *Liberty Tree*, *Fortnight* **196**: 19.

— 1986 *Poetry in the Wars* Bloodaxe, Newcastle upon Tyne.

— 1987 (November) Opening Up: A New Pluralism *Fortnight* **256**: 24–5.

— 1988 Putting on the International Style *The Irish Review* **5**: 75–81.

— 1990 *From Cathleen to Anorexia: The Breakdown of Irelands* Attic Press LIP Pamphlet, Dublin.

— 1990a Undermining Assumptions: The Irish Poem *The Irish Review* **9**: 55–7.

— (ed.) 1991 *Culture in Ireland: Division or Diversity?* Institute of Irish Studies, Belfast.

— 1991a (September) Way Down Upon the Susquehanna, review of *Madoc: A Mystery*, *Irish Times*: 9.

— 1992 (9 January) Belfast Diary *London Review of Books* **14** (1): 21.

— 1992a (August) Thrashing Away Sharply, review of *Colonial Consequences*, *Fortnight* **308**: 29.

— 1993 (Spring) Conference Abstract: Light Verse *The Honest Ulsterman* **95**: 21.

— 1994 *The Living Stream: Literature and Revisionism in Ireland* Bloodaxe, Newcastle upon Tyne.

Longley M 1969 (November) Strife and the Ulster Poet *Hibernia* **33** (21): 11.

— (ed.) 1971 *Causeway: The Arts in Ulster* Arts Council of Northern Ireland, Belfast.

— 1994 *Tuppenny Stung: Autobiographical Chapters* Lagan Press, Belfast.

Lucy S 1977 (April) Irish Writing: A New Criticism *Hibernia* **41** (7): 18.

Lundy J, MacPóilin A (eds) 1992 *Styles of Belonging: The Cultural Identity of Ulster* Lagan Press, Belfast.

MacDermott D 1985 (8 February) Deane Spells Out Field Day's Role *The Derry Journal*: 9.

MacKinnon L 1990 (October) A Dream Diffused in Words, review of *Madoc: A Mystery*, *Times Literary Supplement* **4585**: 26.

— 1991 (June) A Responsibility to Self, review of *Seeing Things*, *Times Literary Supplement* **4601**: 28.

Maguire WA 1993 *Belfast* Keele University Press, Keele.

Mahon D 1979 *Poems 1962–78* Oxford University Press, Oxford.

de Man P 1986 *The Resistance to Theory* University of Minnesota Press, Minneapolis.

Mangan P 1979 (May) In Defence of Northern Poets *Hibernia* **43** (20): 19.

Marrinan P 1973 *Paisley: Man of Wrath* Anvil Books, London.

McCormack WJ 1986 *The Battle of the Books: Two Decades of Irish Cultural Debate* Lilliput Press, Dublin.

McCurry J 1992 (Fall) 'S'Crap': Colonialism Indicted in the Poetry of Paul Muldoon *Eire–Ireland*: 92–109.

McDiarmid L 1991 (28 July) From Signifump to Kierkegaard, review of *Madoc: A Mystery, New York Times*: 14.

McGilchrist I 1982 *Against Criticism* Faber & Faber, London.

McLiam Wilson R 1989 *Ripley Bogle* Blackstaff Press, Belfast.

McLuhan M 1994 *Understanding Media: The Extensions of Man* Routledge, London.

Moloney E, Pollak A 1986 *Paisley* Poolbeg Press, Dublin.

Montague J 1961 *Poisoned Lands* MacGibbon & Kee, London.

— 1970 (Summer) Foreword *Threshold* **23**: 1.

— 1972 *The Rough Field* Dolmen Press, Dublin.

— 1977 *Poisoned Lands* rev. edn, Dolmen Press, Dublin.

Moore G (1911) 1985 *Hail and Farewell* ed. R Allen Cave. Colin Smythe, Gerrards Cross.

Moriarty G 1993 (28 April) Field Day future Uncertain as Board take 'Sabbatical' *Irish Times*: 1.

Muldoon P 1980 *Why Brownlee Left* Faber & Faber, London.

— 1983 *Quoof* Faber & Faber, London.

— 1986 *Selected Poems 1968–83* Faber & Faber, London.

— 1987 *Meeting the British* Faber & Faber, London.

— 1990 *Madoc: A Mystery* Faber & Faber, London.

Mumford L 1961 *The City in History* Secker & Warburg, London.

Newmann K 1993 *Dictionary of Ulster Biography* Institute of Irish Studies, Belfast.

Ni Dhonnchadha M, Dorgan T (eds) 1991 *Revising the Rising* Field Day, Derry.

Nietzsche F 1967 *On the Genealogy of Morals* trans. W Kaufmann, Vintage Books, New York.

Noble JR 1990 *Reflexive Narrative in the Poetry of Medbh McGuckian and Paul Muldoon* unpublished master's thesis, Queen's University of Belfast: 52–66.

Norris C 1982 (7 October) 'Faculty at War' letter *London Review of Books* **4** (18): 4.

— 1990 *What's Wrong With Postmodernism: Critical Theory and the Ends of Philosophy* Harvester/Wheatsheaf, London.

O'Brien CC 1975 (25 September) A Slow North-East Wind, review of *North, The Listener*: 23–4.

O'Brien F (1939) 1989 *At Swim-Two-Birds* Penguin, London.

O'Brien P 1991 (Fall) A Poem of Disturbing Originality, review of *Madoc: A Mystery, Irish Literary Supplement* **10** (2): 29–30.

O'Byrne C (1946) 1982 *As I Roved Out: A Book of the North* Blackstaff Press, Belfast.

O'Faolain N 1991 (11 November) The Voice That Field Day Didn't Record *Irish Times*: 14.

O'Seaghdha B 1989–90 (Winter) And Again. . . *Graph* **7**: 19–20.

O'Toole F 1982 The Man From God Knows Where, interview with Brian Friel. *In Dublin* **165**: 20–27.

Ormsby F 1972 (September) Coping (editorial) *The Honest Ulsterman* **35**: 2–3.

— 1973 (May) Review of *The Long Summer Still to Come, Fortnight* **61**: 18–19.

— (ed.) 1992 *A Rage for Order: Poetry of the Northern Ireland Troubles* Blackstaff Press, Belfast.

Paisley R 1988 *Ian Paisley My Father* Marshall Pickering, Basingstoke.

— 1993 (28 October) A Struggle About Identity, Loyalty, Government and, above all, Territory *Irish Times*: 14.

Parker M 1993 *Seamus Heaney: The Making of the Poet* Gill & Macmillan, Dublin.

Parker S 1989 *Three Plays For Ireland* Oberon Books, Birmingham.

Patterson G 1992 *Fat Lad* Chatto & Windus, London.

Paulin T 1980 *The Strange Museum* Faber & Faber, London.

— 1981 *The Book of Juniper* Bloodaxe, Newcastle upon Tyne.

— 1982 (17 June) Faculty at War – Tom Paulin gives his view of teachers of English review of *Against Criticism, Re-Reading English, London Review of Books* **4** (11): 14.

— 1982a (19 August) 'Faculty at War' letter *London Review of Books* **4** (15): 4.

— 1982b (2 September) Oxford v. Cambridge v. Birmingham etc. *London Review of Books* **4** (16): 22.

— 1983 *Liberty Tree* Faber & Faber, London.

— 1983a (3 February) 'Faculty at War' letter *London Review of Books* **5** (2): 5.

— 1984 *Ireland and the English Crisis* Bloodaxe, Newcastle upon Tyne.

— (ed.) 1986 *The Faber Book of Political Verse* Faber & Faber, London.

— 1987 *Fivemiletown* Faber & Faber, London.

— 1992 *Minotaur: Poetry and the Nation State* Faber & Faber, London.

— 1993 *Selected Poems: 1972–90* Faber & Faber, London.

— 1994 *Walking a Line* Faber & Faber, London.

Pike B 1981 *The Image of the City in Modern Literature* Princeton University Press, New Jersey.

Pollak A (ed.) 1993 *A Citizen's Enquiry: The Opsahl Report on Northern Ireland* Lilliput Press, Dublin.

Ramsey P 1994 (January) One-Night Stanzas *Fortnight* **324**: 44.

Randall J 1979 Interview with Seamus Heaney *Ploughshares* **5** (3): 7–22.

Richards S 1988 (Spring) To Bind the Northern to the Southern Stars: Field Day in Derry and Dublin *Irish Review* **4**: 52–58.

Richtarik M 1995 *Acting Between the Lines: The Field Day Theatre Company and Irish Cultural Politics, 1980–84* Oxford University Press, Oxford.

Said EW 1975 *Beginnings: Intention and Method* Basic Books, New York.

— 1988 *Nationalism, Colonialism and Literature: Yeats and Decolonization* Field Day Pamphlet 15, Derry.

Samson A 1992 *F.R. Leavis* Harvester/Wheatsheaf, London.

Scammell W 1991 (Summer) Interview with Derek Mahon *Poetry Review* **81** (2): 2–6.

Simmons J 1968 (May) Editorial *The Honest Ulsterman* **1**: 2–3.

— 1968a (June) Editorial *The Honest Ulsterman* **2**: 2–4.

— 1968b (August) Revolutionary Advice Part 4 *The Honest Ulsterman* **4**: 2–3.

— 1971 (August) English in Schools *Fortnight* **22**: 27.

— 1973 *The Long Summer Still to Come* Blackstaff Press, Belfast.

— 1986 *Poems: 1956–1986* Gallery Press, Oldcastle.

— 1993 *Sex, Rectitude and Loneliness* Lapwing Press, Belfast.

Smith S 1982 *Inviolable Voice: History and Twentieth-Century Poetry* Gill & Macmillan, Dublin.

Smyth D 1992 (September) Totalising Imperative, review of *The Field Day Anthology of Irish Writing, Fortnight* **309**: 26–7.

Spice N 1982 (15 July) 'Faculty at War' letter *London Review of Books* **4** (13): 4.

Spufford F 1992 (20 February) Patchwork of Ulster Memories, review of *Fat Lad, Guardian*: 23.

Stokes G 1987 (Summer) Field Day Tours America *An Gael*: 29–31.

Tomkins J 1985 *Sensational Designs: The Cultural Work of American Fiction* Oxford University Press, Oxford.

Ulster Folk and Transport Museum Visitors' Broadsheet, 1994 Cultra.

Ulster Museum Souvenir Guide 1993 Ulster Museum, Belfast.

Walker B 1992 (Spring/Summer) 1641, 1689, 1690 And All That: The Unionist Sense of History *The Irish Review* **12**: 56–64.

Warnock E 1965 (9 March) Letter *The Derry Journal*: 5.

Washington P 1989 *Fraud: Literary Theory and the End of English* Fontana/Collins, London.

Waterman A 1979 (26 April) Ulsterectomy *Hibernia* **43** (17): 16–17.

Weir A 1973 (4 May) Review of *The Long Summer Still to Come, Fortnight* **61**: 18–19.

Wellek R 1937 (March) Literary Criticism and Philosophy *Scrutiny: A Quarterly Review* **5** (4): 375–83.

— 1937a (September) Letter *Scrutiny: A Quarterly Review* **6** (2): 195–7.

Whelan K 1991 (second quarter) Come All You Staunch Revisionists: Towards a Post-revisionist Agenda for Irish History *Irish Reporter* **2**: 23–26.

Whyte J 1991 *Interpreting Northern Ireland* Clarendon Press, Oxford.

Wichert S 1991 *Northern Ireland Since 1945* Longman, Harlow.

Widdowson P (ed.) 1982 *Re-Reading English* Methuen, London.

— 1982a (30 December) 'Faculty at War' letter *London Review of Books* **4** (24): 4–5.

Williams R 1977 *Marxism and Literature* Oxford University Press, Oxford.
— 1983 *Keywords: A Vocabulary of Culture and Society* rev. edn. Fontana/Collins, London.
— (1958) 1993 *Culture and Society: Coleridge to Orwell* Hogarth Press, London.
Wills C 1993 *Improprieties: Politics and Sexuality in Northern Irish Poetry* Oxford University Press, Oxford.
Wright P 1991 *On Living in an Old Country: The National Past in Contemporary Britain* Verso, London.
Yeats WB (1955) 1987 *Autobiographies* Macmillan, London.

Index